Teenagers and Community Service

Teenagers and Community Service

A Guide to the Issues

Maureen E. Kenny and Laura A. Gallagher

Contemporary Youth Issues
Richard M. Lerner, Series Editor

Westport, Connecticut
London

Library of Congress Cataloging-in-Publication Data

Kenny, Maureen.
  Teenagers and community service : a guide to the issues / by Maureen E. Kenny and
Laura A. Gallagher.
    p. cm. — (Contemporary youth issues)
  Includes bibliographical references and index.
  ISBN 0-275-97976-8 (alk. paper)
  1. Teenage volunteers in social service—United States. I. Gallagher, Laura A.
II. Title. III. Series.
HN90.V64K44   2003
361.3'7'08350973—dc21   2002193034

British Library Cataloguing in Publication Data is available.

Library of Congress Catalog Card Number: 2002193034

ISBN: 0-275-97976-8

First published in 2003

Praeger Publishers, 88 Post Road West, Westport, CT 06881
An imprint of Greenwood Publishing Group, Inc.
www.praeger.com

Printed in the United States of America

The paper used in this book complies with the
Permanent Paper Standard issued by the National
Information Standards Organization (Z39.48–1984).

10 9 8 7 6 5 4 3 2 1

Contents

Series Foreword

Contemporary Youth Issues is a series of volumes that provides new and important educational materials for the youth and adults involved in middle schools, high schools, and public libraries. Volumes in the series offer accessible information about the nature of the issues facing contemporary youth (children in the first two decades of life), parents, and youth-serving professionals—for example, teachers, practitioners, and governmental and nongovernmental organization personnel.

Both the challenges to healthy development confronting contemporary youth and the assets or strengths of adolescents and of the communities that contribute to their positive development are represented. Each book in the series reviews current knowledge about these challenges and assets, directs youth and adults to current community resources available to address challenges or enhance assets, and discusses key issues of policy and program design pertinent to improving the lives of the diverse youth of the United States and the world.

THE CONCEPT OF THE SERIES

Childhood and adolescence are developmental periods during which most of a person's biological, cognitive, psychological, and social characteristics are changing from what is present at birth to what is considered adultlike. For children and adolescents, and for the parents, friends, and teachers who support and nurture them, the first two decades of life are a time of dramatic challenge requiring adjustment to changes in the self, in the family, and in the peer group. In contemporary Western society, youth experience institutional changes as well. Infants and young children leave the home for preschool and then elementary school. Among young adolescents, there is a change in school setting, typically involving a transition from elementary school to either junior high school or middle school; and in late adolescence, there is a transition from high school to the worlds of work, university, or childrearing.

Given the changes and challenges of the first two decades—especially now when issues of youth population growth; insufficient economic, energy, educational, and employment resources; inequalities of opportunity; and violence and war affect hundreds of millions of young people daily—childhood and adolescence are periods replete with the possibilities of developmental problems. Indeed, because of the strong connection (correlation) that exists among the several problems of youth, and as a consequence of the high rates of these problems, the combined challenge to healthy child and adolescent development exists today at historically unprecedented levels.

As well, however, childhood and adolescence are periods wherein there is a great potential for positive and healthy behavior and development. Children and adolescents may possess considerable physical, psychological, and interpersonal abilities. These strengths may be coupled with the assets provided by friends supporting healthy choices, by parents providing authoritative guidance, and by caregivers, teachers, and communities creating opportunities for positive contributions and leadership. When the individual and ecological strengths, or assets, of youth align, developmental thriving can result. Instead of possessing a set of problem behaviors (associated with unsafe sex, substance use, crime, violence, educational failure, poor health, and poverty), the possession of developmental assets can result in youth who are marked by competence, confidence, character, connection, and caring/compassion.

Accordingly, this series is aimed at issues pertinent to both the challenges to and the opportunities for healthy development among contemporary youth and presents both the problems and positive potential of youth. In each volume in this series young people and the adults charged with promoting their healthy development are informed about:

1. The key concepts and substantive issues pertinent to each issue of concern in a given volume in the series;

2. The important events in the development of the issue, of knowledge about it, and of policies and programs pertinent to it;

3. The biographical backgrounds of key people who have worked and/or are working to address the issue;

4. Contemporary data pertinent to the incidence, impact, or developmental course of the issue;

5. The key organizations, associations, and national and international governmental and nongovernmental organizations addressing the issue;

6. Key, annotated print and nonprint resources pertinent to the issue; and

7. The terms important for understanding the issue, presented in glossary form.

Each book in the series also includes a name and subject index.

Across the volumes in the series, the scholarship that is presented focuses on the advances of the last several decades in the medical, biological, and social scientific study of childhood and adolescence, and in the corresponding advances made by youth-serving professionals and practitioners in the design, delivery, and evaluation of programs that are effective not only in preventing youth problems but, in turn, in promoting the positive development of young people. In short, each volume in the series integratively presents the best "basic" and "applied" information currently available about the physical, psychological, behavioral, social, and cultural dimensions of a contemporary issue relevant to the adolescent period.

All volumes inform youth and their adult caregivers about the richness, challenges, and positive potentials of this dynamic developmental period. The volumes illustrate the diversity of child and adolescent life found across different physical, behavioral, racial, ethnic, religious, national, and cultural characteristics; emphasize the numerous (diverse) life paths that may result in positive, healthy development; present the key social relationships (e.g., involving peer groups, siblings, parents, extended family members, teachers, or mentors) and institutional contexts (e.g., schools, community organizations, faith institutions, and the workplace) that influence the development of today's youth; and discuss and evaluate the policies and programs useful for alleviating problems, for preventing problems, and for promoting positive and healthy development among contemporary youth.

Preface

Community service is increasingly recognized by psychologists, educators, human service professionals, and policy leaders as an important vehicle for promoting positive development among teenagers. Engagement in community service provides youth with opportunities to connect with caring adults and peers in making a difference in their communities. Through community service, teenagers can develop personal, social, civic, and academic skills. Through interaction with persons of different age groups, races, and cultures, they can gain understanding of persons who are different from themselves and gain skills for effective communication. By working alongside adults in different service activities, young people can be exposed to different career opportunities and develop sound work habits. Service-learning has grown as a method of educational reform that links academic learning with the solution of real-life problems in the community. As a result of the contributions teenagers make to the community, adults can gain a greater appreciation of youth as community assets. All community members can potentially benefit from the results of community service initiatives.

The knowledge base concerning community service and service-learning has grown exponentially in recent years, as has the number of organizations, programs, and available resources that support community service. These programs and organizations have grown both on the national and local levels. According to recent polls, however, many Americans do not know what service-learning is or understand the benefits of community service and service-learning for youth and the community. Once they are explained, however, the vast majority of Americans support service initiatives.

This book is intended to provide teenagers, their parents, teachers, and other professionals and concerned adults with current information on community service and service-learning. We have included resources for the complete range of adolescence, including programs and ideas for middle and high schoolers, as well as college or university students. Teenagers can find resources on the types of service programs available and on ways to volunteer and be actively involved in their communities. Teachers and other professionals who are involved in developing or running service programs can find a wealth of information on how to develop and improve their programs. All readers will find valuable information and be able to increase their knowledge and keep abreast of further developments in this rapidly growing field.

The first chapter provides an overview of community service and service-learning, with current examples of community service programs, the diverse goals of service programs, and knowledge concerning the outcomes of service. All service programs do not achieve the same goals or the same level of success. Thus, we examine the characteristics of effective programs and consider who engages in service and who benefits from this activity. Practical strategies for adults and young people interested in joining, starting, or improving their service programs are provided, and current controversies in the field, such as the issue of mandatory service, are briefly explored. The Chronology presented in chapter 2 provides a historical context for understanding the current status of community service and service-learning. We review the critical events that have occurred over the past century that have led to the growth and popularity of youth service. Leading figures in the field are introduced in chapter 3. The range of individuals profiled includes scholars and researchers who have been instrumental in developing the knowledge base about the service programs, political leaders who have helped to draft and support legislation for service programs, and practitioners and community organizers who have developed and/or directed service programs at the local and national level. Chapter 4 provides definitions of community service and service-learning, standards for the development of effective programs, and findings from recent surveys and reports concerning the level of youth involvement in community service and service-learning, the results of community service involvement, public knowledge of community service, and challenges in the development of service programs in both community, high school, and college settings.

Chapter 5 presents a list of organizations related to community service and service-learning. These public and private organizations offer support for individuals, groups, and schools interested in developing community service programs and provide opportunities for teenagers to become involved in community service. We present a range of local and national organizations for teenagers of all ages to find potential volunteer or service opportunities. Many of the organizations provide recognition for young people who provide exceptional service and many offer training opportunities for teenagers to develop leadership and service skills, as well as enhance social and academic development. Some of the organizations partner with others in supporting service initiatives. Other organizations presented provide valuable resources for teachers and community agency staff to help to develop and improve existing programs. Chapter 6 presents a selected annotated bibliography of print and nonprint resources. Books written primarily for parents and professionals are presented separately from those intended as resources chiefly for teenagers. Key articles from periodicals are also summarized and videos are described, along with their sources. Internet sites are described, which can be particularly helpful in learning about new developments in the field. Some of the Internet sites are most helpful for teenagers seeking opportunities for involvement in service programs, whereas other sites are intended for parents and professionals interested in developing or improving service programs in their schools and communities. Some Internet sites offer searchable databases to find volunteer opportunities or other service resources.

We hope that this volume will provide a solid foundation concerning current knowledge and issues related to teenagers and community service and will provide resources to guide you in exploring the topic in greater depth and breadth. Community service, when carefully conceptualized and implemented, has tremendous potential for shaping future citizens to lead our nation and communities with competence and conscience. The development of service programs that effectively serve communities and contribute to the development of varied skills among diverse groups of teenagers is not a simple task. This book is intended to highlight the promises of community service, to provide an introduction to the complexity of this task, and to acquaint readers with the vast array of organizations and resources through which they can develop expertise to develop exemplary programs. We hope that awareness of these resources will engage more teenagers and caring adults in community service and will contribute to the growth of effective service programs. The growing knowledge base and resources pertaining to this topic should contribute to the development of service programs that will effectively enhance the development of teenagers representing varied communities across the country and will provide tangible and intangible benefits to the sponsoring schools and communities.

Acknowledgments

We would like to acknowledge the contributions of Boston College Lynch School of Education undergraduate students Kathleen Wack and Katherine Fleming and graduate students Kevin McKay, Molly Jilek, and Jennifer Grossman for their assistance in completing the research that provides the foundation for this volume. Thanks to Michael Kurgansky for assistance in preparing the tables in chapter 4.

1

Overview

with Jennifer M. Grossman

Through this overview on teenagers and community service, you will be introduced to major issues in the field. We consider, first of all, how community service meets the developmental needs of adolescents and identify factors that have contributed to the rise in popularity of youth service programs. A range of program types and goals is presented, along with examples of service programs designed to meet a variety of community needs and produce a variety of youth outcomes. Ways for youth to become involved in service and considerations for adults who wish to develop programs are presented. Research findings are examined to determine the effectiveness of service programs in meeting their espoused goals. Characteristics of youth volunteers and effective service programs are discussed, as well as considerations in making service programs more responsive to the needs of culturally diverse youth, especially in urban settings. We conclude with a discussion of several controversies in the field, including political philosophies underlying varied models of service and the debate on whether service should be required in public schools.

COMMUNITY SERVICE AND ADOLESCENT DEVELOPMENT

Throughout the 1990s, the popular press, as well as scholarly research, documented the risks that are faced by contemporary teens. Hechinger

(1992), for example, reported that the state of adolescent health is in "crisis proportions" (p. 21), with depression, suicide, use of illegal drugs and alcohol, unprotected sexual activity, cigarette smoking, inadequate nutrition, and exposure to violence either as a victim or perpetrator being widespread among youth as young as ten to fifteen years old. The 1999 report of the U.S. Surgeon General emphasized the prevalence of mental health problems among school-aged children and adolescents (U.S. Department of Health and Human Services, 1999). By age fifteen, 25 percent of adolescents have engaged in one or more high-risk behaviors (Hechinger, 1992). A variety of negative social experiences, including victimization (physical and sexual abuse), parental addiction, social isolation, negative peer pressure, and unstructured and unsupervised time have been linked with adolescent mental health problems and engagement in risky behaviors (Benson, 1993). Adolescence is unquestionably a time of significant risk for many teens (Carnegie Council on Adolescent Development, 1992).

Adolescence can also be a time of "opportunity" (Carnegie Council on Adolescent Development, 1992, p. 9) and "hope and promise" (Hechinger, 1992, p. 24). Interest in identifying ways to help teens navigate the risks of adolescence to achieve a productive and healthy adulthood has grown over the last decade, as exemplified by the first White House Conference on Teenagers held in May 2000 (Roth & Brooks-Gunn, 2000). Whereas poverty, unemployment, neighborhood disintegration, community violence, and family disorganization increase the risks encountered during the adolescent transition, good schools, the presence of caring and supportive adults, and involvement in constructive activities are known to reduce risks and enhance the opportunities, hopes, and promise of the adolescent years (Blum, Beuhring, & Rinehart, 2000; Carnegie Council on Adolescent Development, 1989, 1992, 1996).

During the last decade, researchers have learned a great deal about what is needed to promote healthy adolescent development. In order to be prepared for the future, adolescents need to be more than free of problems. They must develop competencies to interact effectively with the world and to achieve academically, socially, and vocationally. Lerner, Fisher, and Weinberg (2000) identified five attributes that contribute to positive adolescent development. These attributes are: social, academic and vocational competence; confidence or positive sense of self; healthy connections with family, peers, and community; positive values or character; and a sense of compassion or caring. Research conducted by the

Search Institute in Minnesota identified twenty internal and twenty external assets that contribute to positive youth development (Benson, 1997). Internal assets or personal qualities include a positive commitment to learning, positive values, social competencies, and positive identities. External assets, which are the supports and attributes provided by the environment, include support from parents, neighbors, adults at school or other nonparental adults, opportunities to contribute meaningfully in the community, clear boundaries and expectations at home and at school, and constructive use of leisure time. The Search Institute has furthermore identified ways in which programs including service-learning can be organized and implemented to increase the presence of these assets in the lives of youth and thereby enhance positive youth development (Mannes, 2002; Search Institute, 2000).

Community service is one activity that has been recognized as a means of reducing youth risks and promoting positive youth development (Kenny, Simon, Kiley-Brabeck, & Lerner, 2002). The expected goals of community service and service-learning are remarkably similar to the competencies and assets associated with positive youth development (Mannes, 2002). Community service seeks to promote positive self-identity, character, and a sense of caring and compassion. Through engagement in service activities with peers and caring adults, service can enhance healthy connections with others, offer constructive use of leisure time, and provide chances for youth to contribute in meaningful ways to their communities. Well-designed service activities also develop competencies in academic, social, and vocational domains.

Recognition of the large number of teenagers who give to their communities through service activities attests to the moral and psychological well-being of the large majority of contemporary youth. Too often events related to the difficulties of teens are highlighted in the media, with relatively little attention to young peoples' accomplishments and contributions to society. As a result, the majority of American adults believe that teenagers do not respect adults, get into more trouble today than they did in the past, face a crisis in morals and values, and pose a greater threat than any foreign nation to the future of our country (Kimball-Baker & Roehlkepartain, 1998). Youniss and Yates (1997) believe that teens have been unfairly demonized and suggest that community service offers a way to recognize the strengths of youth and provide them with meaningful social roles. Community service can offer youth a way to connect with older generations, help them to understand their current experiences in a broader social and historical context, invite active participation in social problem solving, and create optimism for social change and a better future (Youniss & Yates, 1997). When society focuses on the problems of youth and is preoccupied with ways to prevent those problems, adults tend to set low expectations for young people. Participating in service, in contrast, recognizes the strengths of youth, sets high expectations, and seeks to use those strengths in contributions to society (Zeldin & Tarlov, 1997).

A number of authors (Andersen, 1998; Conrad & Hedin, 1987; Kenny et al., 2002; Mannes, 2002; Schine, 1989) have pointed out ways in which the needs and developmental tasks of adolescents can be met and furthered through involvement in community service. Community service provides opportunities for youth to learn side by side with peers and adults about community problems and ways to solve them. Youth learn the social and communication skills needed to work effectively with a variety of persons. They gain opportunities to solve real problems and envision themselves as contributing members of society. They also can learn to appreciate diversity and reduce intergroup tensions while working towards a common goal (Andersen, 1998). Further, they may participate in career exploration and observe the attitudes and behaviors of the world of work. In the past, youth learned these skills by observing and participating with family members in the home and workplace. In today's busy society, there is greater age segregation, with young people having much less opportunity to observe and learn through the daily activities of their elders. Some youth feel isolated, alienated, and even neglected. Scholars have claimed that many youth lack the important social connections with adults that are critical in passing on "social capital" from one generation to the next (Coleman, 1987; Putnam, 1995). Community service can provide teenagers with support and care from adults, as well as guidance in building skills and competencies needed to understand successfully their community and prepare for their futures (Andersen, 1998). On a theoretical level, at least, there appear to be many benefits to youth involvement in community service as a means to reduce risks and enhance positive development.

COMMUNITY SERVICE AND SERVICE-LEARNING

Throughout the United States, people of all ages have provided service to members of their local, national, and international communities since the nation's founding. The Chronology in chapter 2 of this book provides more detailed information on the history of community service.

Here, we discuss elements of service-learning that make important impacts on youth development. In the last ten to fifteen years, interest in community service among teenagers, parents, educators, and local and national leaders has skyrocketed. Youth service has developed into a nationwide movement committed to providing youth of all ages with service opportunities through which they can simultaneously develop as citizens and contribute to their communities. Many factors have led to this movement, including concerns discussed above about the risks faced by adolescents as well as the recognition that adolescents possess many skills that can be applied productively to improving their communities. Scholars have also begun studying the impact of community service on youth development and have identified some of the factors that distinguish service involvement that truly makes a difference in the lives of youth from service experiences that have little impact. Later in this chapter, we will present a summary of recent research findings.

Research has found that all service experiences are not the same. Structured time for reflection and evaluation has been found to enhance greatly youth learning from service experiences. Spending time talking and writing about a service experience is key to gaining insight from the experience, and it is this learning or insight that positively affects youth development (Roehlkepartain, 1995). This finding has contributed to the growing popularity of service-learning, which links service to the community with student learning in ways that contribute to the growth of the student and benefit the community (Learn and Serve, 2001). The term *service-learning* originated in the late 1960s to describe an internship program in which college students gained academic credit for service endeavors linked with the school curriculum (Sigmon, 1979). The idea has evolved over time, but one of the essential components of service-learning that has remained consistent over the years is the provision of structured time for students to reflect on their service experience. Definitions of service-learning can be found in the Facts and Data chapter of this volume. You may want to examine the similarities and differences across these definitions to gain a better understanding of what is meant by service-learning.

Although learning is a critical part of service-learning, these programs are not limited to school settings. Many community and faith-based youth organizations, in addition to schools, develop service-learning programs. In schools and colleges, learning goals are generally linked to the academic curriculum. Community organizations may emphasize learning goals that relate to the development of practical skills, civic responsibilities, or personal development, such as self-esteem. In both school and community settings, the service experience is coordinated by the sponsoring organization, with the expectation that the experience will enhance the learning goals established by that organization. Youth service programs that follow guidelines for good practice, including the identification of goals for social, civic, or moral learning and the incorporation of reflection to further that learning, are identified as service-learning programs, because they arrange service experiences to promote youth development or learning (Cairn & Kielsmeier, 1995).

Since reflection is a central component of service-learning, it is important to have a clear understanding of this concept. During reflection, young people think about what they did, what it meant to them, and what action or next steps they will take as a result (Roehlkepartain, 1995). Reflection helps young people to gain meaning from their experience. For example, young people can be helped to think about what they have observed and the reasons or root causes for the social problems that their service seeks to address. In this way, reflection can also be critically important in correcting misperceptions or stereotypes about the persons being served. In fact, service experience that lacks reflection can result in undesirable, rather than positive, effects. When appropriate reflection experiences are not provided, young people can develop negative views, reinforcing stereotypes about the people they are trying to assist (Search Institute, 2000).

Reflection can take the form of writing, speaking, multimedia, or student-developed activities (Cairn & Kielsmeier, 1995). Journal writing, the development of scrapbooks and portfolios, creating collages, drawings or sculptures, small and large group discussions, writing a letter about the experience to a parent, friend, or newspaper, researching social issues or public policies related to the experience, running a workshop or training session for other youth and creating a video or slide show about a service project are just a few examples of the methods used for structuring and carrying out reflection (Search Institute, 2000). Reflection can focus on teens' cognitions or thought processes, on affect or feelings, and on the steps or processes involved in carrying out the service project. All three types of reflection are recommended for optimal learning. Through cognitive reflection, youth examine skills, knowledge, and new perspectives gained from the service experience, especially as related to the academic curriculum. Through affective reflection, youth examine their emotions and how their feelings, thoughts, and motivations have changed through the service experience.

Through reflecting on the process, youth examine the steps in which they engaged, such as planning, decision-making, and working with others, as well as what was learned as a result (Close Up Foundation, 2000).

Reflection can be integrated throughout the entire service experience. Before participating, youth assess community needs and strengths, identify and select a problem, and develop a plan to achieve the desired results. They can reflect on the origins of the problem, their expectations concerning the solution, and how their previous life experiences impact their attitudes and hopes about what they might accomplish. During the process of completing the service activity, youth often document their activities through writing, photography, or video. They also engage in reflection that involves sharing their thoughts and feelings with other youth and group leaders in ways that lead to constructive learning and problem solving. Reflection involving participants representing a variety of racial, ethnic, and socioeconomic backgrounds can be particularly helpful in facilitating understanding and reducing prejudices and other barriers to communication (Andersen, 1998). Reflection also helps youth to evaluate the roles they play in the community, their feelings about the project, and their attitudes towards other people involved in carrying out the project. Ongoing reflection provides students with opportunities to adjust their behavior so as to improve the quality and effectiveness of the service experience. Following project completion, reflection focuses on analyzing, understanding, and celebrating outcomes and providing a closure experience (Andersen, 1998; Close Up Foundation, 2000). It is generally best to plan the reflection activity immediately after each service experience, so that the experience is still fresh in the young persons' minds (Search Institute, 2000). Effective reflection exercises need to be based on clear objectives or rationale, must be planned and organized, and should be interesting for the youth. Those programs that involve youth in planning the exercise, require youth to think critically, and include a variety of methods are often successful in engaging youth interest. Reflection exercises should also be informed by academic lessons and make academic learning more clear, relevant, and meaningful to the students (Cairn & Kielsmeier, 1995).

FEDERAL AND PRIVATE SUPPORT FOR SERVICE-LEARNING

During the latter half of the 1980s, interest in community service grew throughout the country. Growing grassroots efforts to develop service programs contributed to the passage of the National and Community Service Act of 1990. This act created a private, nonprofit organization devoted to the promotion of volunteerism, called the Points of Light Foundation, as well as a new federal agency, the Commission on National and Community Service. The commission provided grants and national coordination to states, schools, and community organizations for four types of service initiatives: service-learning for school-aged children and youth, service programs in higher education, youth corps programs, and national service demonstration projects.

National enthusiasm for these programs grew. A second federal service act, the National and Community Service Trust Act, was introduced into Congress by a bipartisan coalition and was signed into law in September of 1993. This legislation expanded the initiatives of the National and Community Service Act of 1990 and authorized funds for every state to incorporate service-learning into its schools. The 1993 legislation also created the Corporation for National Service to administer three initiatives: Learn and Serve America, AmeriCorps, and the National Senior Services Corp. Learn and Serve America supports service initiatives in community organizations, K–12 schools, and in higher education. AmeriCorps is a national service program for young adults, and the National Senior Services Corps engages older Americans in community service. Learn and Serve America has had a tremendous impact on focusing interest and attention on community service and service-learning among school-aged youth and college students and has aided in the expansion of service programs. Grants are given to create new programs, to replicate existing programs, and to provide training to staff, teachers/faculty, and volunteers. Thus, although funds are provided on a national level, programs are developed and controlled on a local level. All Learn and Serve America projects are required to match federal funds with local community resources, thus assuring a commitment to project success among local leaders and citizens (Learn and Serve, 2001).

Growth in community service and service-learning cannot be credited solely to federal support. As previously mentioned, a large number of grassroots organizations and private foundations have been instrumental in furthering community service among youth. The National Youth Leadership Council and the Search Institute have supported the development of community service and service-learning for almost two decades. The American Institute for Public Service, founded almost thirty years ago to encourage youth involvement in public and community service, initiated in 1989 National Youth Service Day, which encourages youth to engage in service projects each spring. The Close Up Foundation has sought for three decades to promote youth participation in democratic processes and now serves to connect the National Service-Learning Clearinghouse with national civic organizations. Traditional youth organizations, such as 4-H and scouting, have a strong focus on youth service and leadership. Newer organizations, such as Do Something, emerged in the 1990s, with a focus on inspiring youth to make a difference in the world. Through its Learning In Deed: Making a Difference Through Service-Learning initiative launched in 1998, the W. K. Kellogg Foundation added to the support it had provided for more than a decade in promoting service-learning as a means to increase youth engagement in their communities. The Campus Outreach Opportunity League (COOL) and Campus Compact, which emerged in the 1980s, have had a huge impact on the growth of community service and service-learning on college campuses. Campus Compact, in particular, has experienced phenomenal growth in membership and influence in the past decade.

PROGRAM GOALS

This brief introduction reveals that an array of goals has been associated with involvement in community service programs. We will first describe each of these goals in greater depth and then describe the kinds of service activities that might be designed to achieve them.

A number of goals focus on the benefits of service for participating youth. Individual youth goals can be divided further into those emphasizing personal and social development, those emphasizing civic responsibility, those impacting student academic learning, and those impacting career exploration and aspirations. Goals can also focus on school-wide changes, including improving methods of instruction, enhancing relationships between students and teachers, and improving understanding and peer relationships among students. They can focus as well on increasing students' feelings of connection to the school and their perceptions of school as a positive environment. Goals for service programs also include benefits to the community and improved perceptions by community members of the school and of the teenage youth who are performing service activities (Billig, 2000a).

To support student personal and emotional development, programs are often expected to enhance student self-esteem, that is, to help students to feel more positively about themselves because they have accomplished something worthwhile. Youth are also expected to become more caring and empathic towards others and to show an increasing sense of responsibility for the welfare of others. Goals for personal growth also include interpersonal development. Through involvement in service activities, youth learn to work with adults and other teens who may be similar and different from them. As a result, they are expected to develop skills in interpersonal communication and increased awareness and acceptance of cultural differences. Weah, Simmons, and Hall (2000) identify four ways in which service-learning can effectively teach students about race and culture. First, by actively engaging with people who are different from themselves, students gain the opportunity to explore new perspectives beyond their own. Further engagement with racial and cultural issues comes from opportunities for reflection. In this context, students can ask questions and challenge their own and each others' ideas and perceptions about race and culture. This early exploration may support long-term positive change in students' attitudes and behaviors. Service-learning also provides opportunities to work through cultural differences within a context of respect for diverse values and beliefs. Finally, service-learning can create space for multiple student and community voices, in which all involved people can be a part of creating positive "solutions." Helping youth to feel connected to their communities, schools, and families is also known to reduce high-risk behavior. By deterring youth from engaging in "at-risk" behaviors and supporting youth investment in constructive activities, service involvement is expected to reduce behavioral problems, including unprotected sexual activity and teenage pregnancy, violence, and records of arrest.

In terms of civic development, service learning is expected to increase awareness of the complexity of social and political problems and to teach youth that these problems can be solved through the efforts of engaged citizens. As a result, students are expected to become more committed to their responsibilities as citizens, believe their voices can make a difference, and participate in community service and voting in the future. They learn about the workings of government and other sociopolitical systems and ways to engage in the political process and assume leadership roles. When civic outcomes are desired, a service activity should be selected that will provide opportunities for this type of learning to take place. Furthermore, the adult facilitator or teacher needs to guide youth in making connections between their experience and social or citizenship issues. For example, if youth were involved in a voter registration drive, they might be guided in understanding the reasons why some segments of the population are less likely to register to vote than others (Billig, 2000a).

In terms of student academic learning, service-learning is expected to enhance the acquisition of academic skills and knowledge as students see and experience the real-world applications of what they study at school. Since this method of learning and teaching is more active and problem-focused, students are expected to develop problem-solving skills and to be engaged and motivated in their academic studies. Students also take responsibility for their own learning, rather than expecting knowledge to come from the teacher. The connections between academic learning and the service experience must be designed carefully for academic learning to be enhanced. For example, geometry skills can be linked with the construction of a wheelchair ramp (Billig, 2000a). In order to enhance cognitive development, reflection activities must also be designed to develop advanced critical-thinking skills. Because service activities occur mostly in community settings that offer exposure to career opportunities, students are expected to make gains in career awareness and exploration and in developing positive work-related behaviors and attitudes. This does not happen automatically, however. When career awareness is a desired goal, the activity must build connections to job skills, job knowledge, or career paths (Billig, 2000a).

Community service programs are also expected to impact the institutions and organizations that partner in service programs. For example, community service and service-learning programs that develop in school settings are expected to impact the overall school climate. To the extent that students work cooperatively with teachers and school administrators in designing and carrying out service activities, the relationships between students and faculty are likely to improve. As students perceive school learning as more relevant to their lives and to the solutions of real problems, they may gain increasing respect for the learning that their teachers provide. Teachers also observe the competency, creativity, and compassion of their students as they interact in solving real problems and offering service to others, and thus may gain increased respect for student skills and talents. The agencies and communities that are served are also expected to change. Not only do they obtain needed services, but they may also come to perceive youth in more positive ways. Youth at school may become less isolated from the community. Through service, communities can reconnect with schools and youth. Partnerships that develop between schools, community organizations, and other agencies lead to a sharing of knowledge, information, and resources that changes everyone involved.

SERVICE OPTIONS

What exactly is it that students do in community service and service-learning that serves to promote the described goals? This is not a simple question to answer because service can take on many shapes and strategies.

First of all, the ways in which youth can become involved in community service are quite varied. These variations, described by Cairn and Kielsmeier (1995), range from service organizations or clubs, to community service classes, to community service as a school-wide theme. Historically, a common way in which faith-based and community organizations and schools have encouraged community service is through clubs or co-curricular programs. Scouting, 4-H, and service clubs, like Key Club, are examples of co-curricular service activities. These types of programs do not offer academic credit, are not linked with the academic curriculum, and generally do not take place during school hours. Clubs and co-curricular activities traditionally have not included participant reflection as part of their service activity. However, reflection components can be integrated with these youth service programs to enhance personal, social, civic, and academic growth among participating youth. The learning goals and reflection activities may vary, however, depending upon the sponsoring institution. For students involved in cleaning up a river or lake, the learning goal at a school may focus on scientific understanding. For a community youth organization, the learning goal may be appreciation of nature or the development of responsible attitudes towards the environment (Search Institute, 2000).

Many schools and colleges also operate a volunteer clearinghouse as a means for students to learn about opportunities for volunteer service in their communities. This is a resource for students who are interested in making a contribution to their community, and in this context, service is completely voluntary and is not linked with academic study. Some schools and youth organizations require students to complete a community service requirement often specified as a certain number of service hours. Internet sites are now also available to help youth identify service opportunities. The school may set aside one day per week or per month for students to participate in service activities. School-wide and community-wide service projects, such as a community-wide blood drive or a seasonal clean-up project, offer some distinct benefits, such as drawing positive attention to youth accomplishment and providing opportunities for individuals across ages to work cooperatively. Another option for service development is when one or more students design an independent proposal for a service project that is approved by a teacher or service coordinator. All of these service experiences have the potential to build in involved youth a sense of personal efficacy or confidence in one's ability to make a difference, social responsibility, personal productivity, and interpersonal skills.

OPTIONS FOR LINKING SERVICE WITH LEARNING

Within school settings, options for linking service to the school curriculum are also varied. For example, individual teachers may decide to build a service project into an existing class. These service projects can also take many forms. For example, products that students create in class might be used elsewhere in the school, in local businesses, or in nursing homes. A class, thus, might contribute a product, such as art, to a community organization. Alternately, as students examine a social issue, such as child care, in their class, the teacher might help them think about ways to address the issue. They might, for example, write to their legal representatives requesting changes in child care regulations. In this way, students apply what they have learned in the classroom to address a real concern. Direct service, such as working at a nursing home, and community education, such as teaching a foreign language to elementary school children, can also be linked with the school curriculum. For example, students can teach what they have learned at school to younger children, the elderly, or the disabled. Often, the skills learned in a class can be helpful to people outside of the school. An English class, for example, might practice literacy skills by helping a community organization to develop and distribute a newsletter. A social studies class might work with new immigrants to prepare them for citizenship tests, or a math class might carry out the computations needed in designing and specifying the dimensions of equipment to be purchased for the new park playground. These class projects are examples of ways in which the academic skills taught in a classroom can be applied, reinforced, and made relevant through involvement in community service. Sometimes the service is completed at school and then turned over to the community, and sometimes students leave the school to perform service at a community location.

Within existing courses, students may also complete individualized service options as a way of obtaining extra credit or fulfilling class requirements. A student may choose to work at a homeless shelter or food bank, for example, while completing a research project on world hunger. The student might write a paper in which she compares what she had learned through library research with what she learned through her community experience. A student in a science class may be studying water pollution and work with the local health department in collecting and testing water samples. Some schools structure opportunities for cross-age tutors and counseling, in which older students provide support for younger students. Peer counselors might also be available to help students who are new to the school make the transition to a new setting. Through these activities, students may acquire leadership, interpersonal, or problem-solving skills or develop increased empathy in understanding the perspectives of others. For those who are tutors, academic skills are reinforced when teaching others. Sometimes, specific classes are designated as community service classes, in which students devote a significant portion of class time during school to community service. If students are completing service during school hours, community service classes are often scheduled for a longer time block to allow sufficient service time.

Rather than having service reflected in isolated courses, community service-learning can also be infused throughout a school's curriculum. This infusion approach enables students to continue service-learning involvement over many years. Some authors maintain that this is the most effective way to support real and lasting gains (Cairn & Kielsmeier, 1995). Some schools adopt a particular community service project as a school-wide theme. The particular theme chosen by the school may vary from year to year. Literacy might be a theme one year, with environmental issues being a focus another year. Students in a variety of courses may complete projects that relate to the selected theme. Schools that adopt community service as a school-wide theme may develop a partnership with a community organization, such as the Red Cross, United Way, or the League of Women Voters. The community organization may rely on ongoing student volunteers to fill a number of positions and provide supervision and mentoring to youth in return. Small or large groups of students might complete their own assessment of community needs and, in collaboration with their teachers and community liaison, develop and carry out a plan to remedy a perceived problem. This latter type of activity can be powerful in increasing problem-solving skills, enhancing feelings of personal and group effectiveness, and developing leadership skills because youth learn how to identify and work towards solving a community problem. Working in a group to identify a problem and develop and carry out a proposed solution has the potential to enhance interpersonal skills in cooperating and negotiating as a team member. An advantage of school-wide programs is that student involvement in service is ongoing. Service involvement does not take place on one day or in one class, but through a series of classes and over a series of years. In this format, the lessons of service programs are more likely to become integrated with students' broader school experiences. As a result, the benefits for students, the school, and the community are more likely to be substantive.

Options for Service Activities

Numerous types of service opportunities exist, and different types of youth services offer different benefits. Direct service, indirect service, social advocacy, and education for change represent four types of service activities that are expected to yield different benefits for the youth and the communities that they service (Search Institute, 2000).

In terms of direct service (working directly with service recipients), tutoring is a common service activity that addresses some of the academic challenges presented to teachers in the schools. Older students can motivate younger students to become more active learners. Younger children look up to older students and learn that it can be "cool" to know things and to succeed in school (Andersen, 1998). Teens can also come to value knowledge and academic learning in a new way as they teach others. Tutoring can be provided as part of the growing number of after-school programs or can be offered during school hours. Peer mentoring and buddy programs are also popular forms of direct service that connect younger children with older peers. Mentoring from an older child builds feelings of belonging and trust for the younger child and enhances feelings of competence and self-esteem for the older youth. Peer mentoring can be linked with tutoring and thus fulfill multiple purposes. Providing a direct service, such as tutoring or mentoring a young child, supports opportunities for developing personal relationships with others and thereby increases interpersonal and multicultural understanding. Through ongoing and direct work with persons different from themselves, students gain personal ties to social justice concerns (Search Institute, 2000). When students connect the lives of specific persons with social issues that they have read about, the issues often become more real and pressing. Direct service activities are not easy to carry out, however, because they require substantial and ongoing time commitment on the part of the youth volunteer. Relationships are built over time and the benefits of this type of service take time to accrue. If mentors and tutors begin to develop relationships with younger children and then lose interest, they may do more harm than good to the children they hoped to help.

Indirect service activities offer services, but without substantial contact with the recipients of those services. These options can fulfill important community needs without requiring an ongoing time commitment from involved students. Organizing a food drive, staffing a food distribution center for the homeless, participating in environmental clean-up or beautification and recycling projects, creating care packages to send in response to needs in other parts of the world, and participating in fundraisers for various charitable political organizations are examples of indirect service. These activities can help youth to build a sense of efficacy. There are limitations to the benefits of indirect service, however. Since there is no sustained contact with the recipients of service, youth have limited opportunities to learn through interaction with others who differ from themselves. Stereotypes about others' disadvantages can be reinforced rather than challenged.

Social advocacy projects can be important in teaching youth about broader social and political systems and in increasing their understanding of systemic factors that contribute to social inequities and injustices (Search Institute, 2000). Participation in boycotts, voter education and registration drives, communication with politicians and media representatives, and participation in local, regional, and national political forums, such as town, state, or congressional meetings, are examples of social advocacy. Social advocacy can sometimes be structured to provide opportunities for youth to collaborate with members of other ethnic, racial, and socioeconomic groups. Advocacy activities can be important in engaging youth in political processes. Youth can set realistic goals and observe the success of their efforts, thus increasing the likelihood that they will engage in social advocacy in the future. Often, however, results are not achieved quickly. It is critical, therefore, to help youth to sustain interest and not become disillusioned when gains are not made in a short period of time.

In service activities focusing on education for social change, youth teach others about social issues that they have studied. By teaching others, youth hope to stimulate dialogue about important social issues and help to effect social change. Whereas tutoring involves teaching others specific academic skills, education for change seeks to share information and knowledge with a community group. Public presentations on health issues, such as domestic violence, sexual harassment, or HIV/AIDS education, can be directed towards changing public attitudes and behavior. These activities build positive perceptions of youth as resources in their communities, enhance youth leadership skills, and often build community knowledge important for involvement in advocacy activities. Direct contact with persons in need of services or diverse populations may not be involved. These activities may thus not include the kinds of direct experiences that enhance social understanding of complex issues. It is, therefore, often desirable to link the academic study and teaching of a social problem with direct contact with persons who have experienced that problem. Talking to people with different views on social issues can also help students to understand better the complexity of the issues they have studied.

PROGRAM EXAMPLES

Over the past decade, the number and variety of youth community service programs across the country have proliferated. The quality of these programs has also increased with the development of standards to guide the development and implementation of community service and service-learning programs. These standards are summarized in chapter 4 of this book. With the advent of the Internet, communication and sharing of information across programs is now accomplished easily and frequently. The National Youth Leadership Council leads the Learn and Serve America Exchange through which schools and community organizations can be linked with peer mentors who provide assistance in the implementation of service-learning programs.

The National Youth Leadership Council, with sponsorship by the Corporation for National Service, has identified exemplary middle and high school programs across the country that integrate civic education, youth leadership development, and technology and include youth and adults in the governance of the programs. These are called the Youth F.E.L.L.O.W.S. Model School Project. In addition, five states (California, Maine, Minnesota, Oregon, and South Carolina) are currently participating in a Policy and Practice Demonstration Project (PPDP) sponsored by Learning In Deed and managed by the Education Commission of the States (ECS), a national organization that assists state leaders in shaping educational policy. Through its website, Learning In Deed also provides examples of Service-Learning in Action and identifies service curricula available on the web. In order to provide the reader with a further understanding of quality youth service programs, we will describe some of the programs in the Youth F.E.L.L.O.W.S. and PPDPs, as well as those presented through the Service-Learning in Action links.

Malcolm Shabazz City High School in Madison, Wisconsin, is an alternative public school that serves a diverse, multicultural community. In this school, service is linked with courses across a variety of curriculum areas, including commercial art, journalism, English, history, and science. Projects involve a variety of service activities, including community education, direct and indirect service, and social advocacy, as described above. A video project on teenage pregnancy is an example of community education. In this project, high school students conduct interviews and collect data pertaining to the topic of teenage pregnancy. They write a script and produce and edit a video that is given to community agencies and public schools to educate other teens. The project reinforces the research, literacy, and communication skills of the teens producing the video, while providing an opportunity for teens to engage with a topic that is vital to their lives. By sharing their video production with other schools and agencies, the students enable other young people to learn from the material presented in the video.

Another example of community education is a course on social justice that examines misperceptions, fears, and stereotypes about persons with disabilities. Students learn about the history of the Americans with Disabilities Act (ADA), study disability rights and terminology, and participate in "inclusion" exercises, which provide insights into the experience of being disabled. At the conclusion of their studies, students develop a project that teaches others at their school and in the community about disabilities.

In an example of direct service activity, students in another course at Shabazz High study the issue of poverty in America at the local and national levels. Readings, videos, and guest speakers inform their academic understanding of the prevalence, causes, and impact of poverty in the lives of Americans. Students go into the community to provide services to the poor in Madison, Wisconsin. The opportunity to link readings and discussion with direct interaction with those persons experiencing poverty allows students, under the guidance of their teacher, to confront stereotypes concerning the poor and to examine the societal structures that contribute to economic inequality.

Direct service through mentoring other students is exemplified by projects in writing and illustrating stories for children. High school students from courses in English and art conducted a survey of first-grade students to learn about their favorite animals, colors, and activities. The high school students also studied existing children's literature with a focus on art mediums, the vocabulary of early readers, and other methods for writing and illustrating books. Pairs of students from art and English classes worked together to write and illustrate a first-grade reading book. Each first-grade student was presented with one of the books, related to the young student's favorite animal or activity. The presentation of their personal book developed by the high school students is intended to increase reading interest and motivation among the first-grade children. (Descriptions of service courses at Shabazz High can be found at their website: http://www.madison.k12.wi.us/shabazz/.)

Advocacy is practiced in courses at Malcolm Shabazz, at White River High School in Buckley, Washington, and at the Sharon Middle School in Sharon, Massachusetts. Shabazz students study immigrant populations by researching areas of the world from which local citizens have left through exile or escape. Students interview members of their community to learn more about immigrants' experiences in their homelands and in their new community. Following this, the students write letters to public officials advocating for international human rights and an end to the violence that many refugees experience in their homelands. This type of project enhances communication skills and empathy, as well as knowledge of history, geography, and political processes.

At White River High School, science students helped to save the Chinook King Salmon, which was nearing extinction. This project combined advocacy, community education, and youth mentoring. Student efforts to help preserve the fish included DNA fingerprinting and stream monitoring using Calculator-Based Laboratory Systems. In terms of community education, the students wrote a newsletter that informed community members about the status of local rivers and streams. They were involved in advocacy by presenting their findings to the local city council. In terms of youth mentoring, they worked with younger students at the local elementary school to teach them about the salmon and what needed to be done to save them. More than 1,000 Chinook King Salmon now return to the local hatchery every year. This project enabled students to see a direct relationship between what they were learning in their science class and a concern of their local community. Furthermore, the students learned the powerful lesson that they could do something about this critical concern through community education and political advocacy.

Service-learning is infused throughout all grades in the Sharon Public Schools in Massachusetts. Eighth-grade students became involved in studying local and national political issues and decided to write editorials, expressing their views on important topics. Editorial writers from state and local newspapers visited the school and discussed editorial writing with the students. Writing mentors at the high school worked with middle school students to improve and refine what they had written. The completed editorials were sent to local newspapers. This type of project teaches students the skills and methods to become active and engaged citizens. They learn to develop their opinions and communicate them effectively and learn that their voices are important. Some may have been exposed to new career options and many likely gained in feelings of personal and political efficacy. (Further description of this and other service courses can be found at the following website: http://www. LearningInDeed.org/tools/examples.html.)

Through the Ordinary Heroes project, students at the Sharon High School partner with fifth-grade students to identify and interview local citizens who have made "extraordinary contributions" to the community. The project takes place over the course of an entire academic year, during which time small groups of cross-age students (three fifth-graders and three ninth-graders) meet to develop criteria for identifying "ordinary heroes" and to generate interview questions. The activity ends with a formal ceremony attended by all of the students during which eight to ten "ordinary heroes" and their families are honored by local state representatives and town officials. Students gain pride in their community and a better understanding of local civic issues and learn how ordinary people can do something that makes a difference. This project is one of fourteen community service lessons published by the Massachusetts Department of Education, Learn and Service America, and the Massachusetts Service Alliance, in a guide entitled, "Community Lessons: Promising Curriculum Practices," by Julie Bartsch and contributing teachers. (This guide can be obtained by writing to the Massachusetts Department of Education Learning Support Services, 350 Main Street, Malden, MA 02148.)

Waterford High School in Connecticut began to provide community service learning just six years ago, and the number and quality of offerings have increased rapidly. A Learning Through Service Committee is composed of students, who are active in inspiring, designing, and consulting with teachers on service-learning projects. This school has taken seriously the belief that youth have many skills to offer and that youth choice in planning and selecting service activities enhances student outcomes. Guided by these beliefs, the school has created a student-run committee that has a substantial voice in the development of service offerings. One example of Waterford's service offerings is the production of a "Meet the Candidates" video by students in a Contemporary Affairs class. The video presented every candidate running for office on the Waterford ballot and was broadcasted by local television stations throughout the election season. Through this type of effort, the students became informed about political issues and choices and provided a service that educated the public at large, with the potential of increasing voter participation in the elections. This type of student product also provides a positive view of youth to the community at large. Another noteworthy community service undertaking is "Friends Forever," an intergenerational oral history project in which ninth-grade students and local senior citizens share their ideas on the meaning of life. The project concludes with a dinner, coordinated by the students, which celebrates all of the participants. From an academic perspective, this project enhances student literacy. From a personal growth perspective, student understanding and empathy can be increased. From a community perspective, students gain increased respect for the knowledge and life experiences of the senior citizens, who receive affirmation, companionship, and recognition.

Spring Valley High School in South Carolina, a Learning In Deed Policy and Practice Demonstration Project (PPDP), provides an example of how service can be integrated with foreign language learning. Students studying Spanish become immersed in Spanish language and culture through work with Hispanic migrant communities. Students work in teams to learn of the needs of migrant families and develop proposals (written in Spanish) for assisting them. Students prepare healthy meals to share with the families they are visiting. Funds to support the projects are solicited through local businesses and through fundraisers. At the end of the projects, students and migrant families enjoy a festive gathering that includes food, worship, gifts, and games. Throughout the course, students write about their work with the families, what they are learning, and how it is affecting them and the participating family members. The students' writings are submitted to their class as part of a portfolio presentation.

Among PPDP schools in Oregon, students at Crook County High School learn about the practical applications of mathematics, whereas students at Powers High School learn about practical applications in the life sciences. The Ochoco Dam in Crook County had experienced soil erosion and water displacement. Crook County students applied math skills to measure water displacement. After converting this data into equations and developing charts and graphs, students presented findings to the community and local officials on the impact of erosion on water levels. Powers High students developed research skills in biology as they studied the beneficial aspects of bats and their biological and physiological make-ups. The students built bat houses and placed them in suitable community habitats in order to increase the bat population to a desirable level. Students wrote up the findings of their research and observations for publication in *Bat Conservation Magazine*. (See http://www.Learning InDeed.org/ppp/ for further description.)

The application of science to the solution of local environmental concerns has also been a focus of several service-learning initiatives among PPDPs in the state of Maine. In Wells, physics students are studying coastal erosion and have found their knowledge of wave mechanics to be pertinent to understanding erosion issues. The impact of harbor dredging and the construction of jetties by the Army Corps of Engineers are controversial issues in the local region and the students have become knowledgeable experts, contributing important technical information to inform this debate. Seventh-graders in Fort Kent conducted studies of water quality and environmental impact at DeBoulie Mountain. In Lubec, students adapted an abandoned cannery for use as an aquaculture research center. (See http://www.LearningInDeed.org/ppp/ for further description.)

In Minnesota, another PPDP state, Public Achievement, a division of the Center for Democracy and Citizenship in Minneapolis, provides a civic education program that is offered at the Andersen Open School for youth from the ages of eight to fourteen. The program promotes community-based learning as students become involved in planning and creating products that are of value to the community and make the accomplishments of youth visible and prominent to community members. Through the process of developing and carrying out these projects, youth are taught skills in teamwork, intergroup communication, planning, responsibility, and accountability that are critical for effective participation in democratic processes. (See http://www.LearningInDeed. org/ppp/ for further description.)

Examples of service-learning curriculum can be easily accessed through the Internet. This is a great and free resource for persons developing service-learning programs. According to Learning In Deed, curriculum examples can be found on the websites of the following organizations: America's Promise, Close Up Foundation, Earth Force, and others. More information on each of these organizations, including their website addresses, can be found in the organizations chapter of this book. Through the Boston Teachnet website (http://boston.teachnet. org), the Boston Public Schools provides examples of service curricula that can be adapted by teachers and students everywhere. Each of the examples is linked with Learning Standards as specified by the Boston Public Schools and the commonwealth of Massachusetts and with examples of classroom, community, and career activities. Mary Ellen Bower, the School-to-Career Coordinator at West Roxbury High School in Boston, has developed a course for high school students who are enrolled in the Teach Boston career pathway, which provides students with exposure to careers in education. Through a project entitled "Literacy Leaders—Cross-School Mentoring," high school students tutor and mentor elementary school students, designated as "Book Buddies." The high school students schedule five read-aloud sessions with the younger students, complete reflection journals on the mentoring process, write a Reading Letter to the parents of the young children, organize and conduct a Literacy Poster Contest, and participate in a Teacher Shadowship Day, during which they learn more about the daily activities of the teaching profession. The range of activities offered in this project enhances the literacy skills of the students and develops school-to-career competencies. Mrs. Bower and her students have presented their work at a statewide Department of Education conference, have testified before the Massachusetts State Legislature, and received an All-Stars 2000 award for community service presented by Fleet Bank (http:// boston.teachnet.org/).

FOR YOUTH: HOW TO GET INVOLVED IN SERVICE

Through service, teens all over America have achieved great accomplishments that they may not have thought possible. Ten million young people who volunteer each year have made a difference in areas such as health, education, the environment, hunger, and politics (DiGeronimo, 1995). Teens have built parks, cleaned up toxic waste, sponsored food and clothing drives, and taught children to read. These are only a few of the many possibilities for teens who want to make a difference through volunteering. Teenagers often hear that they are too young or inexperienced to participate in various projects with adults, but they can apply their enthusiasm and talents in constructive ways through community service. Volunteers come from diverse backgrounds and families. They may do well in school, or may not like academic work (DiGeronimo, 1995). They may enjoy physical activity or prefer to figure out problems in their heads. There is a volunteering activity that is a good fit for every teenager who wants to be involved.

Most young people recognize the numerous benefits of volunteerism. They see volunteering as a way to make a difference, have fun with friends, and meet other teens with similar interests. They also feel good about themselves for contributing to their communities. Teens further recognize that volunteering provides opportunities to increase skills and experience in areas of interest and make connections with their community, gain new insight, and grow to love the work that they do (Prudential, 1998; DiGeronimo, 1995).

We will now offer suggestions on how to choose a volunteer activity and effectively carry it out. We will identify existing organizations that youth can join and will provide tips for starting volunteer groups and projects.

There are several questions teens should ask themselves in order to identify volunteer opportunities for which they are best suited. First, think of an activity that you enjoy. Volunteering should be fun and you are more likely to stay involved in a project that you like. Think about your interests and what types of problems in your community concern you. What would you like to change? Next, think about what you are good at. For example, if you are good with animals, you may want to volunteer at the Humane Society, whereas if you are good at sports, you may want to volunteer as a coach for a community sports team. But do not worry if you cannot think of a talent you can use in volunteer work. Many organizations offer training to help you contribute more effectively to their organization and to succeed in volunteer work (Lawson, 1998).

Within any given area of concern, there are multiple opportunities for involvement. For example, if you are interested in protecting the environment, you can address issues of water or air pollution, forest preservation, global warming, or helping endangered species. Skills in biology, chemistry, law, politics, engineering, and education can all be used in volunteer efforts related to the environment. Environmental protection may include work in an office, such as making phone calls and writing letters to public officials. It may involve outdoor work such as collecting soil and water samples, planting trees, or cleaning trash from a public park. It may also include scientific analysis in a laboratory. Finally, people who enjoy teaching can help to inform and educate others about environmental issues. Therefore, people with diverse interests and talents can find ways to volunteer to help solve environmental problems (DiGeronimo, 1995).

Another setting in which teens often volunteer is health care. There are many reasons to volunteer in this area. Maybe you hope to be a nurse or doctor someday. Perhaps someone close to you has been sick and you would like to help others in the same situation, or maybe you have never spent time in a hospital and are curious to see what it is like. All of these are good reasons to volunteer. As with the previous example, people with many different skills and interests can volunteer in the health field. If you like to work with people, you may be able to help with patient admissions, sit with patients in recovery, deliver flowers, or help transport patients in their wheelchairs. If you prefer less direct contact with patients, you could help in a lab or mailroom or work in reception. For volunteer work in health care, compassion and responsibility are important qualities. However, if you feel uncomfortable around people who are ill, this may not be a good match for you. You can contact your local hospital or clinic to find out more about volunteering in the health care area (DiGeronimo, 1995).

Your school, local church or synagogue, YMCA, or other service organizations in your community can be helpful resources for learning about service opportunities. Many teens are involved in service-learning programs through their schools. Ask your parents, friends, and teachers if they have any suggestions for you, or read the local newspaper for ideas. Depending on your interests, you could find volunteer opportunities at hospitals, homeless shelters, day care centers, homes for the elderly, or at your town or city hall. Most communities have many ongoing volunteer projects that you may not know about until you ask. National organizations, such as the American Red Cross and the Corporation for National Service, also offer information about volunteer opportunities. You can receive information about these organizations by writing to them or going to their Internet website. The contact information for these specific organizations, as well as several others, is available at the Internet site http://www.prudential.com/community. We have also profiled many of these agencies in the organizations chapter of this book. For more volunteering ideas and information, see the Internet sites section of chapter 6 of this book.

Once you decide where you would like to volunteer, it is a good idea to find out about the structure of the organization and the expectations of volunteers. Before you commit yourself to a volunteer organization, it is important to consider how much time and effort you are willing to invest as a volunteer (Prudential, 1998). It is easy to over-commit yourself and become overwhelmed with your volunteer obligations, so it is a good idea to begin with a few hours and gradually increase your time commitment when you understand the expectations for your involvement.

Some youth are able to find a group or organization that is a good match for their volunteering interests and talents. For other youth, existing organizations may not be consistent with what they hope to accomplish. If available opportunities are not a good match, or if you have identified a specific problem that you would like to address, creating your own volunteer project might be a good option.

The Kid's Guide to Service Projects (1995) and *The Big Help Book* (1994) identify steps to consider in creating your own service project. First, choose a project that addresses an issue important to you and find out as much as you can about that issue. Think about the potential benefits of a project and what you will need in order to accomplish your goal. Second, gather a group of people to help you with the project, as it is hard to complete a project on your own. You may recruit friends, parents, or others who share your interests and concerns. To check in with project volunteers and discuss the progress of the project, you may want to establish a regular meeting time. Third, you may need a responsible adult to sponsor your project. Fourth, you need a plan for your project, which includes setting specific goals and assessing their feasibility, establishing a timeline, and estimating the costs of your project. Step five involves finding out how the recipients of service feel about your project. At this stage, it is important to talk to the people you believe will benefit from your project to find out more about their needs and concerns, to ask how they would like to be involved, and to make sure that they feel that your project will be helpful. If the recipients do not think your plan will be helpful, you may want to use their suggestions to rethink your goals and develop a project that better matches their needs. Step six is deciding where your service project will take place. Step seven involves getting permission to perform your service activity. This will vary depending on your age and the type of project, but you may need permission from adults such as your parents, teachers, school principal, or other involved adults. Steps eight and nine involve publicizing your project and raising the funds needed to complete it. You may want to make flyers or put an ad in your school or com-munity newsletter to let people know about the project and to gain sup-port for your work. Local organizations or businesses may also provide needed money or other support. The tenth and final step is to evaluate your project. You may want to evaluate it at several points during your volunteer involvement, as well as after completion, to determine how your project is going and to identify any needed adjustments that should be made. This evaluation can involve talking to those perform-ing the service as well as to those receiving the service. You may also take time to reflect on your experience and how it has affected you. The evaluation will help you explore your own growth throughout the proj-ect, as well as to understand what you have done well and what you might want to change for your next service project.

FOR ADULTS: HOW TO ORGANIZE A YOUTH SERVICE PROGRAM

The following section provides concrete steps that may be helpful for adults in developing service-learning programs. In coordinating a ser-vice project, adults, like youth, have the option of joining an existing ser-vice project or organizing their own. Both options will be presented, with suggestions that are relevant to adults in schools, youth service agencies, and faith-based institutions who are thinking about involving youth in community service.

Clearly, there are advantages to joining an established service program because of the existence of established structures and supportive mech-anisms. In Conrad and Hedin's *Youth Service: A Guidebook for Devel-oping and Operating Effective Programs* (1987), the authors outline three basic steps to follow in collaborating with established service-learning programs. This guidebook is a classic in the service-learning field and contains ideas of ongoing relevance. The first step involves identifying local programs and agencies with which to collaborate. Con-tact people you know who are connected with already established ser-vice projects. Explore your neighborhood and local community centers to learn more about the problems facing your community, as well as opportunities currently available for youth volunteers. Accessing com-munity directories and newspaper/newsletter listings as well as contacting service agencies, churches, synagogues, and local government agencies to better assess community needs and opportunities can be helpful in this process. The second step involves contacting agencies about your interest in partnering in a service-learning effort. Conrad and Hedin (1987) recognize that the choice of whom to contact is important in determining the success of your efforts. Ideally, your first contact in an organization should be with someone you know or with whom you have a previous connection. This individual will likely be responsive to your interest and may help you strategize your approach with other organization members. If you do not have any connection to an organization, you may want to begin by proposing an initial visit or brief project that involves little risk or investment on the part of the organization. You should also emphasize the ways in which your proposal will benefit the organization. At this initial meeting, you should convey the central goals of your program, the characteristics of youth participants, the available time commitment, and so on. Communication with partnering organizations should be clear as to the nature of potential student service activities. Agencies need to be made aware that youth involvement should be challenging and meaningful, as these aspects of service are critical to maintaining youth interest and involvement. The authors' final recommended step is to explore the interests and skills of involved youth. While this step is listed last, it may occur at any point in the project development process and may be useful in determining agencies of interest for service participation. This step will help to ensure a match between the abilities and interests of youth and the ongoing projects identified in local agencies. Youth can brainstorm project ideas that incorporate their skills and interests. Agencies can then be contacted that are a good fit with the ideas developed by the group.

When there is no obvious fit or availability with an existing service program, you may seek to establish a new service-learning program within the structure of an existing organization. To begin this process, a typical first step is to perform a needs assessment of the local community. Exploring your neighborhood and accessing community centers and local directories may be helpful in identifying community needs. In addition, you may want to conduct interviews or administer a formal survey to assess general needs or to gain information on a specific issue. You should design your survey so that it provides concrete information that can help direct the action of your service project. (More information on survey use and development is available in Conrad and Hedin's guidebook.)

In order to develop a service-learning program that will become an ongoing, integrated part of an organization, a strong infrastructure that grounds service programs within the organization should be established. To accomplish this, service-learning programs need to develop strong leadership as well as a base of support from within the organization. The Search Institute (2000) provides recommendations for establishing this structure. First, a program coordinator should be designated, who will be responsible for bringing people and resources together around a core vision for community service. This person will also make sure that program tasks are distributed and accomplished. Next, a leadership team of youth and adults who will take responsibility for the design and implementation of service-learning projects should be put together. This team may consist of youth, organization staff, parents, community members, and others invested in the success of the program. Third, the Search Institute recommends developing a program vision that is consistent with the mission of the overall organization. A service program will be more successful and gain greater institutional support if it fits with organizational values and ideology. In order to accomplish this, you must clarify organizational goals, shape your program to fit with organizational strengths and priorities, identify obstacles, and determine how best to begin your service program. Fourth, find ways to tie your service program to existing activities of the organization. Service-learning may be integrated with existing projects. This will reduce the effort involved in creating an entirely new program and will strengthen existing organizational initiatives. Fifth, support from organizational leaders is critical to the success of any service program. These leaders can support service projects by sharing enthusiasm, providing time and resources for program planning and implementation, making community connections, and recognizing service accomplishments. Support from other stakeholders, such as youth, teachers, community members, and parents, may also help to expand the resources and support for service projects. They may provide assistance with the interpersonal, logistical, and financial needs of your program. Finally, it is important to plan for long-term change. Do not expect organizations to change overnight. Develop long-term goals and plans for implementation that recognize realistic limits and speed of change (Search Institute, 2000).

Once you have identified core goals for your service program and established a base of institutional support, you can begin planning specific service activities. This involves identifying the nuts and bolts of service, such as what your project will be, where it will take place, and who will be involved. Before involving youth, it may be helpful to create a list of possible service options that have the greatest potential for youth growth, learning, and contribution to a chosen area (Search Institute, 2000).

Recruitment of volunteers is an essential part of service projects. Conrad and Hedin (1987) present several steps for effective recruitment. First, be specific in your recruitment messages. Youth are more likely to respond to a specific issue than to a general invitation to volunteer. Next, convey that volunteering is both fun and challenging. Adults often underestimate the desire of youth to engage in meaningful challenges. Youth respond positively to challenges that match their interests and abilities. Recruitment should be an ongoing process. Consistent efforts to publicize service-learning and to reach out to new and diverse groups of volunteers are central to sustaining service projects. School and community newsletters, presentations by current volunteers, bulletin boards, and brochures can be used to keep youth and others in the community informed and excited about current service activities (Conrad & Hedin, 1987).

Preparation of youth for volunteer service is another critical element in successful program development. Youth should be informed of previously established project goals and learn about those persons who will be the recipients of their service. Youth should have opportunities to learn about the involved communities, what to expect from their service involvement, and how to behave appropriately in their service contexts. They should also be prepared with the skills and understanding necessary to be effective service participants. Ideally, youth should also be included in the identification and acquisition of needed resources for the project, assessment of realistic project goals, and planning for their roles in project implementation. Adult leaders, particularly those unaccustomed to working with youth, should be prepared for work with young people. This can be accomplished by recognizing and challenging negative assumptions about youth and by building intergenerational relationships with participating youth (Search Institute, 2000). Youth should also be invited to take ownership of their involvement by assuming leadership roles in project design and planning.

Once a project is underway, the focus shifts from preparing youth for service to providing support throughout the service experience. Continued supervision and training are necessary to help youth cope effectively with on-site changes and difficulties and maintain ongoing enthusiasm for the project. For example, youth may need ongoing support and education for their interactions with people who differ from themselves. Whether differences are cultural, socioeconomic, or intergenerational, youth may need support to adjust to unaccustomed roles and new connections. In this stage, it is important to balance youth service contributions with a focus on youth learning and development (Search Institute, 2000). Adults coordinating service projects should ensure that service sites provide ongoing opportunities for youth development. Establishing a forum in which youth can address multiple interpersonal issues that arise through their service work is critical to learning. A powerful way to support youth growth during a service project is through the process of reflection. Reflection entails setting aside time and space for youth to think about and discuss their service experiences and serves to reinforce the connection between concrete service activities and youth learning. Through this process, youth focus on how their project makes a difference, how it feels to engage in service work, and how this experience might impact other aspects of their lives (National Institute on Out-of-School Time, 1999). (Further discussion of the reflection process can be found earlier in this chapter.)

Periodic recognition of youth service efforts is another important support for youth participation. Recognition can come in many forms, such as verbal support and encouragement, celebratory activities, certificates of completion, or public recognition. Celebration of youth accomplishments can be integrated with discussions of youth goals and expectations for their continued work on a project. When youth have made extraordinary contributions for their service, adults can nominate them for national awards, such as The Prudential Spirit of Community Awards (sponsored by Prudential Insurance Company and the National Association of Secondary School Principals), the Congressional Awards given by the U.S. Congress for volunteer public service, the President's Student Service Challenge given by the White House for outstanding community service, the Colgate Youth for America Award, and the Angel Soft Angels in Action. More information on service awards can be found on the SERVEnet website (see the Internet resources listing in chapter 6).

At all stages of service participation, keeping youth safe is a central concern of service-learning programs. A benefit of service-learning is that it allows youth to experience new environments and relationships. However, the exploration of new environments also requires care in minimizing risk to involved youth. Conrad and Hedin (1987) emphasize that while there are few cases involving negligence or abuse of youth in service programs, preventative planning is central to the creation of a positive and safe environment. Adults experienced in coordinating service-learning programs can be helpful in identifying areas of concern and suggesting preventative action. Implementing clear guidelines and policies for youth participation, providing regular opportunities to share questions and concerns, and training youth and adults to recognize and address risky situations can contribute to safe and healthy service experiences (Search Institute, 2000). Parents/guardians of involved youth should also be informed as to the specifics of youth volunteer participation and permission for youth participation should be obtained. It is also important to be aware of the insurance policies specific to involved organizations, relating to transportation and to insurance coverage of volunteer sites and participating schools or agencies (Conrad & Hedin, 1987).

EVALUATION OF COMMUNITY SERVICE AND SERVICE-LEARNING PROGRAMS

Program evaluation for service-learning and community service programs is a recent but fast-growing area of inquiry. Due to the increase of service-learning and community service programs and funding for such programs, many stakeholders and decision-makers are demanding to know if these service programs are effective. The proponents of service-learning and community service programs make claims about the success of these programs. Teachers and administrators hope that engaging youth in community service will have certain benefits, such as enhancing citizenship and social responsibility, promoting personal development, developing academic skills, and increasing school engagement, as well as having a positive impact on the community. However, anecdotal evidence is rarely sufficient for funders, such as the federal and state government, foundations, and school districts. In an era of increasing school and government accountability, programs have to be able to document whether service programs meet their desired goals. The increasing call for the evaluation of service programs requires teachers and administrators to be aware of and familiar with the process of program evaluation.

This section reviews and addresses issues related to conducting program evaluations for a service-learning or community service program. Although an extensive discussion of this topic cannot be completed in this limited space, additional resources are provided for teachers and administrators interested in learning more about program evaluation. Research on service-learning and community service provides evidence about whether participating in service is beneficial, who benefits from engaging in service, and the types and aspects of programs that are most likely to contribute to beneficial outcomes. Evaluation research on service-learning and community service for youth specifically examines the development, implementation, and outcomes of particular programs to determine whether such programs are effective (Waterman, 1997). Evaluation can range from assessment of an individual's performance in a service program to the formal and systematic evaluation of a school or district-wide service-learning program. In addition, evaluations can be formative or summative. Formative evaluation answers questions regarding whether the program is doing what it says it is doing (i.e., the process of the service program). Summative evaluation answers questions regarding the extent to which a program's goals are being met or the impact the program is having on its participants, schools, and community (i.e., the outcome of the service program). Evaluations help identify highly successful programs, as well as programs that are not so successful. In addition, evaluations can be conducted throughout the course of the program in order to monitor the program and to facilitate necessary mid-course corrections to improve the program.

Evaluations are primarily conducted to answer questions raised by teachers, administrators, and funders. However, program evaluation is relevant to participants at all levels of the community service or service-learning project, including community members, parents, and participants. External audiences, including policymakers, educators, practitioners, and the media, may also be interested in program evaluation. Evaluation studies can provide reasonable hypotheses about expected outcomes or benefits of similar programs and also assess whether the benefits of a proposed program outweigh the costs of implementation. For example, parents of students in service-learning or community service programs can learn about the expected outcomes or benefits their children would receive from participating in the program. Considering the results of many evaluation studies collectively can be helpful in providing information for developing new programs or improving existing programs (Waterman, 1997). However, before assuming that findings from previous research can be applied to your program, the similarity between the programs evaluated and your program, including the type of program, the method of implementation, and the characteristics of the program participants (e.g., age, race/ethnicity, socioeconomic status, and so on) should be taken into consideration.

As noted previously, service-learning and community service programs may have wide-ranging goals and desired participant outcomes. For example, a school-based service-learning program may be designed to promote certain educational objectives and to provide opportunities for youth to reflect critically upon their experiences, whereas a community service program at a youth service agency may focus more on social development of youth and meeting community needs. An effective program evaluation assesses how well the program has achieved clearly articulated goals. Although many program goals include attitudinal changes, such as instilling an appreciation of diverse groups (e.g., the elderly and homeless), there is an increasing emphasis on examining behavioral outcomes (e.g., grades, hours of service provided, engagement in risk behaviors). Unfortunately, short-term service programs often do not result in large changes in behavior. Thus, it is important to identify realistic expected outcomes for a service program of a given length. An evaluation strategy must take into account what questions one wants answered, the purpose of the evaluation, the amount of funding allocated toward the evaluation, and the audience for the evaluation (Bradley, 1997).

Formal evaluation of service programs can be a complicated process, requiring technical skills, knowledge of research design, and the ability to perform statistical analysis. Often, it is difficult to discern the impact of the service program from the impact of other events that are happening at the same time (e.g., maturation, involvement in extracurricular activities). Evaluations can be conducted by people internal or external to the organization. Internal evaluations, which are completed by someone inside the organization or institution (e.g., a teacher or program administrator), offer an insider's perspective on the program and are generally less expensive. However, many teachers or program administrators at community agencies are not familiar with and have not received education or training to conduct program evaluations. Often outside or external funders may question the validity of the results and the objectivity of an internal evaluator. External evaluators generally are more costly than internal evaluators, but offer a third-party, objective perspective on the impact of the program. If a school or community organization either does not have sufficient evaluation expertise among its staff or if hiring an external evaluator or consultant is too costly, many resources and guides exist online and in libraries to assist program administrators in conducting evaluations. Teachers or community agency staff who are interested in conducting an evaluation of their program can form partnerships with or receive consultation from social scientists at colleges or universities who have knowledge and expertise in program evaluation and research. In addition, teachers who are responsible for leading service-learning courses can evaluate their programs by engaging in what is called action research. The *Action Research and Evaluation Guidebook for Teachers* (1998), edited by Jay Smink and Marty Duckenfield and sponsored by the National Youth Leadership Council, comprehensively discusses how teachers can engage in action research to evaluate their service-learning courses.

After deciding whether to conduct an internal or external evaluation of a service program, the next key step is determining what assessment data to collect in order to determine whether, and to what degree, the program goals are being fulfilled. Bradley (1997) outlines several key issues for evaluators to consider, including whether a service-learning program is meeting student goals, the quality of the community-school partnerships, the appropriateness of the program design and goals, the nature of reflection activities, the integration of service into the curriculum, the type of service experience at the community site, and the degree of support from teachers, schools, and parents. The number and complexity of issues to be considered make it important for the program coordinator (either teacher or community agency staff member) to meet with the evaluator before the program has been initiated in order to ensure that the procedures for data collection are in place. This meeting can also help to define more clearly the goals of the program. Other principal members of the project, such as students, community members, and parents, can also offer valuable input in the development of evaluation plans.

Program evaluation can focus on many different factors, such as the performance of service participants, the extent to which the school or agency supports service learning, and the impact on the school, community agency, and community at large. Because the majority of evaluation studies largely consist of survey measures that address short-term attitude change, Robert Serow (1997) has called for "holistic" assessment to evaluate more comprehensively outcomes of service programs. Holistic assessment evaluates the multifaceted dimensions of the service experience from multiple perspectives (including the perspectives of students, teachers, supervisors, service recipients, and community members).

Assessment data can be quantitative or qualitative. Quantitative data are generated through the use of surveys or other sources of program data, such as program and school records indicating the number of hours of service completed, attendance in service courses, number of clients served, grade point averages, and so on. Quantitative evaluation optimally follows rigorous methodological procedures, including the use of reliable and valid measures (instruments). Often quantitative studies use pretest/posttest designs (i.e., assessing variables of interest prior to participation in a program and then again after completion of a program) to assess change in attitudes and behaviors. In addition, the use of a control group (i.e., an equivalent group of students who are not participating in the service program or a group of students on a wait list), and, if possible, random assignment of youth to service and control groups are desirable to determine whether changes are, in fact, due to participation in the service program. Once data are collected, statistical analyses are conducted to look at the magnitude of changes in attitudes or behaviors.

Qualitative data are usually generated through open-ended or semi-structured interviews with participants. Qualitative research designs are often used to illustrate the experiences and perspectives of the participants in the program that are not readily captured by multiple choice or closed-ended survey questions. Interviews can be conducted with students, service recipients, teachers, community members, and administrators. Process observations and analysis of meeting minutes are other ways evaluators can collect information on whether the program is doing what it proposes to be doing. In his advocacy of the use of holistic assessment, Serow (1997) recommends the evaluation of student portfolios to document student performance and service impact. Portfolios represent the cumulative body of work that students produce while they are engaged in the service program and can serve as a means to identify which aspects of the program are working and which need improvement. Examples of products that are included in student portfolios are essays, journal writing, drawings, photographs, certificates or awards, research projects, term papers, computer projects, and other multimedia projects. Serow suggests that portfolios can also include testimonials from supervisors, community members, and service recipients about their experiences and the impact of the program.

Student outcomes have been the predominant focus of service-learning and community service program evaluation. Conrad and Hedin (1987) provide some considerations for assessing student outcomes. They note that student performance is often difficult to assess, especially when the service provided by students is not under the direct supervision of the community staff supervisor or the teacher. Programs should, first of all, keep track of where students volunteer, how many hours they spend or how often they volunteer, the type, quality, and amount of supervision or training the site provides, and the quality of the students' work. Teachers often consider the benefits of student service as intangible, and thus difficult to directly observe or evaluate. Teachers are often uncertain about whether they should assign letter grades or credit for hours served. If teachers decide to give letter grades, they must then decide which aspects of students' performance should determine the grade. Service-learning programs sometimes require student self-assessments to gain a better idea of the students' perceptions of their performance and engagement in the service activity. Overall, in order to assess student outcomes, a detailed and organized record-keeping system is needed (Conrad & Hedin, 1987).

The Search Institute (1994) developed a set of pretest and posttest surveys entitled Learning through Service, which can be used for the evaluation of service-learning programs. In addition to collecting basic demographic information on students, the surveys assess the number of hours students spend in various activities (including homework, band, sports, clubs, religious activities, and volunteer work), school performance and engagement, school attendance, risk and problem behaviors, self-efficacy, personal and social responsibility, acceptance of diversity, and future volunteer plans. In addition to some of the previous questions, the posttest questionnaire asks the students specifics about their service experiences, including number of hours, type of program, what type of duties and service students provided, and questions regarding how students perceived their service experiences in relation to other aspects of their lives. A number of additional instruments have been developed to assess a range of student outcomes. When using existing instruments, it is important to consider the instrument's psychometric properties, including its reliability and validity (i.e., whether it measures the construct in a consistent manner and whether the instrument is really measuring the construct of interest), as well as whether the instrument is appropriate for the age and developmental level of participants in the program. For example, a survey developed for college students may not be appropriate for students in the ninth grade.

Many school-based service-learning programs also assign written work as a means of encouraging student reflection on service experiences. As previously stated, written assignments can be used as qualitative data to assess the extent to which students are able to integrate their experiences doing service with the material learned in their classes. Yates and Youniss (1996), for example, evaluated the reflection essays of high school juniors who were volunteering in a soup kitchen and found that participation in community service enhanced students' abilities to think critically and abstractly about social, political, and moral issues. In addition to written reflection, students may be asked to participate in group or classroom discussions about their experiences, their perspectives about social issues, or how their service experiences relate to what they have learned in class. Students' participation in the discussion could then be assessed by the teacher or leader.

In addition to the student surveys, the Search Institute has also created the National Learning through Service Teacher/Staff Survey, which is completed by the coordinator of the service program. This survey assesses the goals of the program, types of service activities, the role of the coordinator, the planning and implementation of the program, and specifics about the program (e.g., number of years in operation, structure, location, amount of service performed, and percentage of student reflection time). This survey also assesses the coordinator's attitudes about service-learning and its impact (e.g., as a teaching method, whether it meets community needs, impact on school, and so on). More information on the Search Institute and available assessment instruments is provided in the organizations chapter and at the Search Institute website (http://www.searchinstitute.org).

Another assessment instrument that has been developed for evaluating service-learning programs is Shumer's Self-Assessment for Service-Learning (2000), which is available online with additional information and instructions through the National Service-Learning Clearinghouse (http://www.nicsl.coled.umn.edu). The instrument can be used for a specific course or a school- or district-wide program. The administrator answers a series of questions concerning program goals and activities, and then responds to twenty-three statements, which are "desirable goals for effective service-learning." Administrators rate their programs from "weak" to "strong" on five dimensions: context and culture; the rationale or purpose of the program; policies and structures; the role of teachers, students, community members, and administrators in the implementation of the program; and evidence that the program is meeting its goals. Therefore, this instrument helps the program administrator or evaluator to identify areas that need improvement. Moreover, it can be used at any phase of the development and implementation to both monitor and evaluate a program. The Compendium of Assessment and Research Tools (CART) is also an excellent online resource for program evaluators to find information on various assessment tools (http://cart.rmcdenver.com).

Supervisors at the community service site are also potential valuable sources of assessment data. Supervisors are often asked to complete checklists, ratings, or open-ended questions that evaluate students' performance, level of participation and level of engagement. Community members, who are service recipients, should also be consulted during an evaluation to assess the impact of the students' performance and the program as a whole on the community.

After the results are completed, the evaluator is responsible for communicating and disseminating the findings to all stakeholders in a timely manner and in a format that is appropriate for the targeted audience. The language of the report should be user-friendly and should explain how the findings relate to existing research and to the delivery of service-learning programs. The evaluator has many outlets for disseminating the findings, including online databases and clearinghouses, local and national conferences, and newsletters and professional journals. In addition, the program evaluator, in conjunction with the program administrator, can hold a workshop or in-service for teachers, parents, community members, and other administrators regarding the nature of the findings and implications for program improvement.

Overall, evaluation and research on service-learning is a dynamic and growing field. For more information on evaluation, please consult the National Service-Learning Clearinghouse (http://www.nicsl.coled.umn.edu) and the UCLA Service-Learning Clearinghouse Project (http://www.gseis.ucla.edu/slc/research.html). Funding is also available for service-learning research. The Learning In Deed website has posted links to potential funders and resource centers for individuals interested in acquiring funding for service-learning research (http://www.Learning InDeed.org/research/fndngsrv.html).

WHAT CAN BE ACCOMPLISHED THROUGH COMMUNITY SERVICE

Given the increasing emphasis on accountability and evaluation, a growing body of research has examined the varied hoped-for outcomes of service-learning and community service for youth. Stakeholders (parents, school administrators, teachers, community members, agencies, and funders) want some assurance that this activity or educational strategy has positive effects. In addition, they may want to know whether the services youth provide are making a difference for the community at large. Teachers, school administrators, and parents may also wonder whether school-based service-learning activities that take students away from classroom learning detract from student achievement.

In order to address these issues, several national studies have systematically examined the impact of service-learning programs. These studies lend support for some positive effects of service-learning and community service for youth. One national study (Melchior et al., 1999), completed at Brandeis University for the Corporation for National Service, investigated the outcomes of community and school-based service Learn and Serve America programs (more detail on this study can be found in chapter 4: Facts and Data of this book). Seventeen programs identified as well designed or "upper tier" were chosen to be included in the study and thus are not representative of all service-learning or community service programs in operation. Students primarily participated in education and human services projects (e.g., tutoring, service in nursing homes), with some students also involved in environmental and public safety projects. Another national study, which evaluated the Learn and Serve America Higher Education programs (Gray, Ondaatje, & Zakaras, 1999), also documented positive effects for student, community, and school outcomes (for further information on Gray and associates' study, see summary in chapter 4). The Learn and Serve America Higher Education programs seek to involve students in addressing community needs; improve student academic achievement, civic engagement, and social responsibility; and increase opportunities for students to serve through well-designed service-learning courses at the college level. The majority of students completed their direct service (either tied to a course or an extracurricular activity) in the field of education, including tutoring, mentoring, or serving as teacher aides.

Impact on Students

A report completed by Shelley Billig for Learning In Deed (2000a) examined the outcomes of school-based service-learning for students, schools, and communities. Student outcomes for service-learning and community service activities were categorized into personal and social development, civic engagement, academic skills and achievement, and career development outcomes. Some research has also examined the impact service-learning and community service have had on schools and communities.

Personal and Social Development

Overall, many research studies have examined the impact of service on students' personal and social development, including self-esteem, personal and social responsibility, social competence, and problem and risk behaviors. One of the earliest and most widely cited studies that examined outcomes of service-learning programs was conducted by Dan Conrad and Diane Hedin. In this national study of twenty-seven school-based service programs, Conrad and Hedin (1982) found that adolescents' level of moral reasoning, personal and social responsibility, self-esteem, and problem-solving increased. In general, research findings suggest that involvement in service-learning increases students' sense of self-efficacy, self-confidence, and self-esteem (Cognetta & Sprinthall, 1978; Yates & Youniss, 1996). Rutter and Newmann (1989) reported in their study of eight school-based voluntary community service programs that students gained on measures of personal development, but they did not increase in their level of civic responsibility. Other research has documented improvements in problem-solving, pro-social reasoning, and cognitive skills among college undergraduate service participants (Batchelder & Root, 1994; Eyler, Root, & Giles, 1998). While not all research has found significant differences in quantitative measures of self-esteem for middle school students, qualitative assessments (e.g., journal entries, essays, and interviews) have supported the notion that service activities increase student self-esteem (e.g., Johnson & Notah, 1999).

In one of the first large-scale studies that used quantitative measures to assess a range of outcomes for a number of service programs, Blyth, Saito, and Berkas (1997), of the Search Institute, completed an evaluation of the National Service-Learning Initiative and the Generator Schools project, which found mixed results over a range of outcomes. Regarding personal and social development, the majority of students reported that they were able to get to know the people they worked with at least somewhat well and 68 percent of the students built relationships with other youth in the program. The majority of students (56 percent) also reported that it felt good to help people through participation in service. Surprisingly, Blyth and colleagues found that self-esteem of student participants significantly decreased, and there were no changes in their self-efficacy. In addition, this study found that students who participated in service-learning programs exhibited less socially responsible attitudes concerning the environment and less responsibility toward others in need than those individuals who did not participate. The authors noted that students had relatively positive attitudes on these measures to begin with, so it was difficult to effect positive change. Limitations of this study, including varied programs and the lack of control or comparison groups, decrease confidence in the findings. More recently, the Brandeis study (Melchior et al., 1999) of well-designed Learn and Serve America

programs found that the overall group of participants did not show significant changes in social and personal development compared to a
group of students who were not participating in service-learning programs.

Another goal associated with many service-learning programs is
increasing student appreciation of diversity (Yates & Youniss, 1996).
Research has found that students' attitudes improve toward the groups
they serve (Conrad & Hedin, 1982). In the Brandeis Learn and Serve
America study (Melchior et al., 1999), students also exhibited significant
short-term increases on acceptance of cultural diversity. However, Blyth
and colleagues (1997) did not find increases overall in youth's acceptance
of diversity. One exception was a program involving sixth-graders, which
did reveal significant changes, perhaps indicating either a greater impact
for younger children or that the program was more effective in promoting this goal. The Learn and Serve America Higher Education study
(Gray et al., 1999) found some modest positive outcomes for undergraduate service-learning participants on measures of interpersonal skills and
an increase of appreciation for diversity.

In addition, research supports that participants in service-learning
programs tend to report lower levels of alienation and behavioral problems than nonparticipants (Stephens, 1995; Yates & Youniss, 1996).
Eccles and Barber (1999) also found that adolescents who participated
in prosocial activities (including church and volunteer activities) were
less likely to be involved in risk behaviors, including drug use and tru-
ancy. Furthermore, the evaluation of a national school-based, volunteer
service program indicated that the program achieved its goals of reducing rates of teen pregnancy and school drop-out (Allen et al., 1997). A
study by Hart, Atkins, and Ford (1998), using data from the National
Longitudinal Survey of Youth, also found that teens who volunteered
were less likely to engage in five out of seventeen problem behaviors
during the course of the year. Similarly, O'Donnell and colleagues (1999)
found that participation by middle school students in a community
service-learning course integrated with the health curriculum was associated with decreases in violence and unprotected sexual activity.

However, not all studies have found that service programs decrease
risk or problem behaviors. Blyth and colleagues (1997) found no significant differences on six measures of risk behaviors after students participated in a service-learning program. More recently, the Brandeis study
(Melchior et al., 1999) found that service participants across all age levels did not demonstrate significant reductions in problem behaviors.

However, middle school students engaged in service programs were less likely to have been arrested in the past six months than the comparison group of middle school students.

Civic Engagement and Volunteer Service

Overall, research indicates that service-learning and community service can provide students with opportunities to develop civic and social responsibility, including concern and responsibility for one's community, identification and involvement with community institutions, and awareness that one can make a difference through individual and collective action. In the Brandeis Learn and Serve America study (Melchior et al., 1999), high school service-learning students demonstrated significant positive increases in service leadership and civic attitudes (including appreciation of diversity, leadership in service, and social and personal responsibility), although middle school students did not exhibit any increase in civic engagement. Overall, increases in civic attitudes were relatively small because most participants began the program with strong and positive civic attitudes. Service leadership, including awareness of the needs of the community, knowledge of how to develop and implement a community service project, confidence in one's ability to make a difference in the community, and current and expected future level of commitment to service, increased more than other civic attitude measures.

Hamilton and Zeldin (1987) also examined the effects of service-learning among high school students who were assigned to a placement in a government office. Students completing service in the government offices showed significant increases in their self-reported political efficacy (i.e., competence in doing political work, respect for government, and belief that government is responsive to people's needs). In several studies, however, community service did not result in gains in civic involvement (Blyth et al., 1997; Rutter & Newman, 1989).

Youniss and Yates (1997) completed an in-depth qualitative case study of 160 parochial high school students who were participating in a required year-long social justice program through which they provided twenty hours of volunteer work at a soup kitchen for the homeless. Overall, their findings indicated that the school-based service program provided opportunities for students to become more politically aware, develop a political identity, and increase feelings of social responsibility. Regarding future service, 80 percent of the students indicated that they were going to continue to engage in service the following summer. In addition, follow-up of former students who had completed the social justice program revealed that 44 percent of the students performed some type of voluntary service after completion of the program and 45 percent completed service since high school graduation. Other research has also supported that students who are participating in service-learning reported that they are likely to continue to volunteer in the future (Conrad & Hedin, 1981, 1982). In a review of the literature examining longitudinal studies to uncover how service involvement is related to civic participation and engagement in adulthood, Youniss, McLellan, and Yates (1997) found that high school students who took part in community service or volunteered for school government were more likely than students who did not participate to be actively involved in community organizations and to vote fifteen years later or more.

These findings are also supported with college students. Astin and Sax (1998) found in their study of community service participation by undergraduates at forty-two colleges that students who participated in community service exhibited increases in civic responsibility and development of life skills, as well as increases in understanding community problems. The Learn and Serve America Higher Education survey (Gray et al., 1999) found that students who participated in service-learning reported higher levels of civic responsibility, including an increased likelihood that they would volunteer in the future and actively attempt to make social change than students who did not participate in service-learning. Another national study of twenty undergraduate service-learning programs with approximately 1,500 students also found significant changes in civic efficacy and attitudes (Eyler & Giles, 1997). Giles and Eyler (1994) also found that undergraduates' commitment to volunteer service increased during the semester following participation in community service. In another study, Markus, Howard and King (1993) randomly assigned undergraduates to a political science course that required twenty hours of community service and found that students exhibited increased political efficacy. Other research also indicates that the majority of youth in service-learning programs feel as if they can make a difference in their communities (Billig & Conrad, 1997; Scales & Blyth, 1997).

Student Academic Learning

Student academic learning is a critical goal for many service-learning programs as educators seek to help students better understand abstract academic material by making it relevant to the real world. Some research has found that students' grades do improve when they are involved in service-learning courses (e.g., Dean & Murdock, 1992; Markus, Howard, & King, 1993; O'Bannon, 1999; Shumer, 1994). Eccles and Barber (1999) found that adolescent participation in prosocial activities (including a broad range of activities, such as church and community services) was associated with positive academic outcomes. Johnson and colleagues (1998) found that ninth-grade students who volunteered had higher grades than student who did not volunteer. Some research also suggests that attendance is better at schools offering service-learning (O'Bannon, 1999), and that students who participate in service-learning have higher attendance rates than students who do not participate (Shumer, 1994).

The Brandeis study (Melchior et al., 1999) also investigated educational outcomes and found that participants, as a group, showed increases in school engagement and math grades compared to nonparticipants. Middle school students were more likely to have higher social studies grades and high school students were less likely to have failed one or more courses over the year and had higher math grades than nonparticipants. Overall grades (core grade-point average) did not significantly change, however. Therefore, it is difficult to conclude that service-learning participation has a considerable impact on academic achievement, but this study reveals some modest beneficial effects on student learning.

In higher education, overall, research findings on academic indices are mixed. In the UCLA study (Astin & Sax, 1998), service-learning participants exhibited increases in grade-point average, as well as more contact with faculty, higher educational aspirations, and higher self-reported academic self-concept. Another study, which used random selection to control for selection effects, also found that undergraduates in the service-learning course had higher grades than students not enrolled in a service course (Markus et al., 1993). However, the Learn and Serve America Higher Education study (Gray et al., 1999) did not find any significant differences between the group of service-learning participants and comparison group on measures of academic skills, including writing, quantitative reasoning, and analytical skills.

It appears that it is more likely that students will learn more in service-learning courses if their service experiences are tied to the academic content of the course. For example, Hamilton and Zeldin (1987) found that students participating in a service placement within government increased their knowledge about politics and local government more than students in a wait-list control group. Similarly, among college students, Cohen and Kinsey (1994) found that communications students who participated in service demonstrated greater knowledge of mass communications and the relevance of the material to the real world compared to students in the same course without the service component. Use of reflection activities has also been associated with student learning and increased problem-solving skills for students who are engaged in service activities (Conrad & Hedin, 1981, 1982; Eyler, 1993). Among college students, reflection and integrating service with course content have also been associated with better career preparation skills, conflict resolution skills, increased interaction with faculty members, and increased knowledge of community and social problems (Sax & Astin, 1997). As Stukas, Clary, and Snyder (1999) have contended, research supports that service-learning promotes student understanding when combined or integrated with systematic reflection activities and specific course content.

Career Exploration and Aspirations

Less research has focused on examining the impact of service-learning programs and community service activities on career development processes. However, a few studies indicate that students can gain knowledge and awareness of careers through service-learning. For example, students who participated in service-learning reported engagement in career exploration and development of career skills (Billig et al., 1999). Johnson and colleagues (1998) found that students who volunteered had higher educational aspirations, plans, and intrinsic work values than nonvolunteers. Also, in the Brandeis study (Melchior et al., 1999), teachers reported that service-learning increased student knowledge of different careers. However, the Learn and Serve America Higher Education study (Gray et al., 1999) did not find any significant differences between the group of service-learning participants and the comparison group on decisions about college majors or careers.

Impact on Schools

Although few studies have directly assessed the impact of service-learning programs on schools, some positive impacts have been documented. A study of service-learning programs in California has found that students and teachers increased in mutual respect, and the relationships and cohesiveness among peers and with teachers increased (Weiler et al., 1998). Furthermore, research suggests that service-learning can improve the overall school climate (Billig & Conrad, 1997; Weiler et al., 1998).

The Brandeis study (Melchior et al., 1999) indicated that, in general, teachers and administrators largely supported the service-learning programs in their schools. For example, 90 percent of the teachers reported that service-learning programs can be utilized as a means to improve students' social development and attitudes toward school. In addition, the majority of teachers (80 percent) reported that service-learning can help to improve student achievement.

The Learn and Serve America Higher Education study (Gray et al., 1999) also reported benefits for the university or college, including enhancing community-university partnerships. Community agencies were very involved in helping to design and implement the service programs with the universities or colleges, and many community agencies reported that the partnerships improved the relationships with the university or college. In approximately one-half of the agencies, faculty and staff consultation increased, participation on committees increased, the number of joint projects increased, and the use of community staff as instructors or consultants for college classes increased. Overall, institutional support for service-learning at the colleges and universities increased.

Impact on Communities

Only a few studies have examined the direct impact of youth service on communities, but some promising research findings in this area are emerging. In general, community members tend to view youth who serve in the communities as valuable contributors to the community (Billig & Conrad, 1997; Kingsland, Richards, & Coleman, 1995; Weiler et al., 1998). In the Brandeis Learn and Serve America study (Melchior et al., 1999), staff at the community agencies where students were involved in service activities were interviewed and almost all stated that their experience with the program was good or excellent. The majority of staff at the community agencies (96 percent) stated that they would have students volunteer again at the agency. The average rating of student performance was 8.6 on a scale from 1 (unacceptable) to 10 (best possible). In addition, 90 percent of the community agencies stated that students helped to improve the services of the agency to the community and 68 percent of the agencies stated that the students helped to increase service to the community by taking on new projects. Further-more, the staff at the community agencies reported that the services the youth provided resulted in direct benefits to the clients or members of the community that the agencies serve. Examples of such impacts on clients include improving the quality of life and mood and providing social interaction to the elderly in nursing homes. Having the students volunteer in the community agencies also resulted in more positive staff attitudes toward youth and toward working with the public schools. The Learn and Serve America Higher Education study (Melchior et al., 1999) also provided information on the impact of students' service on the communities. The majority of community agencies in this study were very satisfied with the service students provided. In addition, one-third of the staff at agencies reported that students contributed to an increase in services offered to the community and another third reported that students served as good role models for others.

Research on Long-Term Effects of Service

Overall, there is limited research on long-term effects of service-learning, as the majority of studies examine outcomes soon after the completion of service. One of the only national studies that examined long-term effects was the Brandeis study of the Learn and Serve America K–12 programs (Melchior et al., 1999). In this study, researchers examined whether the impact on civic engagement and school performance was sustained at a one-year follow-up. The find-ings of this study revealed that the majority of the impacts that were found in the short-term assessment did not persist one year later. How-ever, positive impacts on service leadership and science grades were sustained over time among high school students. In addition, the Bran-deis Learn and Serve America study (Melchior et al., 1999) examined whether or not students who continued to participate in service-learning activities during the following year showed any long-term impacts. The findings reveal significant positive impacts on school engagement, hours of volunteer service, and service leadership for students who continued to engage in service-learning. Clearly, additional research is needed to assess the impact of engaging in service-learning and com-munity service. Research on the outcomes of service should occur over periods of time that one would expect to see changes in attitudes and/or behaviors and should include both short-term and long-term assessments.

Limitations and Future Research

The majority of research that has attempted to document the effectiveness of and to inform best practices for service programs has been based on anecdotal evidence, qualitative accounts, or nonexperimental designs. However, recently service-learning and youth development researchers have begun to fill in the gaps with more structured research designs. In view of the fact that research on the outcomes of service-learning and community service is still relatively new, several limitations of this body of research should be considered.

Many studies are correlational in nature, which means that conclusions cannot be drawn with certainty that service experiences caused the outcomes. Studies are also limited by self-selection of students into service programs (Waterman, 1997). That is, students who choose to participate in service-learning or volunteer at a community agency may have certain personal and social characteristics, such as greater awareness and concern for social and political issues, that are related to the outcomes being assessed. Thus, when volunteers and nonvolunteers are compared, the differences may reflect preexisting personal characteristics, rather than effects of service participation. Furthermore, it is also important to consider that the results of many of these studies represent a group average of participants in each program or programs, and thus individual differences in outcomes are not reflected. In addition, caution should be taken in generalizing findings from studies with small numbers of participants or evaluations of a program at a single site to other populations and programs.

In evaluating research findings, consideration also needs to be given to the type and quality of service program being evaluated. Program structures vary in many different respects, including the number of hours of service expected, voluntary versus mandatory service, quality of supervision, amount of reflection, level of autonomy and responsibility given to volunteers, quality of program implementation, type of service activity, and so on. Research has begun to examine these factors, rather than assuming that all types of service programs have similar outcomes. Certain factors or elements of service programs have been identified that increase the likelihood of more beneficial outcomes (Stukas et al., 1999). For example, service-learning programs that give students more responsibility and autonomy in their service activities are more likely to have positive outcomes (Conrad & Hedin, 1981; Shumer, 1997). In addition, the duration and intensity of the service are thought to be important in producing positive outcomes (Eyler & Giles, 1997). (See chapter 4:

Facts and Data for a summary of recent findings concerning characteristics of effective programs.)

In addition, measurement of outcomes should be improved with future
research. Researchers should use instruments that have been developed
with sound psychometric properties to produce reliable and valid results.
Instruments must also be sensitive to the kinds of changes produced by
service experiences. Many studies indicate that students began the program with relatively positive attitudes on numerous measures, making it
difficult to obtain significant increases. Moreover, the majority of
research uses self-report measures in which individuals indicate whether
their attitudes or behaviors have changed. Although self-report measures
are useful in assessing individuals' attitudes and perceptions, multiple
sources of information obtained in different ways are important to assessing change. For example, students may report high levels of school
engagement, yet their teachers may report poor attendance and low levels of participation in class. Although students may be assured of the con-
fidentiality of their responses to evaluation questionnaires, they may still
believe that teachers or community partners will see their responses,
which might affect their grades in a service-learning course. Thus, students may be more likely to endorse prosocial behaviors and attitudes
than they are to actually engage in them or believe them.

Using rigorous research designs will help to determine whether or not
the service program is actually causing the desired outcomes. More longitudinal studies with experimental designs, using random assignment to
a service program or control group, are needed to assess the impact of
service on teens. As previously mentioned in the discussion of program
evaluation in this chapter, outcomes should be assessed that are relevant
to the goals of the service program. Unless the service-learning course is
explicitly designed to build academic skills, one should not expect to see
improvements in academic grades across the board. However, if a
service-learning component is integrated within a science course, such
as an ecology or environmental studies course that helps monitor water
supply or natural habitats in the community, then one should expect an
increase in students' knowledge of environmental issues that may be
reflected in their science course grades.

WHO VOLUNTEERS AND WHY

There is much that we have learned about who is most likely to participate in service activities. Research on the demographic characteris-

tics of volunteers, for example, reveals the ethnicity, sex, and socioeconomic status of volunteers. Personality characteristics and motivational
factors are also associated with volunteer involvement. What follows is a
summary of this information, as well as discussion of ways to increase
youth involvement and commitment to service work.

Results from two 1996 surveys, the National Household Education
Survey (NHES) of 7,940 students from sixth to twelfth grade and an
Independent Sector (IS) survey of 1,007 adolescents of ages twelve to
seventeen, provide a profile of youth involvement in volunteerism.
These surveys reveal that between 50 percent and 60 percent of youth
had volunteered at least once over the past year (Brown, 1999; Ward,
1997). According to the surveys, those who volunteer appear to differ
from those who do not volunteer based on individual, school, and community characteristics. A student who volunteers is likely to come from
a school that either requires or provides opportunities and support for
volunteering. Teen volunteers are most often in the eleventh or twelfth
grade and are involved in a variety of school activities. Teen volunteers
are more likely to live in communities with high economic resources,
high rates of home ownership, and low poverty levels. They will likely
have two parents/guardians living with them as well as an adult model
who performs community service. According to one study (Fitch, 1987),
78 percent of volunteers indicated that their parents were also involved
in volunteering. Adolescents who are female, White, and middle to
upper class are most often volunteers (Brown, 1999).

Although the above surveys reveal higher rates of volunteerism among
White, middle and upper class students, Cook (1999) suggests that volunteering is prevalent within African American and Latino communities
but is underreported. In the process of compiling a bibliography on service among African American and Latino youth, Cook contacted many
organizations that were practicing youth service but that had no official
records of volunteer activities. Much of the research on volunteerism
assesses student service involvement only within school settings. For
youth of color, volunteerism may take place in the context of community
organizations such as church groups, which are less likely than schools to
keep records of volunteer participation. Cook suggests that the oral traditions of minority cultures result in little written documentation of volunteer work. Some research suggests that urban minority youth
volunteer more than is typically documented. Lewis (1992), for example,
found that among urban tenth-graders, African Americans volunteered
at higher rates than any other ethnic group.

The confounding of race and social class complicates interpretation of data concerning the volunteer involvement of minority teens. Data from the National Longitudinal Study of Youth (NLSY), collected from 7,000 youth between 1986 and 1994, reveals that although 40 percent of White teens reported volunteer involvement, only 15 percent of Hispanic teens and 17 percent of Black teens reported involvement in volunteer activity. Hart and colleagues (1998) noted that these findings are surprising given the strong expressed commitment of urban minority adolescents to the welfare of others; they believe that this inconsistency can be explained by considering the social class of many urban minority youth. In the NLSY study, net family incomes of youth who volunteer averaged at $34,800, while those of youth who do not volunteer averaged at $24,000. Research of the U.S. Department of Education has also shown lower rates of volunteering among high school youth from low-income families (Search Institute, 2000). Families living in poverty may have fewer opportunities for formal involvement in volunteer activity. Having the internal and external resources to support service involvement may be critical in determining who gets involved. Poverty, rather than minority status, may thus explain commonly cited racial differences in rates of youth volunteerism.

Volunteerism is also related to school opportunities, which vary by socioeconomic status. One important finding from the IS and NHES surveys is that students attending a school that coordinates opportunities for volunteering are more likely to volunteer (Cook, 1999). A service-learning evaluation by the National Center for Educational Statistics (Skinner & Chapman, 1999) explored school volunteer opportunities in relation to student social class and ethnicity. Schools with at least 50 percent of students receiving free or reduced-price lunch were less likely than other schools to offer or organize community service or service-learning. Schools with over 50 percent minority enrollment were also less likely to provide service activities than were other schools. These findings suggest that minority students and students of lower socioeconomic status may be offered fewer opportunities for school participation in service activities. Schools with fewer resources may also be less likely to document their student activities, therefore appearing to have fewer volunteer opportunities than are actually available.

Gender differences in volunteerism are also worth noting. Typically, studies of youth volunteers show that girls are more likely to volunteer than are boys. While there appear to be consistent gender differences in rates of volunteering, these differences are often small and less predictive of volunteering than race and class distinctions. Findings of gender differences in volunteer involvement are consistent with research describing girls as more prosocial than boys (Rosenthal, Feiring, & Lewis, 1998). These findings raise questions about the socialization of boys and girls for volunteerism, which is not widely addressed by youth volunteer organizations.

Understanding motivations for youth volunteerism can be useful in thinking about ways to involve youth in volunteer efforts, to sustain volunteer involvement over time, and to improve the experience of youth involved in service projects. The desire to give to others and to help those in need is a commonly understood motivation for volunteer involvement. However, research suggests that there is no single motivation; instead, volunteer motivations are varied and complex (Serow, 1991). Motivational goals can be categorized as altruistic, egoistic, and social obligation. Altruistic goals involve a commitment to supporting the welfare of others. Egoistic goals related to one's own welfare, such as increasing one's skills, employment opportunities, or recognition. Social obligation goals involve repaying a debt owed to society (Fitch, 1987). A combination of altruistic and egoistic motivational categories is the most commonly documented motivation (Waterman, 1997). Commitment to volunteering requires both altruistic and egoistic motivations, which can be understood as a balance of costs and benefits (Fitch, 1987). People need to perceive themselves as gaining something from an interaction (such as service participation) in order to stay involved in the activity. Volunteer programs may be most effective in retaining volunteers when they focus on both altruistic and egoistic goals for participants.

Research on volunteer motivation can be applied to the practice of matching volunteer motivations with the goals, structure, and presentation of the volunteer organization. Sergent and Sedlacek (1990) suggest that organizations should review their own goals, objectives, and structures to understand better the type of opportunities offered to volunteers. Second, organizations should seek to recruit volunteers who have motivations that match the goals of the organization. Alternatively, if organizations hope to appeal to persons who have not traditionally been involved in volunteering efforts, they may want to adapt their programs to fit with the known motivations of these groups. Finally, the authors suggest that if the organizational structure is similar to the identified motivations of volunteers, volunteers are likely to be satisfied and continue their volunteer work (Sergent & Sedlacek, 1990). Research (Clary & Snyder, 1999) indicates that when recruitment messages are matched with the motivations of potential volunteers, individuals are more likely to volunteer. When volunteer activity matches the motivational reasons for volunteering, volunteers are also more satisfied with their experiences (Clary & Snyder, 1999).

Waterman (1997) describes several applications of knowledge concerning volunteer motivations. First, programs should be aware of the motivations of participating students, so as to help make volunteering meaningful to involved youth. Second, a broad range of motivational goals should be promoted, so as to meet the needs of diverse volunteers. Third, if programs have limited space for volunteer involvement, those whose motivations are consistent with program goals should be the first enrolled. Fourth, to the extent possible, volunteers should be matched with activities that are consistent with their stated motivations. Finally, volunteer programs should include periodic reviews of the extent to which volunteer activities meet the volunteers' expectations and assess changes in volunteer motivation over the course of a service project (Waterman, 1997).

Evidence presented throughout this book shows clearly that volunteerism benefits involved youth in multiple ways, developmentally, academically, and interpersonally. However, research also suggests that some youth may have greater access to volunteer opportunities than others. Service-learning projects can be valuable in urban contexts by bringing together students of diverse backgrounds in an environment of validation and empowerment (Keith, 1997). The next section of this chapter will consider ways to extend service opportunities to urban and low-income students.

SERVICE-LEARNING AND URBAN YOUTH

Although adolescence introduces new stressors into the lives of many teens, the challenges can be particularly great for teenagers who live in urban environments and attend inner-city public schools. Urban youth represent diverse ethnic/racial and linguistic backgrounds and typically have limited access to economic resources. In comparison with youth attending more affluent suburban high schools, urban high school students are at increased risk for negative social and school outcomes such as high drop-out rates, poor academic performance, alienation, and early sexual activity (Brown, 2001). Poor school performance has been associated with poorly funded schools, poor communication between the school and community, and pressure for students to assimilate to majority models in school (Maybach, 1996). In recognition of the unique challenges confronting urban high school students, service-learning has been identified as a promising way to engage positively urban youth in school and contribute to their academic and social development.

Many characteristics of effective service-learning programs are consistent with educational practices that have been found to be effective with urban students. For example, personal interaction and collaboration with teachers and other caring adult figures (Brown, 2001; Vasquez, 1994), student responsibility in designing and carrying-out service-learning interventions (Newman, 1991), adult perceptions of youth as capable and worthy of trust (Schine, 1997), and opportunities for critical reflection on social issues (Weah et al., 2000) are elements of service-learning practice that are effective in work with urban minority youth. Another characteristic that is increasingly recognized as important to the effectiveness of youth service in both traditional and urban settings is "student voice." Student voice means that students have active input in shaping their service experiences. Evidence suggests that when adolescents feel that they have helped to design and implement aspects of their own education, they also feel more invested in their learning. This need may be particularly salient for urban students, whose schools are often highly controlled, with little room for individual input into their academic experiences (Schine, 1997). Opportunities for students to gain voice in designing their own education may enhance school engagement and commitment. (For more information on youth voice, see the section on Integrating Youth Voice in Service-Learning in chapter 4: Facts and Data.) Collaborative projects can help students to feel more engaged with their schools and communities and with the process of their education (Keith, 1997).

Despite the apparent "fit" between the learning needs of urban youth and characteristics of effective service-learning programs, service-learning programs have also been criticized for failing to meet the needs of diverse youth, especially as pertaining to issues of racial and ethnic inequality (Weah et al., 2000). Although many youth struggle with alienation and dis-empowerment within school and social systems, these issues may be particularly salient for urban minority youth. The gap between school and community life has been identified as a critical problem for youth in urban schools (Schine, 1997). Students may experience little, if any, connection or communication between their lives at home and at school. Schools may have little understanding of students' home lives and may not recognize the importance of home and community connections to school success. Therefore, schools may inadvertently separate students from their natural support systems and force them to choose between school success and home and peer acceptance (Keith, 1997).

Research indicates, however, that connections among family, community, and school are important to student success and school engagement (Dornbusch, Ritter, & Steinberg, 1991), especially among African American adolescents (Slaughter & Epps, 1987). If community service programs seek to increase their effectiveness with urban adolescents, consideration must be given to building connections among the local community, the family, and the school. Service programs that provide a "family-like environment" have been associated with positive outcomes for urban youth (McLaughlin, Irby, & Langman, 1994). School personnel, students, family members, and community representatives may collaborate in designing community service programs that focus on issues within students' communities and involve community members. We will discuss this further in our presentation of the "change" model of community service.

Adult perceptions of urban youth, both in and outside of school environments, present another barrier to success. Teacher expectations for minority and low-income youth are often lower than for White, middle class students (Keith, 1997). Societal perceptions of urban youth as dangerous and potentially criminal rather than capable of positive outcomes also emphasize the deficits of urban youth and contribute to low expectations (Hart et al., 1998). Earlier in the chapter, we mentioned that society holds negative images of teens, but this is particularly prevalent for urban minority youth. McLaughlin and colleagues (1994) identify four myths that characterize negative social perceptions of urban youth. The first myth is that some youth are beyond hope. This suggests that negative outcomes are inevitable for struggling teens who are identified as "bad kids." The second myth is that urban youth are lazy. This myth suggests that youth problems result from negative, individual characteristics rather than from unjust social systems. The last two myths describe urban youth as constantly rejecting of discipline and as uninterested in any type of organizational involvement. These myths reinforce negative stereotypes and limit service approaches that offer the potential to engage urban youth in healthy and constructive ways (McLaughlin et al., 1994).

Schools often fail to recognize the strengths that youth carry from their cultural values and experiences (Keith, 1997; Maybach, 1996).

Within many schools, mainstream groups are recognized as the "holders of culture and knowledge," while those from different cultures or races are not acknowledged as possessing legitimate or valuable knowledge (Keith, 1997). To counteract these negative expectations, service programs should value the "local knowledge" or "culturally relevant learning" that youth possess. Acknowledging student "local knowledge" may connect students to their education and make learning more relevant to all students (Keith, 1997; Maybach, 1996). One example of a culturally relevant service initiative is a service-learning project instigated by sixth-graders in Washington Heights, New York City. Dominican students addressed a problem within their own community, using their "local" and cultural knowledge. After a fatal police shooting in their neighborhood, these students determined that the language barrier between White police and Dominican youth contributed to hostility between these groups. As part of their Spanish class, Dominican students developed games to teach police officers Spanish language skills. As well as improving police officers' Spanish, this effort increased communication and cooperation between youth and the police (Schine, 1997). It also provided urban youth with a chance to address a problem within their own community and to see themselves as capable of initiating positive change.

Service-learning programs also need to focus on social barriers of inequity and discrimination. This may involve conversations with students about inequities in social systems. Youth should also be supported in developing service efforts that seek social change. Social advocacy and education for change, as described earlier in this chapter, may be more relevant for effecting social change than direct or indirect service. Programs that connect academic learning to the potential for social change may engage urban students in learning that is relevant to their own lives and futures (Fine, 1992). One example of a service effort that resulted in social change took place at the Camden campus of Rutgers University, where Latina students began a project that supported the economic success of local Latina women who were heads of households and living in poverty. Students studied the social and political issues relevant to these women and then proposed a bill, which was signed into law, called the Hispanic Women's Demonstration Resource Center Act, providing institutional support for the success of this group. Participating students were involved on local and state levels and continually met to reflect on their experiences and to assess their progress (Weah et al., 2000). Through their service activities, students learned about social systems and successfully promoted social change that was meaningful both for themselves and for members of their local community.

A recent report completed for the Academy for Educational Development and the National Youth Leadership Council Service-Learning Diversity Project emphasizes the importance of adopting a "conception of service" that will foster diversity (Fine, 2000). Evidence suggests that a "change" or "empowerment" model of service-learning may be most useful for urban minority adolescents. This model contrasts with a more traditional "charity" model of service-learning. We will describe the charity model of service-learning in order to clarify some underlying goals of traditional service-learning programs, which may not always be stated explicitly. This examination is critical, because the underlying philosophy of a service-learning program strongly influences the ways in which students and communities experience service projects. This traditional service-learning model will then be contrasted with a "change" model, which may be particularly well suited to urban settings.

MODELS OF SERVICE

Through community service, students learn about their potential to change the world around them. The charity and change models teach different lessons about the power of youth to make a difference and are related to political and social debates about the goals of service and the desirable solutions for social problems.

Charity Model

Service programs are often designed to assist communities or individuals that are under-served or identified as "needy" or "at-risk" in some way. While the needs of these groups are certainly real, there is a risk of identifying the recipient group as weak and needy and identifying the service providers as strong and capable. This approach to service is sometimes referred to as the "charity model" (Westheimer & Kahne, 1999). Goals of traditional service-learning programs that teach youth to care for and aid people with symptoms of need are consistent with the charity orientation (Maybach, 1996).

While charity service-learning programs provide valuable opportunities for youth to engage with their communities and provide needed services, this approach has been criticized for supporting divisions between those who provide service and those who receive service. Community service programs have traditionally allowed little voice for the people who receive services (Maybach, 1996). Decisions about the services to be provided are sometimes made by institutions that often have little knowledge or understanding of community needs. Programs may focus solely on the experiences of service-learning participants (Westheimer & Kahne, 1999), suggesting that community members receiving service have little to contribute to the service-learning process (Weah et al., 2000). The charity model has also been criticized for increasing divisions across race and ethnic lines, given that services are often provided by White students to persons of color (Keith, 1997; Westheimer & Kahne, 1999).

Change Model

The "change" approach promotes an alternative relationship between the provider of service and the recipient of service that may be more empowering to diverse participants. This approach incorporates a number of the elements that we discussed as important in designing service programs for urban adolescents. The change model recognizes strengths of the communities being served and understands service as a reciprocal relationship, in which participants and recipients of service alike learn and benefit from one another. Students should be taught not only compassionate caring, but also how to participate in mutually empowering and supportive service relationships (Maybach, 1996).

The tool of critical reflection can be used to examine the ways in which social systems have contributed to social difficulties, which can then be addressed through service-learning interventions (Westheimer & Kahne, 1999). This model thus emphasizes student qualities of "critical analysis...and transformative educational experience" (Westheimer & Kahne, 1999, p. 37). Service participants are encouraged to combine a caring attitude with a broader understanding of social systems and social change (Ward, 1997) and to carry out interventions that address the root causes of need, rather than focusing solely on symptoms.

Service-learning thus has the potential to expand participants' world-views and to challenge both students and community recipients to reassess their roles in the broader communities that surround them. By forming partnerships with communities and allowing community voices into the process, service programs can recognize the strengths and self-knowledge of communities. Such partnerships acknowledge not only direct needs for material aid, but also recognize the broader social issues and barriers that have prevented communities from obtaining essential resources. Through collaborative work with communities, students and participating school staff can learn to value community voices and approach service through shared power and respect for multiple perspectives. This approach may also change the ways recipients view themselves. For recipients of service, who have been historically identified as unable to contribute positively to their communities and society as a whole, a revised understanding of self as an active, competent contributor to success may result. Collaborative interventions can change the way schools and communities see themselves and each other while helping to remove systemic barriers to student and community health and success (Maybach, 1996).

In order to meet community needs, the voices of community members need to be represented throughout all phases of the service project. Since community members best understand their own communities, community and program leaders must collaborate to identify the needs of communities and the focus of the service program. Evaluation must also include community participants. Program evaluation has traditionally focused on student outcomes, rather than on outcomes for individual and community recipients of service (Keith, 1997; Maybach, 1996). Neglect of the effects of service-learning on recipients of service has multiple implications. First, it means that we have little information on how recipients respond to service programs. Programs demonstrated to be effective for involved students may not be as positive or effective for service recipients (Ward, 1997). Second, the exclusion of recipient voices in the evaluation of service-learning suggests that the impact of service on the student/provider is more important than the impact of service on recipients. This imbalance sends a message to student participants about the meaning of service, and their roles in service-learning in relation to the communities in which they serve.

Implementing the change approach to service-learning is not easy (Ward, 1997). Service participants need to learn as much as possible about the community and individuals with whom they will work. Service participants should also understand the broader political and social contexts of the problems that recipients of service face, rather than only focusing on their immediate needs. Many community problems cannot be solved on an individual level. Students must also examine their own values and biases and gain an understanding of the impact of these views on their service work.

One way to enhance racial and cultural understanding in service-learning is to increase the diversity of those involved in service programs. The Service-Learning Diversity Project was developed by the National Youth Leadership Council, with support from Learning In Deed, to increase diversity in service-learning. To understand better effective ways to enhance diversity among students, practitioners and advocates of service-learning and staff from a broad range of organizations were interviewed about their diversity efforts (Fine, 2000). Results reveal several necessary conditions for strengthening diversity within service programs. First, a common understanding of what is meant by diversity should be developed. A set of diversity goals that fits with the mission of the organization should then be produced. A plan must be developed for reaching these goals on multiple levels of the organization. Last, diversity goals must be understood as ongoing. Progress and barriers should be periodically assessed and plans should be revised accordingly.

MANDATORY SERVICE

We conclude our overview of community service and service-learning with attention to the debate on whether service should be required, especially in school settings. Schools have varied approaches to service, with some schools requiring student service and others offering voluntary service opportunities. There has been controversy as to whether there should be school-wide, citywide, or even statewide mandates for service among K–12 students. The Institute for Justice estimates that only 8 percent of school districts require service as a requisite to graduation. Several cities such as Chicago and Philadelphia, as well as the state of Maryland, require service in order to advance within the public school system (Education Commission of the States, 1999). Legal issues and court cases related to mandatory service are presented in chapter 4: Facts and Data. Educational and legal questions have been raised in the controversy over mandated service. Potential benefits and drawbacks of mandatory service are discussed here.

Several issues are often raised in debates concerning the effects of mandatory service. One concern is whether service that is required is as beneficial to students as voluntary service. Student autonomy has been repeatedly linked to positive student outcomes for service (Clary & Snyder, 1999). Thus, one concern about mandatory service is that students may feel a loss of autonomy and experience negative attitudes toward service. In one research project, college students who participated in mandatory service reported less intent to continue service in the future than students involved in voluntary service (Raskoff & Sundeen, 2000). The term "mandated community service" also carries a negative association for many people who associate the term with punishment for criminal activity (Andersen, 1998; Education Commission of the States, 1999). Changing the terminology used in referring to service requirements may reduce negative responses. Concerns regarding student autonomy and resistance may also be reduced by offering student choice within service programs. Students can be given options in choosing their service sites and their own roles within a service project. The provision of sufficient autonomy within the context of a service requirement may serve to reduce significantly resistance and negative attitudes among youth and parents.

One argument in favor of mandated service is that students who may not otherwise participate in service will have opportunities to learn and grow through service involvement. This argument may be particularly relevant given findings that students who are the least likely to participate in service may reap the most benefits from participation. Students who are marginalized for various reasons often find unique opportunities for leadership and success through service participation (Search Institute, 2000). However, an additional finding challenges this argument. The Education Commission of the States (1999) reports data from a 1996 Independent Sector survey, indicating that among students ages 12–17 who were offered volunteer opportunities, close to 93 percent reported getting involved in service. Similar findings from a 1998 study by the U.S. Department of Education indicate that rates of volunteering for schools requiring service are almost identical to those for schools providing voluntary opportunities for service involvement (Education Commission of the States, 1999). If asking students to participate is sufficient, mandatory service may not be needed. Instead, efforts to invite service participation from all students may be critical to increased student involvement. Andersen (1998) argues that schools should strive to make service-learning programs appealing to all students by encouraging rather than requiring them to participate. Service opportunities can be exciting and engaging for youth. Hence, school, faith-based, and community programs might focus efforts on improving the quality of service programs rather than requiring them.

A final consideration regarding mandatory service concerns the community recipients. Andersen (1998) suggests that participation should be voluntary for all participants, including recipients of service. Just as we should invite student participation, those who are served should be asked about their needs and desire for service. Andersen suggests that service only lives up to its name if the recipients value the assistance provided.

CONCLUSION

This chapter provides a wealth of practical, research, and theoretical information pertaining to teenagers and community service. This information summarizes information that is available from a wide array of print and Internet resources and from the growing number of organizations that support community service. We hope that you will use the resources listed throughout this volume to examine in greater depth the topics that are of interest to you and to find the answers to questions that you might have about engaging in community service.

REFERENCES

Allen, J. P., Philliber, S., Herrling, S., & Kuperminc, G. P. (1997). Preventing teen pregnancy and academic failure: Experimental evaluation of a developmentally based approach. *Child Development, 68,* 729–742.

Andersen, S. (1998). *Service-learning: A national strategy for youth development.* Washington, DC: The Communitarian Network and George Washington University.

Astin, A. W., & Sax, L. J. (1998). How undergraduates are affected by service participation. *Journal of College Student Development, 39,* 251–263.

Batchelder, T. H., & Root, S. (1994). Effects of an undergraduate program to integrate academic learning and service: Cognitive, pro-social cognitive, and identity outcomes. *Journal of Adolescence, 17,* 341–355.

Benson, P. L. (1993). *The troubled journey: A portrait of 6th–12th grade youth.* Minneapolis, MN: Search Institute.

Benson, P. L. (1997). All kids are our kids: *What communities must do to raise caring and responsible children and adolescents.* San Francisco: Jossey-Bass.

Billig, S. H. (2000a). Learning In Deed, The impacts of service-learning on youth, schools, and communities: research on k–12 school-based service-learning, 1990–1999. Retrieved February 7, 2001, from http://www. LearningInDeed.org/research/slresearch/slsrchsy.html.

Billig, S. H. (2000b). Research on K–12 school-based service-learning: The evidence builds. *Phi Delta Kappan, 81,* 658–664.

Billig, S. H., & Conrad, J. (1997). *An evaluation of the New Hampshire service-learning and educational reform project.* Denver, CO: RMC Research Corporation.

Billig, S. H., et al. (1999). *An evaluation of Jefferson County school district's school-to-career partnership program.* Denver, CO: RMC Corporation.

Blum, R. W., Beuhring, T., & Rinehart, P. M. (2000). *Protecting teens: Beyond race, income, and family structure.* Minneapolis, MN: Center for Adolescent Health, University of Minnesota.

Blyth, D. A., Saito, R., & Berkas, T. (1997). A quantitative study of the impact of service-learning programs. In A. S. Waterman (Ed.), *Service-learning: Applications from the research* (pp. 39–56). Mahwah, NJ: Lawrence Erlbaum Associates.

Boston Public Schools, "Literacy Leaders ~ Cross-School Mentoring," http://boston.teachnet.org/bower.htm (cited April 6, 2001).

Bradley, L. R. (1997). Evaluating service-learning: Toward a new paradigm. In A. S. Waterman (Ed.), *Service-learning: Applications from the research* (pp. 151–171). Mahwah, NJ: Lawrence Erlbaum.

Brown, B. L. (1998). Eric Digest No. 198, Service-learning: more than community service. Retrieved March 18, 2000, from http://www.stw.ed.gov/products/1379.htm.

Brown, D. F. (2001). The value of advisory sessions for urban young adolescents. *Middle School Journal, 32* (4), 14–22.

Brown, E. (1999). The scope of volunteer activity and public service. *Law and Contemporary Problems, 62,* 7–40.

Cairn, R. W., & Kielsmeier, J. C. (Eds.). (1995). *Growing hope: A sourcebook on integrating youth service into the school curriculum.* Minneapolis, MN: National Youth Leadership Council.

Carnegie Council on Adolescent Development. (1989). *Turning points: Preparing youth for the 21st century.* Washington, DC: Author.

Carnegie Council on Adolescent Development. (1992). *A matter of time: Risk and opportunity in the non-school hours.* New York: Author.

Carnegie Council on Adolescent Development. (1996). *Great transitions: Preparing adolescents for a new century.* Washington, DC: Author.

Clary, E. G., & Snyder, M. (1999). The motivations to volunteer: Theoretical and practical considerations. *Current Directions in Psychological Science, 8,* 156–159.

Close Up Foundation. (2000), Service-Learning Quarterly: Reflection. Retrieved April 6, 2001, from http://www.closeup.org/sl_ef.htm.

Cognetta, P. V., & Sprinthall, N. A. (1978). Students as teachers: Role taking as a means of promoting psychological and ethical development during adolescence. In N. A. Sprinthall & R. L. Mosher (Eds.), *Value development as the aim of education* (pp. 53–68). Schenectady, NY: Character Research Press.

Cohen, J., & Kinsey, D. (1994, Winter). "Doing good" and scholarship: A service-learning study. *Journalism Educator, 4,* 4–14.

Coleman, J. S. (1987). Families and schools. *Educational Researcher, 16,* 32–38.

Conrad, D., & Hedin, D. (1981). National assessment of experiential education: Summary and implications. *Journal of Experiential Education, 4* (2), 6–20.

Conrad, D., & Hedin, D. (1982). The impact of experiential education on adolescent development. *Child and Youth Services, 4,* 57–76.

Conrad, D., & Hedin, D. (1987). *Youth service. A guidebook for developing and operating effective programs.* Washington, DC: Independent Sector.

Cook, C. C. (1999). National Service-Learning Clearinghouse, African-American, Hispanic, and Latino youth in service topic bibliography. Retrieved February 7, 2001, from http://nicsl.jaws.umn.edu/res/bibs/afram.htm.

Corporation for National Service. About us: Legislative history. Retrieved November 10, 2000, from http://www.cns.gov/about/leg_history,htm.

Dean, L., & Murdock, S. W. (1992, Summer). The effect of voluntary service on adolescent attitudes toward learning. *Journal of Volunteer Administration,* 5–10.

DiGeronimo, T. F. (1995). *A student's guide to volunteering.* Franklin Lakes, NJ: Career Press.

Dornbusch, S. M., Ritter, P. L., & Steinberg, L. (1991). Community influences on the relation of family status to adolescent school performance: Differences between African Americans and non-Hispanic Whites. *American Journal of Education. Special Issue: Development and Education Across Adolescence, 99,* 543–567.

Eccles, J. S., & Barber, B. L. (1999). Student council, volunteering, basketball, or marching band: What kind of extracurricular involvement matters? *Journal of Adolescence Research, 14,* 10–43.

Education Commission of the States (1999). Mandatory community service: Citizenship education or involuntary servitude? Retrieved April 26, 2001, from http://www.ecs.org/clearinghouse/14/26/1426.htm.

Eyler, J. (1993). Comparing the impact of two internship experiences on student learning. *Journal of Cooperative Education, 29,* 41–52.

Eyler, J., & Giles, D. E., Jr. (1997). The importance of program quality in service-learning. In A. S. Waterman (Ed.), *Service-learning: Applications from the research* (pp. 57–76). Mahwah, NJ: Lawrence Erlbaum.

Eyler, J., Root, S., & Giles, D. E., Jr. (1998). Service-learning and the development of expert citizens. In R. G. Bringle & D. Duffey (Eds.), *With service in mind: Concepts and models for service-learning psychology* (pp. 85–100). Washington, DC: American Association for Higher Education.

Fine, M. (1992). *Framing dropouts.* New York: Teachers College Press.

Fine, M. (2000). *Creating inclusive communities: An inquiry into organizational approaches to pursuing diversity.* New York: Academy for Educational Development and National Youth Leadership Council.

Fitch, R. T. (1987). Characteristics and motivations of college students volunteering for community service. *Journal of College Student Personnel, 28* (5), 424–431.

Giles, D. E., Jr., & Eyler, J. (1994). The impact of a college community service laboratory on students' personal, social, and cognitive outcomes. *Journal of Adolescence, 17* (4), 327–339.

Goodman, A. (1994). *The Big Help book: 365 ways you can make a difference by volunteering.* New York: Pocket Books.

Gray, M. J., Ondaatje, E. H., & Zakaras, L. (1999). *Combining service and learning in higher education: Summary report.* Santa Monica, CA: RAND.

Hall, M. (1991). Gadugi: A model of service-learning for Native American communities. *Phi Delta Kappan, 72,* 754–757.

Hamilton, S., & Zeldin, R. S. (1987). Learning civics in the community. *Curriculum Inquiry, 17* (4), 407–420.

Hart, D., Atkins, R., & Ford, D. (1998). Urban America as a context for development of adolescent identity in adolescents. *Journal of Social Issues, 54,* 543–530.

Hechinger, F. M. (1992). *Fateful choices: Healthy youth for the 21st century.* New York: Hill and Wang.

Johnson, A. M., & Notah, D. J. (1999). Service-learning: History, literature review, and a pilot study of eighth graders. *Elementary School Journal, 99,* 453–467.

Johnson, M. K., Beebe, T., Mortimer, J. T., & Snyder, M. (1998). Volunteerism in adolescence: A process perspective. *Journal of Research on Adolescence, 8,* 309–332.

Kahne, J., & Westheimer, J. (1996). In the service of what? The politics of service-learning. *Phi Delta Kappan, 77,* 593–599.

Keith, N. Z. (1997). Doing service projects in urban settings. In A. S. Waterman (Ed.), *Service-learning: Applications from the research* (pp. 127–149). Mahwah, NJ: Lawrence Erlbaum.

Kenny, M. E., Simon, L. A. K., Kiley-Brabeck, K., & Lerner, R. M. (Eds). (2002). Promoting civil society through service learning: A view of the issues. In M. E. Kenny, L. A. Simon, K. Kiley-Brabeck, & R. M. Lerner (Eds.), *Learning to serve: Promoting civil society through service learning* (pp. 1–14). Norwell, MA: Kluwer.

Kimball-Baker, K., & Roehlkepartain, E. C. (Summer 1998). Are Americans afraid of teens? *Assets Magazine, 3* (2), 6–8.

Kingsland, S. F., Richards, M., & Coleman, L. (1995). *A status report for KIDSNET, Year One, 1994–1995.* Portland: University of Southern Maine.

Kleiner, B., & Chapman, C. (2000). Youth service learning and community service among 6th through 12th grade students in the United States: 1996 and 1999. *Education Statistics Quarterly, 2,* 34–52.

Lawson, D. M. (1998). *Volunteering: 101 ways you can improve the world and your life.* San Diego, CA: ALTI Publishing.

Learn and Serve. About Learn & Serve: Service-learning. Retrieved January 15, 2001, from http://www.nationalservice.org/learn/about/service_learning,html.

Learning In Deed. Creating inclusive communities: An inquiry into organizational approaches to pursuing diversity. Retrieved May 24, 2001, from http://www.LearningInDeed.org/tools/other/inclusum.html.

Learning In Deed. Policy and practice demonstration project. Retrieved April 28, 2001, from http://www.LearningInDeed.org/ppp/.

Learning In Deed. Service-learning in action. Retrieved March 29, 2001, from http://www.LearningInDeed.org/tools/examples.html.

Lerner, R. M., Fisher, C. B., & Weinberg, R. A. (2000). Toward a science for and of the people: Promoting civil society through the application of developmental science. *Child Development, 71,* 11–20.

Lewis, A. (1992) Urban youth in community service: Becoming part of the solution. *ERIC Clearinghouse on Urban Education Digest, 81,* 1–2.

Lewis, B. A. (1995). *The kid's guide to service projects: Over 500 service ideas for young people who want to make a difference.* Minneapolis, MN: Free Spirit Publishing.

Mannes, M. (2002). Search Institute's evolving approach to community-based human development and the role of service learning. In M. E. Kenny, L. A. Simon, K. Kiley-Brabeck, & R. M. Lerner (Eds.), *Learning to serve: Promoting civil society through service learning* (pp. 423–441). Norwell, MA: Kluwer.

Markus, G. B., Howard, J., & King, D. (1993). Integrating community service and classroom instruction enhances learning: Results from an experiment. *Educational Evaluation and Policy Analysis, 15,* 410–419.

Maybach, C. W. (1996). Investigating urban community needs: Service learning from a social justice perspective. *Education and Urban Society, 28,* 224–236.

McLaughlin, M. W., Irby, M. A., & Langman, J. (1994). *Urban sanctuaries: Neighborhood organizations in the lives and futures of inner-city youth.* San Francisco: Jossey-Bass.

Melchior, A., et al. (1999). *Summary report: National evaluation of Learn and Serve America.* Waltham, MA: Center for Human Resources, Brandeis University.

National Institute on Out-of-School Time. (1999). *Tips for effective service-learning programs in out-of-school time programs.* Wellesley, MA: Center for Research on Women, Wellesley College.

National Youth Leadership Council. FELLOWS Project. Retrieved April 25, 2001, from http://www.nylc.org/fellows/.

Newman, F. M. (1991). Student engagement in academic work: Expanding the perspective on secondary school effectiveness. In J. R. Bliss, W. A. Firestone, & C. E. Richards (Eds.), *Rethinking effective schools: Research and practice* (pp. 58–75). Englewood Cliffs, NJ: Prentice-Hall.

O'Bannon, F. (1999). Service-learning benefits our schools. *State Education Leader, 17,* 3.

O'Donnell, L., Stueve, A., San Doval, A., Duran, R., Haber, D., Atnafou, R., Johnson, N., Grant, U., Murray, H., Juhn, G., Tang, J., & Piessens, P. (1999).

The effectiveness of the reach for health community youth service learning program in reducing early and unprotected sex among urban middle school students. *American Journal of Public Health, 89,* 176–181.

Prudential Insurance Spirit of Community Initiative. (1998). *Catch the spirit: A student's guide to community service.* Newark, NJ: Author.

Putnam, R. (1995, January). Bowling alone: America's declining social capital. *Journal of Democracy, 6,* 65–77.

Raskoff, S. A., & Sundeen, R. A. (2000). Community service programs in high schools. *Law and Contemporary Problems, 62,* 73–111.

Roehlkepartain, E. (1995). *Everyone wins when youth serve.* Washington, DC: Points of Light Foundation.

Rosenthal, S., Feiring, C., & Lewis, M. (1998). Political volunteering from late adolescence to young adulthood: Patterns and predictors. *Journal of Social Issues, 5,* 477–493.

Roth, J., & Brooks-Gunn, J. (2000). What do adolescents need for healthy development? Implications for youth policy. *Social Policy Report, 14* (1), 3–19.

Rutter, R. A., & Newman, F. M. (1989). The potential of community service to enhance civic responsibility. *Social Education, 53,* 371–74.

Sax, L. J., & Astin, A. W. (1997). The benefits of service: Evidence from undergraduates. *Educational Record, 78* (3–4), 25–32.

Scales, P., & Blyth, D. (1997, Winter). Effects of service-learning on youth: What we know and what we need to know. *The Generator,* 6–9.

Schine, J. (1989). *Young adolescents and community service.* Washington, DC: Carnegie Council on Adolescent Development.

Schine, J. (1997). School-based service: Reconnecting schools to youth at the margin. *Theory into Practice, 36,* 170–175.

Search Institute. (1994). *Learning through service survey.* Minneapolis, MN: Author.

Search Institute. (2000). *An asset builder's guide to service-learning.* Minneapolis, MN: Author.

Sergent, M. T., & Sedlacek, W. E. (1990). Volunteer motivations across student organizations: A test of person-environment fit theory. *Journal of College Student Development, 31,* 255–261.

Serow, R. (1997). Research and evaluation on service-learning: The case for holistic assessment. In A. S. Waterman (Ed.), *Service-learning: Applications from the research* (pp. 13–24). Mahwah, NJ: Lawrence Erlbaum.

Serow, R. C. (1991). Students and volunteerism: Looking into the motives of community service participants. *American Educational Research Journal, 28,* 543–556.

Shumer, R. (1994). Community-based learning: Humanizing education. *Journal of Adolescence, 17,* 357–367.

Shumer, R. (1997). What research tells us about designing service-learning programs. *NASSP Bulletin, 81,* 18–24.

Shumer, R. (2000). *Shumer's self-assessment for service-learning.* Minneapolis, MN: Center for Experiential and Service-Learning, Department of Work, Community, and Family Education, College of Education and Human Development, University of Minnesota.

Sigmon, R. (1979). Service-learning: Three principles. *Synergist, 8,* 9–11.

Skinner, R., & Chapman, C. (1999). *Service-learning and community service in K–12 public schools* (NCES 1999–043). U.S. Department of Education. Washington, DC: U.S. Government Printing Office.

Slaughter, V. T., & Epps, E. G. (1987). The home environment and academic achievement of black urban children and youth: An overview. *Journal of Negro Education, 86,* 3–20.

Smink, J., & Duckenfield, M. (Eds.). (1998). *Action research and evaluation guidebook for teachers.* Roseville, MN: National Youth Leadership Council.

Stephens, L. (1995). *The complete guide to learning through community service: Grades K–9.* Boston: Allyn & Bacon.

Stukas, A. A., Clary, E. G., & Snyder, M. (1999). Service-learning: Who benefits and why? *Social Policy Report: Society for Research in Child Development, 13,* 1–19.

U.S. Department of Health and Human Services. (1999). *Mental health: A report of the surgeon general.* Rockville, MD: U.S. Department of Health and Human Services, Substance Abuse and Mental Health Services Administration, Center for Mental Health Services, National Institute of Health, National Institute of Mental Health.

Vasquez, J. A. (1994). Contexts of learning for minority students. In J. Kretoviks & E. J. Nussel (Eds.), *Transforming urban education* (pp. 291–300). New York: Teachers College Press.

Ward, J. V. (1997). Encouraging cultural competence in service learning practice. In J. Schine (Ed.), *Service learning* (pp. 136–148). Chicago: University of Chicago Press.

Waterman, A. S. (1997). The role of student characteristics in service-learning. In A. S. Waterman (Ed.), *Service-learning: Applications from the research* (pp. 127–149). Mahwah, NJ: Lawrence Erlbaum.

Weah, W., Simmons, V. C., & Hall, M. (2000). Service-learning and multicultural/multiethnic perspectives: From diversity to equity. *Phi Delta Kappan, 81,* 673–675.

Weiler, D., LaGoy, A., Crane, E., Rowner, A. (1998). *An evaluation of K–12 service learning in California: Phase III final report.* Emeryville, CA: RPP International with the Search Institute.

Westheimer, J., & Kahne, J. (1999). *In the service of what? The politics of service learning.* In J. Claus & C. Ogden (Eds.), *Service learning for youth empowerment and social change* (pp. 25–38). New York: Peter Lang.

Yates, M., & Youniss, J. (1996). Community service and political-moral identity in adolescents. *Journal of Research on Adolescence, 6,* 271–284.

Youniss, J., McLellan, J. A., & Yates, M. (1997). What we know about engendering civic identity. *American Behavioral Scientist, 40,* 620–631.

Youniss, J., & Yates, M. (1997). *Community service and social responsibility in youth.* Chicago: The University of Chicago Press.

Zeldin, S., & Tarlov, S. (1997). Service learning as a vehicle for youth development. In J. Schine (Ed.). *Service learning* (pp. 173–185). Chicago: University of Chicago Press.

2

Chronology

Community service has a long tradition in American society. A commitment to helping one's neighbor was critical to the survival of American pioneers, who faced dangers and scarcity in their travels across the country. For many years, a number of voluntary associations, including 4-H, Girl and Boy Scouts, and the YMCA, have introduced American youth to the experience of community service. National service programs, such as the Youth Conservation Corps, the Peace Corps, VISTA, and the Job Corps, have also involved youth and young adults in seeking solutions to social and economic problems within our country and abroad. During the social activist period of the 1960s, organizations such as the National Commission on Resources for Youth were also formed to provide youth with socially meaningful roles that would prepare them for adult life. Dating back to the Morrill Act of 1862, our nation's colleges have held a commitment to serving the local community and preparing students to be productive and engaged workers and citizens. Similarly, an important function of the public school system has been to prepare students for future roles as contributing citizens in their communities and nation.

In conjunction with the American commitment to service, Americans have historically demonstrated a high degree of individualism. Intellectuals like Alexis de Tocqueville in the 1830s and John Dewey in the early 1900s noted a potential conflict between social responsibility and individualism in American life. According to de Tocqueville and Dewey, citizens in a democratic society must be concerned for the overall good of

the public, and not only for their individual concerns. Citizens should
have an understanding of the lives of other citizens. Dewey viewed experiential learning and community participation as critical methods for
teaching citizens to understand others, so that they would cast their
votes with an awareness of the public good and would be equipped to
solve the problems faced by a changing society.

Over the past several decades, the conflict between individuality and
public service has been evident in the growing apathy and civic disen-
gagement among young people. In *Habits of the Heart* (1985), for example, Bellah, Madsen, Sullivan, Swidler, and Tipton expressed concern
regarding increased individualism in American life. Political theorists
like Benjamin Barber (1982) and Richard Battistoni (1985) voiced concerns regarding a decline in political participation among youth and
advocated community service as a means to motivate political participation.

The term *service-learning* was first used in 1967 to describe a college
internship program in which students gained college credit for working
on community projects (Sigmon, 1979). Although interest in service-
learning, which links academic study and community service, declined
during the 1970s, interest increased throughout the 1980s. Service was
identified as a means to combat materialism, political withdrawal, and
youth alienation, and to engage youth in meaningful social activity.
College-based organizations, such as the Campus Outreach Opportunity
League (COOL) and Campus Compact were formed and would prove
to have an enormous impact on promoting service-learning. Standards
of sound practice for combining academic study and service were
developed through the Wingspread Conference. The growth of service-
learning and community service programs for those in late adolescence
on college campuses heightened interest in community service among
those working with younger adolescents in school and community settings. Organizations such as the National Center for Service Learning
for Early Adolescents and the National Youth Leadership Council and
events such as National Youth Service Day emerged in the early 1980s to
promote service among adolescents. Service-learning in K–12 school
programs increased during the mid- to late 1980s, and some schools
began to require community service as a high school graduation requirement.

The 1990s witnessed a tremendous surge in interest and participation
in community service. The establishment of the Office of National Service and passage of the National and Community Service Act of 1990

and the National and Community Service Trust Act of 1993 have provided structures and funds to support service initiatives in schools and communities. Private foundations and business organizations have also devoted resources to encourage youth participation in service and to increase knowledge about effective service programs. Service-learning, community service, and positive youth development have grown as areas of scholarly inquiry so that knowledge about the benefits of community service for youth and their communities and knowledge of the characteristics of effective service programs are more evident. In response to concerns that American youth are alienated, uncaring, and uninvolved, developmental psychologist James Youniss (Youniss & Yates, 1997) noted the large numbers of American youth who contribute positively to their communities and participate in community service. Youth involvement in community service may help to challenge negative images of teens as irresponsible or indifferent to community needs. The September 11, 2001 tragedy inspired many of America's young people to engage in service to their communities. Robert Putnam's survey (2002) revealed an increase in civic attitudes and behavior. In January 2002, millions of youth responded to the "Kindness and Justice Challenge" sponsored by Do Something and devoted two weeks to good deeds and volunteerism. President Bush sought to keep this spirit of service alive by forming the USA Freedom Corps that connects potential volunteers with volunteer opportunities.

1862 The Morrill Act is signed into law by President Lincoln in 1862, declaring that each state must have at least one college to promote practical education and apply scholarship to practical problems of society.

1910 The American philosopher William James puts forth the idea of nonmilitary national service in his essay "The Moral Equivalent of War."

1915 The Plattsburg Movement is part of a broader "Preparedness Movement," intended to increase and modernize the U.S. armed forces in response to World War I. This movement is initiated by General Leonard Wood, who believes that citizens can be quickly trained to become soldiers. He creates a volunteer six-week summer training camp to teach youth about the army. These volunteer camps are used to test the potential success of military training centers all across the country, to train college men for future military service, and to provide "moral awakening" to young males through voluntary military training. These camps provide a model for later national service programs.

1916 John Dewey's vision of democracy, presented in *Democracy and Education* (1916), challenges citizens to take part in a form of decision-making that balances the interests of the individual with those of others. According to Dewey, democracy demands that citizens understand the lives and experiences of other members of society so that they can cast their votes with awareness of their effect on others. Dewey's arguments are often cited to support the value of community service for adolescents, in preparation for their role as democratic citizens.

1918 The first National Service Center is established by United Way of America.

1933 The Civilian Conservation Corps, a national service program, is developed to remedy unemployment of the Great Depression. Through the Civilian Conservation Corps, 3 million unemployed men will serve their country. The Civilian Conservation Corps provides a model for the development of other national service programs.

1938 In his book *Experience and Education,* John Dewey promotes the concept of experiential learning. Service-learning programs are grounded in the importance of experience as a basis for learning and on the centrality of reflection to enable learning. Dewey's writings have been influential in shaping service-learning curricula.

1959 The Johnson Foundation, a private foundation that cosponsors conferences on issues of public interest, is established. The Johnson Foundation has sponsored several conferences that have been central in the promotion of service-learning.

1961 The Peace Corps is established by President John F. Kennedy as part of a call to service to all Americans. The Peace Corps is a volunteer program in which American participants spend two years living and working in host countries, mostly countries with needs in education or industrial development. A goal of the Peace Corps is to increase understanding between Americans and the people of other nations. Volunteers receive extensive language and cross-cultural training and work with citizens of host communities to improve education, create economic opportunities, promote health, and increase resources so that the citizens of the host community could better direct their own futures.

1964 Although the idea for VISTA (Volunteers in Service to America) was created by President John F. Kennedy, this program is established as part of Lyndon B. Johnson's War on Poverty legislation. VISTA volunteers work with community agencies to reduce poverty by expanding work opportunities and improving living conditions. Since its founding, there have been over 120,000 VISTA volunteers. Johnson's War on Poverty included the National Teacher Corps, Job Corps, University Year for ACTION, as well as VISTA. The Retired and Senior Volunteer Program (RSVP), the Foster Grandparent Program, and the Senior Companion Program are also developed in the 1960s to involve older Americans in service to their communities. These programs for older Americans are now part of the National Senior Service Corps.

1967 The National Commission on Resources for Youth (NCRY) is founded in New York City, with the goal of encouraging all Americans, especially government officials and young professionals, to recognize the value of children and adolescents as contributors in their communities. "Youth Participation" programs are established to provide young people with opportunities to become involved in the community and the workplace. These programs are designed to facilitate the transition of young people from adolescence to adulthood. Programs sponsored by NCRY, such as Youth Tutoring Youth, Day Care Youth Helper, and the Early Adolescent Helper program, provide American youth with the chance to engage in responsible planning and/or decision-making that can make a difference in the lives of others. NCRY was dissolved in 1986, yet many of the ideas of the NCRY are evident in contemporary service-learning programs that promote community activism for youth.

1967 The term *service-learning* first emerges in the work of Robert Sigmon and William Ramsey at the Southern Regional Economic Board. The term is used to describe an internship program through which college students perform community service for academic credit and/or payment funded by the federal government.

1969   The Office of Economic Opportunity establishes the National Student Volunteer Program, as a subdivision of VISTA. The National Student Volunteer Program, later renamed as the National Center for Service-Learning, is established to encourage school-based service programs by providing small grants, workshops, conferences, and a quarterly journal. Two years later, this program along with VISTA and the Peace Corps, combine to form the federal agency ACTION.

1970   The Youth Conservation Corps provides the opportunity for 38,000 young people between the ages of fourteen and eighteen to work in conservation programs during the summer months. The program is administered by the interior and agriculture departments of the U.S. government and continues until the early 1980s.

1970   The Close Up Foundation is established to promote participation in democratic processes. Based upon the belief that students can learn much about democracy through involvement in activities outside of the classroom, the foundation supports community service and other experiential educational programs.

1971   The report of the White House Conference on Youth calls for linking service and learning.

1971   The Society for Field Experience Education is founded. This society is committed to experienced-based learning in the community. It is reorganized in 1978 as the National Society for Internships and Experiential Education and in 1994 as the National Society for Experiential Education. This society distributes many written resources on community service and service-learning.

1972   The Association for Experiential Education (AEE) is created through a North Carolina educators' conference focusing on how to make education more relevant to people's real-life experiences. This organization's stated goals are to change education in ways that will promote positive change throughout the world. Currently, AEE has a membership of 2,000 educators worldwide.

1972 The American Institute for Public Service is founded by Jacqueline Kennedy Onassis, Senator Robert Taft, and Sam Beard in an effort to encourage youth to become involved in community and public service. The American Institute for Public Service presents the Jefferson Award to community members who have made significant service contributions to their communities.

1974 The Council for Adult and Experiential Learning (CAEL), originally called the Cooperative Assessment of Experiential Learning, is created by the Educational Testing Service (ETS). This organization's mission is to support life-long learning for employees. The belief that involvement in community and public service contributes to critical learning is a premise of service-learning and CAEL.

1976 Governor Jerry Brown establishes the California Conservation Corps (CCC), which is the first statewide youth corps. Its two stated goals are to protect state natural resources and to support youth development. The program targets out-of-school youth who are looking for ways to improve their skills and educational opportunities through community and public service. The California Conservation Corps (CCC) is based on the national Civilian Conservation Corps program of the 1930s. CCC workers are still employed as an emergency response force, to provide assistance in times of natural disasters. The CCC is the most extensive statewide conservation corps in this country, with more than 70,000 participants since its founding. The California Conservation Corps is the inspiration for other youth service programs, including the Program for Local Service in Seattle and the City Volunteer Corps in New York.

1976 Habitat for Humanity, a nonprofit, nondenominational Christian housing organization, is founded. Through Habitat for Humanity, many youth provide service to their communities by helping to construct affordable housing.

1978 The Young Adult Conservation Corps is founded, which provides opportunities for young adults between the ages of sixteen and twenty-three to participate in environmental service programs.

1979 The National Center for Service Learning publishes *Synergist*, a journal promoting service and learning.

1980   The National Center for Service Learning for Early Adolescents and the Early Adolescent Helper Program are founded by the National Commission on Youth Resources. The National Helpers Network/Early Adolescent Helper Program begins at three New York City intermediate and junior high schools. The program is designed to recognize the unique needs of early adolescents (11 to 14 years of age) as well as their capacity to contribute to their communities through volunteer service. Sponsorship of the program is taken over in 1983 by the Center for Advanced Study in Education

1981   Dan Conrad and Diane Hedin publish research indicating the beneficial effects of service experiences to student learning. These findings are important in justifying the link between community service and education.

1982   Ernest Boyer calls for the participation of high school students in community service in his book titled *High School*.

1982   National Youth Service Day is initiated by the American Institute for Public Service. National Youth Service Day, now sponsored by Youth Service America, is the largest service event in the world, involving more than 500,000 youth in service projects across the country during the spring of each year.

1982   The Job Training Partnership Act (JTPA) is signed by President Reagan, eliminating funding for conservation corps.

1982   The Giraffe Project is founded to give recognition to individuals who have taken action to solve social problems in the United States. The project creates a story-based, service curriculum to teach youth about service and to inspire them to take action and benefit others through service activity.

1983   The National Youth Leadership Council (NYLC), a nonprofit organization dedicated to developing service-oriented youth leaders, is founded. The mission of NYLC is to engage students in their schools and communities through innovative learning, service, leadership, and public policy. NYLC leads the Learn and Serve America Exchange, which provides peer-based training and technical assistance to support community-based service programs involving youth in kindergarten through college.

1984   The Campus Outreach Opportunity League (COOL) is a national, nonprofit organization, which uses service as a tool to educate and empower college students. COOL engages diverse students in activist activities in an effort to strengthen our nation. COOL engages with community issues such as homelessness, illiteracy, and the problems in the environment. COOL also sponsors an annual community service conference designed to encourage increased service involvement among college students.

1984   The City Volunteer Corps is founded in New York. This youth service project combines physical labor and human services work. Volunteers receive a weekly stipend, an educational program to meet their specific needs (i.e., ESL or GED classes), and an educational allowance to finance further education upon completion of a year of service with the City Volunteer Corps. This service model is copied in many other cities and serves as a model for the AmeriCorps year of service programs. By the end of the 1980s, nearly seventy youth service programs exist across the country.

1985   National Campus Compact, the only national higher education organization that supports campus-based public and community service, is established by college and university presidents. The organization is formed based upon a commitment to help students develop the values and skills of citizenship through participation in public and community service.

1985   Youth Service America is established, with the goal of increasing opportunities for young people to engage in service and bringing together diverse groups of youth in service activities. This organization advocates for public policy that supports community service programs in middle schools, high schools, and colleges. It acts as a resource center for organizations committed to increasing youth service and seeks to strengthen and sustain youth service organizations.

1985   The National Association of Service and Conservation Corps (NASCC) is formed to revive and network youth conservation corps programs throughout the states.

1985   *Habits of the Heart: Individualism and Commitment in American Life,* written by Bellah, Madsen, Sullivan, Swidler, and Tipton, is published. This volume describes the constant competing pressures in American society between individualism and commitment to the common good. The decade of the 1980s is characterized as narcissistic and individualistic, with decreasing concern for the common good. The philosophical argument set forth in this book raises consciousness among many who seek to decrease individualism through a refocus on the importance of community service.

1986   The Carnegie unit on service is created. Ernest Boyer proposes that students should spend not less than 30 hours a year, and a total of 120 hours over four years, in order to qualify for one Carnegie service unit. This formula provides a means of computing the amount of academic credit to be granted for community service.

1987   The Center for Youth as Resources (YAR) is created by the National Crime Prevention Council, with funding from the Lilly Endowment. YAR involves youth from the ages of five to twenty-one in service projects that address social problems and contribute to community change.

1988   The American Youth Foundation (AYF) begins to develop programs that link service and learning. AYF supports a network of summer camps and other outdoor programs that are designed to promote personal excellence, a balance of physical and spiritual development, and youth service to communities. Their mission is to help youth to realize their "personal best" in a context of safety, respect, and responsibility.

1988   City Year is founded in Boston by Mike Brown and Alan Khazei. Based upon the ideas of the City Volunteers Corps in New York, City Year begins as a summer program in 1988. In the fall of 1989, City Year enrolls fifty young people for nine months of full-time service. City Year provides opportunities for high school graduates to perform a year of national service. City Year volunteers offer a variety of resources to the city of Boston. In 2001, City Year has expanded to thirteen other cities.

1988   President George Bush establishes the Office of National Service.

1989   SCALE (Student Coalition for Literacy Education), a student-initiated literacy program, is founded by Lisa Madry and Clay

Thorpe, two undergraduates from the University of North Carolina. The SCALE project is a national network that provides support and the exchange of ideas among literacy programs in college settings throughout the country. Students primarily serve as community tutors or teachers. SCALE currently provides service such as training, technical support, conferences, and publications.

1989 The National Society for Internships and Experiential Education articulates a set of principles that culminate in a conference hosted by the Johnson Foundation. The conference is held at the Wingspread Conference Center in Racine, Wisconsin, where more than seventy organizations collaborate to produce the Principles of Good Practice for Combining Service and Learning. These principles are to be highly influential in guiding the development of service-learning programs.

1989 Foundation funding for youth service increases, with major funding being offered by the Ford Foundation, Mott Foundation, W. K. Kellogg Foundation, and DeWitt Wallace–Reader's Digest Foundation.

1990 The National and Community Service Act of 1990 creates an independent federal agency, the Commission on National and Community Service.

1990 The Points of Light Foundation, a nonpartisan, nonprofit organization that seeks to increase volunteerism, is created as a result of the National and Community Service Act of 1990. Based upon the premise that disconnection and alienation are at the root of many social problems, the Points of Light Foundation seeks to support community service through the development of youth leadership programs, providing assistance to employers who wish to develop volunteer programs in the workplace, establishing volunteer centers across the nation, and encouraging family members to volunteer together.

1990 The Bonner Scholars Program is created at Berea College in Kentucky in an effort to produce student leaders and to increase student involvement with local communities. This program awards four-year college scholarships to high school students who aspire to college, demonstrate financial need, and have shown a commitment to community service. The Bonner program has expanded since its inception to support 1,500 students annually, who attend twenty-five different undergraduate institutions.

1991 The National Society for Internships and Experiential Education develops a five-year high school service-learning initiative.

1991 The CalServe Initiative is created, with the goal of establishing service-learning programs throughout half of the California public school districts by the year 2004. Through CalServe, the California Department of Education provides funding for thirty-six school-community service partnerships.

1993 *A Call to Service,* written by Robert Coles, is published. Coles is a strong advocate of volunteerism and community service. He maintains that service is part of a natural moral impulse that can bring personal satisfaction and improve the lives of many.

1993 The National and Community Service Trust Act is passed. Through this legislation, the Commission on National and Community Service and ACTION merge to form the Corporation for National and Community Service, referred to as the Corporation for National Service. For twenty years, ACTION has administered VISTA and the three senior corps programs—the Retired and Senior Volunteer Program (RSVP), Foster Grandparents, and Senior Companions. With the establishment of AmeriCorps in 1993, VISTA becomes a part of AmeriCorps. Today, more than 40,000 Americans serve as volunteers through AmeriCorps.

1993 As part of the 1993 Defense Authorization Act, the National Civilian Community Corps (NCCC) is established. The NCCC is a residential national service program modeled after the Civilian Conservation Corps and the U.S. military. NCCC is a part of AmeriCorps that is open to young adults between the ages of eighteen to twenty-four, who serve in volunteer teams of ten to fifteen and seek to meet the critical needs of safety, education, and conservation in urban and rural communities.

1993 The Alliance for Service-Learning in Education Reform is formed by a diverse group of service-learning educators in order to develop a common definition and set of standards to judge service-learning programs.

1993   Community Problem Solvers: Youth Leading Change is established in Queens, New York, through the National Center for Service Learning in Early Adolescence. Groups of early adolescents are assisted in building team skills and completing a needs assessment in their community. Following the needs assessment, the adolescents identify a service or community action project to complete, which is linked to the school curriculum.

1993   The Grantmaker Forum on Community and National Service is formed through leadership provided by the W. K. Kellogg and the James Irvine Foundations to bring together grant makers interested in community service and volunteerism.

1994   The first group of 20,000 AmeriCorps volunteers begins their service in more than 1,000 communities. AmeriCorps volunteers receive post-service educational stipends that can be used either to pay off their educational loans or finance further education or training.

1994   Earth Force is created by Pew Charitable Trusts to help youth become involved in environmental initiatives through service involvement in local government and committees.

1995   A study supported by the IBM Foundation, the Charles A. Dana Foundation, and the James Irvine Foundation reports that the benefits to volunteers and the communities they serve are worth approximately twice as much as every federal dollar invested.

1996   America Reads is launched by President Clinton as part of a comprehensive children's literacy program to ensure that all children can read well and independently by the end of the third grade. As a result of America Reads, many college students become involved in tutoring children through their college community service programs. Work-study funds can be used to pay tutors, thus enabling many college students to simultaneously become involved in community service and fund their college education.

1996   The Charitable Choice Amendment is passed as part of the welfare reform legislation. This amendment provides a means for churches and other faith-based organizations to obtain government funds in efforts to make the poor less dependent upon welfare and more self-sufficient.

1996   SERVEnet.org, the first national database of community service opportunities, is developed by Youth Service America.

1997   The President's Summit for America's Future is held in Philadelphia on April 27–29, 1997, and is attended by more than 4,000 people. Retired General Colin Powell, President Clinton, Vice President Al Gore, former First Lady Nancy Reagan, and former presidents George Bush, Gerald Ford, and Jimmy Carter lead efforts to clean up Philadelphia's Germantown Avenue. The purpose of the summit is to celebrate America's commitment to its youth and to create nationwide interest in volunteerism and community service. At the end of the event, President Clinton signs a Summit Declaration, emphasizing the responsibility that all Americans share for the well-being of all. Representatives from communities across the nation meet in small groups to discuss ways to take the ideas and enthusiasm of the summit back to their home communities, schools, and places of work and worship. The summit is sponsored by the Points of Light Foundation and the Corporation for National Service.

1997   America's Promise, a nonprofit organization, is founded in April of 1997 at the Presidents' Summit. America's Promise seeks to improve the lives of the more than 15 million at-risk youth in the United States. In efforts to achieve this, volunteers are recruited from hundreds of corporations, service agencies, state and local governments, and nonprofit organizations across the country to provide social and economic resources to children in need.

1997   The Education Awards Program increases the scope of AmeriCorps, providing a means for faith-based organizations, nonprofits, welfare-to-work programs, and other organizations to participate in the AmeriCorps network of service programs.

1998   A new initiative of the W. K. Kellogg Foundation entitled, "Learning In Deed: Making a Difference through Service-Learning," focuses on expanding the integration of service experiences and academic curriculum throughout K–12 schools across the nation. This initiative builds on the decade-long support of the W. K. Kellogg Foundation for service learning as a way to engage youth meaningfully in their communities.

1999 Nearly 400 college presidents sign a Declaration on the Civic Responsibility of Higher Education at the Presidents' Leadership Colloquium organized by Campus Compact and the American Council on Education.

1999 The National Society for Internships and Experiential Education brings together university administrators and faculty at the Wingspread Conference Center in Racine, Wisconsin, in an effort to revitalize the commitment of universities to civic engagement. The conference focuses on the potential for university research to contribute to global well-being. Student involvement in the Wingspread conference is supported by the Wingspread Fellows Program, created by Melvin Brorby in the 1970s, in an effort to promote student mentoring for future leadership in education.

1999 The President's Student Service Challenge awards are developed to help schools, colleges, and community organizations recognize young people who provide outstanding community service. The award includes the President's Student Service Awards and the President's Student Service Scholarships. The Student Service Awards are given to students who complete 100 hours of service to their communities that makes a significant impact in meeting local needs. The scholarships are available to two exemplary juniors and seniors from each high school across the country who complete 100 hours of significant service within the last year. The Corporation for National Service provides a $500 scholarship, which is matched by another $500 from the community. These awards are intended to increase youth involvement in community service. Awards are also given to up to 100 high schools and 100 middle schools each year for excellence in community service and service-learning.

2000 The University College of Citizenship and Public Service, a university-wide initiative focused on preparing students as committed citizens and community leaders, is created at Tufts University through the support of a $10 million award from the Omidyar Foundation.

2000 The National Youth Leadership Council (NYLC) and Youth Service America (YSA) form an alliance called Service Learning International. The purpose of this alliance is to increase the participation of youth in service activities in their communities. Innovations in service-learning curricula and technology and a Youth as Decision Makers Institute are a few of the initial initiatives of this alliance.

2001 The National Commission on Service-Learning is formed as an extension of Learning In Deed. The Commission is made up of leaders in K–12 and higher education, government, business, media, youth development, civic action, entertainment, and youth representatives. Former astronaut and former senator John Glenn is chair of the commission. The goal of the commission is to bring a higher level of public awareness and commitment to service-learning.

2001 President George W. Bush creates a White House Office of Faith-Based and Community Initiatives to provide support to faith-based and community organizations. This office works with the Corporation for National Service in recruiting volunteers for secular and religiously based community service projects that seek to meet local community needs.

2001 In the aftermath of September 11, Arizona Senator John McCain praises AmeriCorps and calls for an expansion of the national service program as a vehicle for young people to express their patriotism and commitment to their country.

2001 State Farm Insurance Co. announces a commitment to help expand and strengthen service-learning throughout American public education through work with the National Service-Learning Partnerships.

2001 The Wingspread Summit on Student Civic Engagement was held at the Johnson Foundation in Racine, Wisconsin. The summit was attended by student leaders from twenty-seven colleges and universities, who discussed their civic experiences in higher education.

2002 In his State of the Union address, President Bush asks that each American devote 4,000 hours or the equivalent of two years of their lives to serve others in order to support our communities, extend the compassion felt by Americans to other nations, and to protect our homelands. The USA Freedom Corps was formed to involve Americans of all ages in volunteer service.

2002   The National Commission on Service-Learning releases their report, "The Power of Service-Learning for American Schools," which calls on American schools to use service-learning as a proven mechanism for educational reform that will simultaneously teach citizenship and raise test scores.

2002   The National Commission on Service-Learning releases a report calling for American schools to use service-learning as a means for simultaneously building student skills in academics and citizenship.

REFERENCES

Bellah, R. N., Madsen, R., Sullivan, W. M., Swidler, A., & Tipton, S. M. (Eds.). (1985). *Habits of the heart: Individualism and commitment in American life.* Berkeley, CA: University of California Press.

Bonnen, J. T. (1998). The land-grant idea and the evolving outreach university. In R. M. Lerner & L. A. K. Simon (Eds.), *University-community collaborations for the twenty-first century: Outreach scholarship for youth and families* (pp. 25–71). New York: Garland.

Coles, R. (1993). *The call of service.* Boston: Houghton Mifflin.

Conderman, G., & Patryla, V. (1996). Service learning: The past, the present, and the promise. *Kappa Delta Pi Record, 32,* 122–125.

Corporation for National Service. About us: History of national service. Retrieved February 7, 2001, from http:www.cns/about/leg_history.html.

de Tocqueville, A. (1969) *Democracy in America.* New York: Doubleday. (Originally published in 1835)

Dewey, J. (1916). *Democracy and education.* New York: MacMillan.

Dewey, J. (1963). *Experience and education.* New York: Collier. (Original work published 1938)

Eberly, D. J. (1993). National youth service: A developing institution. *NASSP Bulletin, 77,* 50–57.

Harkavy, I. (1996). Back to the future: From service learning to strategic, academically-based community service. *Metropolitan Universities, 7,* 57–71.

Johnson, A. M., & Notah, D. J. (1999). Service-learning: History, literature review, and a pilot study of eighth graders. *Elementary School Journal, 99,* 453–467.

Kenny, M. E., & Gallagher, L. A. (2002). Service learning: A history of systems. In M. E. Kenny, L. A. Simon, K. Kiley-Brabeck, & R. M. Lerner (Eds.), *Learning to serve: Promoting civil society through service learning* (pp. 15–29). Norwell, MA: Kluwer.

Kinsley, C.W., & McPherson, K. (Eds.). (1995). *Enriching the curriculum through service learning.* Alexandria, VA: Association for Supervision and Curriculum Development.

Kraft, R.J. (1996). Service learning: An introduction to its theory, practice, and effects. *Education and Urban Society, 28,* 131–159.

Lerner R.M., Ostrom, C.W., Miller, J.R., Votruba, J.C., von Eye, A., Hoopfer, L.C., Terry, P.A., Taylor, C.S., Villarruel, F.A., & McKinney, M.H. (1996). Training applied developmental scientists for community outreach: The Michigan State University model of integrating science and outreach for children, youth, and families. In C.B. Fisher, J.P. Murray, & I.E. Sigel (Eds.), *Applied developmental science: Graduate training for diverse disciplines and educational settings* (pp. 163–188). Norwood, NJ: Ablex Publishing Corporation.

McGuckin, F. (Ed.). (1998). *The reference shelf: Volunteerism.* The H.W. Wilson Company. New York.

National Commission on Service Learning. (2002). Learning in deed: The power of service-learning for American schools. Battle Creek, MI: W.K. Kellogg Foundation.

National Youth Leadership Council. Service-Learning International: Two national service nonprofits announce strategic alliance. Retrieved March 31, 2001, from http://nylc.org.news.cfm.

Putnam, R. (2002). Bowling together. *The American Prospect, 13* (3).

Schine, J. (1997). School-based service: Reconnecting schools, communities, and youth at the margin. *Theory into Practice, 36,* 170–175.

SERVEnet. Timeline of service. Retrieved February 7, 2001, from http://www.servenet.org.

Sigmon, R. (1979). Service-learning: Three principles. *Synergist, 8,* 9–11.

Stanton,T.K., Giles, D.E., & Cruz, N.I. (1999). *Service-learning: A movement's pioneers reflect on its origins, practice, and future.* San Francisco, CA: Jossey-Bass.

Youniss, J., & Yates, M. (1997). *Community service and social responsibility in youth.* Chicago, IL: The University of Chicago Press.

3

Biographical Sketches

Many notable leaders have emerged in the field of community service and service-learning. The individuals profiled in this chapter have made outstanding and long-lasting contributions to the field. Although there are many significant people who have been committed and dedicated to promoting community service in the United States, we have chosen a diverse group of individuals to profile. Our group of leaders ranges from politicians and scholars to grass-roots organizers, all of whom share a common thread—a commitment to solving social problems in our communities and our country.

The rationale for youth service and service-learning is often traced back to the writings of philosopher John Dewey, with his work leaving an indelible mark on the field. Educators and scholars, such as Ernest Boyer and Ted Sizer, have been instrumental in recognizing the connection for improving education through student engagement in service. Other scholars, such as Benjamin Barber, have been essential in sparking debate about service and citizenship in a democratic society. In addition, we have recognized a group of researchers the field has grown tremendously through their identification of the benefits and outcomes of service experience and examination of which types of programs seem to be the most effective. The work of these researchers, such as Robert Shumer, Peter Benson, James Youniss, and Dale Blyth, has informed practitioners about the best practices in the field.

Moreover, since many of the programs for youth have been influenced by programs developed at the college and university level, we have included a group of key individuals who have created the structures for service programs and helped to define the best practices in higher education. These individuals, such as Timothy Stanton, Ira Harkavy, Dwight Giles Jr., and Janet Eyler, have been critically involved in developing programs at colleges and universities across the country that provide opportunities for students to participate in service.

Furthermore, we have identified a range of individuals who have been leaders of national service organizations, such as the National Youth Leadership Council, Learn and Serve America, America's Promise, and the National Indian Youth Leadership Project. These leaders, such as James Kielsmeier, Harris Wofford, Colin Powell, and McClelland Hall, have been responsible for bringing national service for youth to its current prominence and popularity. Finally, we have highlighted a few key political leaders, including former presidents Clinton and Bush and Senator Edward Kennedy, who were instrumental in passing legislation that provide the structures and funding for national service programs in the United States.

However, our list of contributors is not exhaustive. Many individuals who are responsible for developing and running programs are not in the public spotlight but are local community members who work for agencies that are vital in providing services to the community. We must also recognize the critical role that teachers and youth leaders have in implementing service-learning programs. These individuals realize the important value that connecting real world experiences with academic material can have for student development and building academic skills, as well as meeting the needs of the community. Finally, we must acknowledge all of the youth who have recognized the value of service and who have developed into leaders in their communities.

BENJAMIN BARBER

Benjamin Barber, a leading political scientist, is primarily known for his writing on civic education and democracy. For many years he served as a professor and director of the Walt Whitman Center for the Culture and Politics of Democracy at Rutgers University in New Jersey. He is the author of *An Aristocracy of Everyone: The Politics of Education and the Future of America* (1992), which examines the connection between public education and public citizenship in the United States. A key component to civic education is community service. His work is also strongly committed to diversity and the belief that diversity has the power to build a society. He has served as consultant to many political leaders and organizations in the United States and abroad, including former President Bill Clinton and former vice president Al Gore. He has also received many honors and awards, including the Guggenheim Fellowship, a Fulbright, and Social Science Research Fellowships. Barber received his Ph.D. in government from Harvard University. Barber has written several other books on democracy, including *Strong Democracy* (1984), *The Conquest of Politics* (1988), and *A Place for Us: How to Make Society Civil and Democracy Strong* (1998). He is also a contributor to many publications, including *Harper's* magazine, the *Atlantic Monthly*, and the *New York Times,* among others. Barber was also a founding editor and the editor-in-chief of the quarterly journal, *Political Theory.*

PETER L. BENSON

Peter Benson is a lecturer, author, researcher, and consultant who is widely recognized in the field of child and adolescent development. His work focuses on strengthening communities and working on public policy to enhance the positive developmental opportunities for youth in America. Benson has worked for the Search Institute since 1978 and has been the president of the organization since 1985. The Search Institute is a nonprofit research organization dedicated to promoting positive and healthy development of children and adolescents through engaging in research on important issues that impact youth, families, and communities. The Search Institute developed the concept of developmental assets, which are factors that help promote healthy development in youth. The organization provides information and resources for individuals, families, community agencies, and other professionals. As president of the Search Institute, Benson directs a large staff that is interested in making a contribution to positive youth development, include promoting opportunities for youth to participate in community service and other prosocial activities. He has contributed to the field as the author of many books on adolescents and how the community shapes their lives. His very informative and practical books include: *Beyond Leaf Raking: Learning to Serve, Serving to Learn* (1993); *All Kids Are Our Kids: What Communities Must Do to Raise Caring and Responsible Children and Adolescents* (1997); *What Teens Need to Succeed: Proven, Practical Ways to Shape Your Own Future* (1998); *What Kids Need to Succeed: Proven, Practical Ways to Raise Good Kids* (1998); and the

Fragile Foundation: The State of Development Assets among American Youth (1999). His work has introduced new thinking in the field of how communities can contribute to raising healthy, successful, and caring adolescents. Benson received his bachelor's degree from Augustana College in Rock Island, Illinois. Later, he earned an M.A. from Yale University and both an M.A. and a Ph.D. in social psychology from the University of Denver. More information on the Search Institute is available in the organizations chapter of this book.

SHELLEY H. BILLIG

Shelley Billig is the vice president of RMC Research Corporation and oversees the office located in Denver, Colorado. She is an expert in the field of education, service-learning, research design, and program evaluation. She directs many large-scale projects on service-learning, including W. K. Kellogg's Learning In Deed Service-Learning Research Network, which is responsible for the creation of a network to disseminate research on service-learning. She is also the codirector of the IASA Federal Programs/ Service-Learning project. She has conducted many other evaluation projects and research studies related to service-learning and education. In addition, she has authored several publications examining the impact of service-learning on youth. She also developed a guide for service-learning in federal programs to help practitioners to develop, implement, and evaluate programs to foster student academic achievement.

Before taking her position at RMC, Billig was an assistant professor at Metropolitan State College, Merrimack College, Regis College, Northeastern University, and the University of Rhode Island. She taught courses on social policy and evaluation, research methodology and statistics, as well as social psychology and sociology courses at the graduate and undergraduate levels. Billig received her B.A. in sociology from Boston University and both her M.A. in Sociology: Organizational Development and Behavior and her Ph.D. in Sociology: Research Methodology, Social Psychology and Family Relations from Tufts University in Massachusetts. More information on RMC Corporation is available in the organizations chapter of this book.

DALE BLYTH

Dale Blyth began his work in the field of community service and service-learning when he was at the Search Institute. Since 1998, Blyth has been the director of the Center for 4-H Youth Development at the University of Minnesota. Blyth is also an assistant director in the University of Minnesota Extension Service, which is associated with the Center for 4-H Youth Development. The center aims to support activities, such as outreach and research, which promote positive youth development and resiliency, as well as to support youth in their communities. His work at the center aims to improve policies and programs for youth. Blyth is also Minnesota's 4-H Program leader, and the cochair of the University of Minnesota's University of Promise. As a researcher, author, and public speaker, Blyth is an expert in putting research findings on community-based youth development into practice at the program and community level. Blyth has extensive experience in evaluating the impact of service-learning programs (Blyth, Saito, & Berkas, 1997). Blyth received his B.A. in psychology and sociology from Luther College and his Ph.D. in sociology from the University of Minnesota.

ERNEST L. BOYER SR. (1928–1995)

During his lifetime, Ernest Boyer was recognized as one of the biggest contributors to the field of education (Carnegie Foundation for the Advancement of Teaching, 1996). His work is thought to have shaped current views on education, as well as emphasized the importance of community service for youth. From 1979 to 1995, Boyer served as the seventh president of the Carnegie Foundation for the Advancement of Teaching. He was a strong advocate for integrating service into education in order for students to become connected to their communities. He recommended and set forth an implementation plan for a Carnegie unit to be added for service hours completed as a requirement for a high school degree. Under his leadership, the Carnegie Foundation for the Advancement of Teaching issued a number of reports on the current status of education at all levels in the United States, including reports on teaching and school reform.

From 1985 to 1990, Boyer was a senior fellow at the Woodrow Wilson School at Princeton University. He also served as the U.S. commissioner of education from 1977 to 1979 and was chancellor of the State University of New York (SUNY) from 1970 to 1977. He was appointed to several national commissions on education during the administrations of Presidents Nixon, Ford, Carter, Reagan, and Bush. Under former president George H.W. Bush, Boyer was appointed to the National Education Goals Panel, which established a set of goals for the nation to achieve in education. He received several national awards, including the

Charles Frankel Prize in the Humanities; the James B. Conant Education Award; the President's Medal from Tel Aviv University; the Horatio Alger Award; and Educator of the Year from *U.S. News & World Report*, among others. Through the Woodrow Wilson National Fellowship Foundation, a scholarship exists in his name for individuals who are dedicated to careers in teaching. Boyer's educational background includes attending Messiah College in Grantham, Pennsylvania and receiving his bachelor's degree from Greenville College in Illinois. He began graduate studies at Ohio State University in 1950 and continued his studies and earned a master's and Ph.D. from the University of Southern California. He received a postdoctoral fellowship from the University of Iowa Hospital in medical audiology, was a Fulbright Scholar in India and Chile and a visiting fellow at Cambridge University. He then began his teaching career at Loyola University in Los Angeles. At Upland College, he became a professor of audiology and speech pathology and served as academic dean.

Boyer was also the author of numerous significant books and articles. His publications were critically influential for educators interested in service-learning and community service for youth. *High School: A Report on Secondary Education* (1983) was Boyer's first major study at the Carnegie Foundation and was a widely read analysis of the problems with teaching and learning in American high schools. This book triggered a school reform movement by making recommendations for improving the nation's schools (e.g., emphasizing excellence for every student, raising graduation requirements, improve teaching training, restructuring the school day). Boyer also advocated the use of community service to connect students' learning to the real world. His book *College: The Undergraduate Experience in America* (1987) was another landmark study, which focused his critical attention on the nation's colleges and universities. Among several recommendations for reform was his suggestion to implement student community service programs, so that students are active participants in their education outside of the classroom. Boyer's other highly influential publications include: *Scholarship Reconsidered: Priorities of the Professoriate* (1990); *Ready to Learn: A Mandate for the Nation* (1991); and *The Basic School: A Community for Learning* (1996).

HARRY BOYTE

Harry Boyte is a senior fellow and codirector of the Center for Democracy and Citizenship at the Hubert H. Humphrey Institute of

Public Affairs and the University of Minnesota. The Center for Democracy and Citizenship aims to engage individuals to become actively involved in public life. Boyte has asserted that although service may have some individual benefits, it may not necessarily serve as a method to increase youth's participation in the political and democratic process (1991). He has proposed that service programs often enhance personal development but fail to teach strategies for effecting social and political change. He has called for a new way to teach politics and to increase youth civic engagement and hopes to achieve these goals through programs at the center. Boyte was also the coordinator for New Citizenship, a program designed to bring citizens and their government closer together, and developed Public Achievement, a civic education youth initiative that now has over forty sites in the United States and Ireland. He participated in a Camp David seminar on the future of democracy, presenting his views to President Bill Clinton and Vice President Al Gore in 1995. Boyte was also a senior advisor for the National Commission for Civic Renewal, directed by former U.S. education secretary William Bennett and former senator Sam Nunn.

Early in his service career, Boyte worked for Martin Luther King Jr. on behalf of the Southern Christian Leadership Conference during the 1960s. He received his doctorate in Political and Social Thought from the Union Institute. Boyte is also a prolific writer. He has authored several books and articles on citizenship and community organizing. In addition, his works have been published in over seventy publications, including the *New York Times* and *Wall Street Journal*. Some of his more influential books include: *The Backyard Revolution: Understanding the New Citizen Movement* (1980), *CommonWealth: A Return to Citizen Politics* (1989), and, with Nancy Kari, *Building America: The Democratic Promise of Public Work* (1996).

ROBERT BRINGLE

Robert Bringle is a scholar whose research focuses on service-learning, personality, close relationships, and the evaluation of social, educational, and health programs. He is currently a professor of psychology at Indiana University Purdue University at Indianapolis (IUPUI) and Director of the IUPUI Center for Public Service and Leadership. Bringle received his B.A. from Hanover College and his M.S. and Ph.D. from the University of Massachusetts at Amherst. Bringle is nationally recognized for implementing service-learning into higher education. He has made significant contributions to the field of service-learning and was recognized for his accomplishments when he received the Thomas Ehrlich Faculty Award for Service-Learning by Campus Compact and American Association for Higher Education in 1998. He is also an editor, with Donna Duffy, of a monograph for the American Association of Higher Education series on service-learning and the academic disciplines (*With Service in Mind: Concepts and Models for Service-Learning in Psychology*) and other publications on service-learning and faculty development.

GEORGE H. W. BUSH

As the forty-first president of the United States, George H. W. Bush was instrumental in the passage of the National and Community Service Act of 1990 and created the Office of National Service. This act created service opportunities that involve school-age youth, the youth corps, service in higher education, and national service demonstration models. This legislation also created the Points of Light Foundation, a private, nonprofit organization that helps individuals engage in service to their communities. In 1992, the Bush administration helped to draft legislation that created the National Civilian Community Corps to use military resources to address domestic social problems.

Bush began his career in the military in 1942 when he became a pilot in the U.S. Navy and fought in World War II against Japan. His plane was shot down in the Pacific, and he was rescued and returned to the United States in 1944. After marrying Barbara Pierce, Bush attended and graduated from Yale University with a degree in economics. George and Barbara had six children, including George W., John, Neil, Marvin, Robin, and Dorothy. Moving his family to Texas, Bush became involved in the oil business and was a millionaire by the age of forty-one. In 1962, he entered local politics and in 1964 ran for Senate as a Republican. Although Bush was defeated, he ran again for the U.S. House of Representatives and won in 1966. He was also reelected in 1968. During his years in the House, he was on the Ways and Means Committee and supported extending voting rights to eighteen-year-olds and the abolishment of the draft for the military. Although he ran for Senate after his two terms in the House, he lost to Lloyd Bentsen. He was then appointed to serve as the U.S. Ambassador to the United Nations from 1971 to 1973. From 1973 to 1974, he was the chairman of the Republican National Committee. From 1974 to 1975, he served as a U.S. envoy to China and then became the director of the Central Intelligence Agency. Although Bush made a bid to become the 1980 Republican presidential nominee, Ronald Reagan prevailed, but asked Bush to be his running mate. He served as vice president from 1980 to 1988. Then, he ran and won the presidency in 1988. During his presidency, Bush was instrumental in the passage of a number of key domestic policies, including the 1990 Americans with Disabilities Act and increasing federal funding for education and child care. After he was defeated for re-election by Bill Clinton in 1992, Bush returned to private life. Bush participated in the Presidents' Summit for America's Future and is the honorary chairman of the Points of Light Foundation.

WILLIAM J. CLINTON

As the forty-second president of the United States, Bill Clinton was a strong advocate of national service (Corporation for National Service, 2001). He supported the Corporation for National Service, which ensured continued funding for national service programs. Bill Clinton's administration worked with members of Congress to create and pass the National and Community Service Trust Act of 1993, which amended the National and Community Service Act of 1990. This act created the Corporation for National Service, which increased and expanded opportunities for citizens to engage in service to their communities through such programs as AmeriCorps and Learn and Serve America. In addition, the act also provided education grants to people ages seventeen years and older who perform community service before, during, or after postsecondary education. President Clinton also presided over the Presidents' Summit for America's Future, which celebrated America's commitment to its youth and promoted a national interest in volunteerism and community service. This summit also launched America's Promise—The Alliance for Youth, which was headed by Retired General Colin Powell. At the end of the event, President Clinton signed a Summit Declaration, which emphasized the responsibility that all citizens share in promoting good for all Americans. More information on the Corporation for National Service, AmeriCorps, Learn and Serve America, and America's Promise is available in the organizations chapter of this book.

Clinton's interest in service and civic participation began when he was in high school. In 1963, as a junior in high school, Clinton was elected as a delegate from Arkansas to Boys Nation, which was a government study program sponsored by the American Legion veterans' organization. During this experience, he debated and advocated for civil rights legislation and had the opportunity to meet then U.S. President John F. Kennedy at the White House. In 1964, Clinton attended Georgetown University and received his bachelor's degree in international affairs. Clinton also interned for the U.S. Senate Foreign Relations Committee. Before attending Yale Law School, Clinton won a Rhodes Scholarship to the University of Oxford in England. At Yale, he met his future wife, Hillary Rodham. Both Bill Clinton and Hillary Rodham were involved in political campaigns. After law school, Clinton taught at the law school at the University of Arkansas. He married Hillary in 1975, and their only child, daughter Chelsea, was born in 1980. In 1974, Clinton began his career in public political service when he ran for office in the U.S. House of Representatives. Although Clinton lost that election, he decided to run and was elected as the attorney general of Arkansas in 1976. In 1978, Clinton ran and was elected governor of Arkansas, but lost reelection in 1980. He ran and won again the governor's office in 1984, 1986, and 1990. Clinton decided to run for president in 1992, campaigning on domestic issues, including a national service program.

ROBERT COLES

Robert Coles is renowned for his work as a child psychiatrist and professor at Harvard University. In addition, Coles has been dedicated to community service and is regarded as an expert in the field of volunteerism and community service. In his own life, he worked for desegregation and the civil rights movement, advocating for human rights, as well as tutoring youth in the inner city. In his compelling book, *The Call of Service—A Witness to Idealism* (1993), Coles explores the nature of idealism and considers social activism as a basic drive necessary to individuals and society. Coles examines his own experiences in serving others and his interactions with other volunteers who have made a difference and changed lives. He also asserts that service should be an essential part of higher education in the United States. Coles firmly believes that through service, a person experiences a great satisfaction that can improve one's life in many aspects. Coles is a prolific writer, and his work has been published in a number of publications, including the *New Republic*, the *Atlantic Monthly*, *New Oxford Review*, and *Teacher* magazine. He also won the Pulitzer Prize for his book *The Spiritual Life of Children* (1990). Other widely read books include: *The Moral Life of*

Children (1986), *The Political Life of Children* (1986), and *The Call of Stories: Teaching and the Moral Imagination* (1989).

NADINNE CRUZ

Nadinne Cruz has been very influential in the field of international and cross-cultural service-learning. She comes from the Philippines, a country she felt was undone by service, and therefore began her career questioning service (Stanton, Giles, & Cruz, 1999). Cruz studied at the University of the Philippines in the late 1960s, but quit to join a peasant organization to learn more outside of the classroom and from the people. She was inspired to advocate for service through her work with the Philippine peasants. Fleeing from martial law, Cruz came to the United States. She earned a master's degree in political science at Marquette University and received her Ph.D. from the University of Minnesota. She was involved in the Alliance for Philippine Concerns and became the director of the Twin Cities' Higher Education Consortium for Urban Affairs for twelve years in St. Paul, Minnesota, where she began to study how education and politics could influence service-based knowledge to help students understand urban environments and how they could become change agents within those environments. Cruz developed and taught the City Arts program, which connected arts to community development and social change. She believed in collaborating with the artists in her program, rather than using traditional, analytical modes of teaching. She has also directed community-based learning programs in Latin America and Scandinavia and was the Eugene M. Lang Professor of Social Change at Swarthmore College.

After serving as the associate director and interim director, Cruz became director of the Haas Center for Public Service at Stanford University, which organizes and supports public and community service by the Stanford community. She continues to see the academic institution as a base from which social change can happen. However, Cruz believes that service is not the same thing as community development or social change (Stanton et al., 1999). She cautions against institutionalizing service-learning, arguing that an expanded, more advanced field runs the risk of diluting service-learning's commitment to unique individual transformation shaped by the society. Educational institutions are part of the larger system that helps to create social problems in the first place. Therefore, direct service can only ameliorate bad situations, not change them. She argues that what is to be learned is not always agreed upon or easy to define and cautions that some academic institutions may view service-learning as outside of the institution's mission, and therefore, a distraction to the commitment to the academic component of the university. Cruz has also been a lecturer in the Urban Studies Program and has developed service-learning courses and programs to support public service.

JOHN DEWEY (1859–1952)

John Dewey is most often credited with developing the concept of experiential education. A philosopher and educator, his writings have been instrumental to the development of the field of service-learning. Advocates of service-learning often credit Dewey's philosophy with the idea that service is a valuable and effective method of teaching and learning (Boyer, 1983; Eyler & Giles, 1997). Although Dewey did not necessarily advocate service per se, his philosophy of education (pragmatism) focuses on learning by doing. Students' experiences come from the interaction between the individual and the environment. Dewey believed that informal learning (i.e., learning that is not a part of the traditional curriculum) is critical to students' learning. He viewed experiential learning and community participation as essential methods for helping individuals to gain an understanding of others and to find solutions to solve community problems.

Dewey attended the University of Vermont in Burlington, Vermont, where he began pursuing his interest in philosophy. After he graduated from the University of Vermont, Dewey taught high school for two years. He enrolled in Johns Hopkins University for graduate school in philosophy. He received his doctorate in 1884, and began teaching at the University of Michigan. In 1894, Dewey took a position at the University of Chicago, where his vision of pragmatism began to take hold. In addition, he founded and directed a laboratory school that gave him the opportunity to apply his ideas on education. In 1904, he resigned from the University of Chicago and took a position in the philosophy department at Columbia University, where he remained for the rest of his academic career. Dewey became a leader in philosophy and education, and was a prolific writer and speaker. Among his great works, the following writings have been most influential on education and service-learning: *The School and Society* (1900), *Democracy and Education: An Introduction to the Philosophy of Education* (1916), and *Experience and Education* (1938).

JOHN DiBIAGGIO

John DiBiaggio is a strong proponent of service-learning and of the role of universities to partner with communities as they prepare students to become active and committed citizens. He is a member of the board of directors of National Campus Compact and helped to draft the Presidents' Declaration on the Civic Responsibility of Higher Education. DiBiaggio exemplifies a strong personal commitment to service and citizenship, having served as the president of the board of the American Council on Education, chairman of the National Campus Compact, member of the International Exchange of Scholars, and on the boards of the National Collegiate Athletic Association (NCAA) foundation, American Film Institute, the Knight Foundation Commission on Intercollegiate Athletics, and the American Cancer Society Foundation.

DiBiaggio has a long history in university leadership, serving as president of Tufts University from 1992 to 2001, president of Michigan State University from 1985 to 1992, and president of the University of Connecticut from 1979 to 1985. While at Tufts, he established, with support from the Omidyar Foundation, the University College of Citizenship and Public Service (UCCPS). The UCCPS was developed to make the values and skills of active citizenship, including a commitment to community participation for the development of healthier communities, a critical component of undergraduate and graduate education at Tufts University. DiBiaggio holds three earned degrees, twelve honorary degrees, and has received numerous prestigious awards for his leadership, vision, and commitment to public service and active citizenship.

DONALD J. EBERLY

Donald Eberly tested the ideas of national service in the early 1950s (as outlined in his 1988 book, *National Service: A Promise to Keep*), which were followed by the establishment of the Peace Corps and service-learning. He is currently the president and cofounder of the Commonwealth Foundation in Pennsylvania, an institute dedicated to civic, democratic, and economic renewal. In addition, Eberly directs the Civil Society Project and serves on the Council on Civil Society and the National Commission on Civic Renewal. He is founder and chairman of the National Fatherhood Initiative, a group dedicated to restoring fatherhood in our culture. Eberly is also an affiliated scholar at the Institute for American Values. Eberly defines national service as service to society that is part of citizenship responsibility. Citizens should be provided opportunities to contribute and make a difference. He views national service as an educational experience for those who serve and has been one of only a few scholars to study national service at the international level. He views national youth service as a democratic, nationwide institution that is a logical outgrowth of the relationship between a nation and its young people. He argues that many young people are prepared to serve and need to be told that they can make a difference, yet lack the necessary support in order to do so full-time.

In order to remain committed to our mission of a civil and just society, he argues that schools and colleges need to recognize the educational value of service experiences and offer opportunities for students to perform a supervised and supported year of national service within the context of their academic degree program. Educators need to understand that service supports education and that service-learning activities can and need to be outlined with learning objectives to measure outcomes. Eberly argues that students need to be provided an opportunity to provide service across many domains (domestic, overseas, full-time, part-time, and so on) and should be compensated for their work and efforts. He further argues that service activities support vocational development and the development of healthy self-sufficiency by linking service with educational opportunities. Moreover, he believes that national youth service is a citizenship responsibility of young people, and substantial support is needed from federal, state, and local government for youth to perform full-time plus paid. In addition, Eberly argues that employers in the private sector as well as within the volunteer sector need to recognize the value of education and work and make opportunities for service available.

Eberly is a prolific writer, with many of his writings centering around the condition of political and social life and what is necessary in order to work towards cultural and civil renewal. Some of his books include: *The Moral Equivalent of War: A Study of Non-Military Service in Nine Nations* (1990), *National Youth Service: A Democratic Institution for the 21st Century* (1991), *Building a Community of Citizens: Civil Society in the 21st Century* (1994), and *America's Promise: Civil Society and the Renewal of American Culture* (1998). He received his M.A. from George Washington University and his M.P.A. from Harvard University. He received his doctoral training at the Pennsylvania State University.

THOMAS EHRLICH

Thomas Ehrlich has made major contributions to the field of service-learning and higher education. As the president emeritus of Indiana University, Ehrlich was a model link between the university and the community. Ehrlich is a senior fellow at the Carnegie Foundation for the Advancement of Teaching, where his work focuses on the values, citizenship, and character in education. He also serves on the board of directors for the Commission of National and Community Service and has served as the chair of the Campus Compact Executive Committee. He has also served as the chair of the 2000–2001 American Association for Higher Education board of directors and is on the board of the Center for Civic Education, Bennett College, National Center for Public Policy and Higher Education, and the Public Welfare Foundation. His continuing efforts to advocate service-learning and civic responsibility in communities led to the Thomas Ehrlich Award for Service-Learning, named in his honor. Currently, Ehrlich is a Distinguished University Scholar at California State University and teaches courses that integrate academics and community service at the undergraduate level. At Stanford University, he is a visiting professor of law, teaching courses on international human rights. Ehrlich has written or edited many books and articles, including *Civic Responsibility and Higher Education* (2000). Ehrlich was also the provost of University of Pennsylvania and dean of the Stanford Law School. He is a graduate of Harvard University and Harvard Law School.

MICHELLE ENGLER

Michelle Engler is the wife of the former Republican governor of Michigan, John Engler. Her main objective as Michigan's First Lady was to encourage people to volunteer and become involved in their communities through public service. Her primary responsibility as Michigan's First Lady was as the chair of the Michigan Community Service Commission, which encourages community service and volunteerism. In 1997, Engler was asked by Retired General Colin Powell to be on the executive board of America's Promise, which recruits mentors for children. The movement is striving to help build and strengthen the character and competence of America's youth. In 1998, Engler was reappointed to the America's Promise board. Engler was in charge of Michigan's branch of the national organization, called Michigan's Promise, which falls under her responsibilities in the Michigan Community Service Commission. In addition, Engler has been a member of the board of directors of the Points of Light Foundation and the Michigan Nonprofit Association and a member of the National Commission on Service-Learning of the Learning In Deed initiative of the W. K. Kellogg Foundation. She was also recently recognized for her work in reducing mortality from breast cancer. Engler's other public service commitments include serving on the board of directors of the Library of Michigan Foundation and participation in the Girlstown Foundation, Artrain, and the Michigan Caring Program for Children, which is a model program that provides preventative health care for uninsured children.

JANET EYLER

Janet Eyler is currently a professor of the practice of education at Vanderbilt University's Peabody College. She earned her bachelor's and master's degrees in education at the University of Washington and received her Ph.D. from Indiana University. Eyler has completed research that focuses on the outcomes of service-learning, such as problem solving, cognitive development, civic engagement, and transfer of learning among university and college students. She also teaches a number of service-learning courses, including a public policy and higher education seminar in service-learning that integrates a weeklong service trip during spring break. Eyler has codirected a national service-learning research project and a Corporation for National Service on learning outcomes at the college level. In 1999, she received the Outstanding Research Award from the National Society for Experiential Education. Eyler has published a number of articles examining internships and service-learning in higher education. She is also coauthor, with Dwight Giles Jr., of an informative book that examines service-learning outcomes in college students, entitled *Where's the Learning in Service-Learning?* (1999).

ANDREW FURCO

Currently, Andrew Furco directs the Service-Learning Research and Development Center at the University of California at Berkeley. In addition, Furco heads up research and evaluation studies and on various issues regarding service-learning at all levels of education, including kindergarten through higher education. He also provides technical assistance and training to K–12 schools and higher education institutions on service-learning issues and creates instruments for program evaluation of service-learning projects in grades K–12 and in higher education. He is also a member of the research advisory committee of Learning In Deed, an initiative of the W.K. Kellogg Foundation. Furco received his doctorate from the University of California at Berkeley.

DWIGHT GILES JR.

In January 2001, Dwight Giles Jr. was appointed professor of higher education and a senior associate at the New England Resource Center for Higher Education (NERCHE) in the Graduate College of Education at the University of Massachusetts in Boston. As a professor, he teaches courses in institutional change and curriculum and learning. Prior to taking his current position, Giles was professor of human and organizational development at Vanderbilt University's Peabody College, as well as director of internships from 1992 to 2001. His research focus has been on student outcomes and engagement in reflection in service-learning in college students. In addition, his academic interests include community development, volunteering, civic participation, participatory action research, university-community partnerships, and higher education reform. He has served as a consultant for experiential education and service-learning programs for colleges and universities, professional organizations, and foundations. In addition, he has been on the board of the National Society for Experiential Education and is currently an invited member of the National Faculty Consulting Corps, sponsored by American Association of Higher Education (AAHE) and Campus Compact. In 1998, Giles received, with Janet Eyler, the Outstanding Research Award from the National Society for Experiential Education. Giles received his master's degree from the Union Theological Seminary in New York. In 1980, Giles joined Cornell University's Field and International Study Program, where he was involved in the development of service-learning programs and building university-community partnerships. Giles then completed his Ph.D. in community development at Pennsylvania State University. He has coauthored books on service-learning research, including: *Where's the Learning in Service-Learning?* (1999) with Janet Eyler, and *Service-Learning: A Movement's Pioneers Reflect on Its Origins, Practice, and Future* (1999), with Timothy Stanton and Nadinne Cruz. He is also currently working on a book entitled, *Designing Effective Service-Learning* with Janet Eyler. Giles is coauthor of many other publications and has presented his work at professional conferences throughout the United States.

McCLELLAND HALL

McClelland Hall has made significant contributions to the education and development of Native American youth. Hall is Native American of the Cherokee/Pawnee tribal affiliation. He is the founder and executive director of the National Indian Youth Leadership Project (NIYLP) headquartered in Gallup, New Mexico. The NIYLP is the pioneer organization of service-learning, experiential education, and leadership development for Native American youth. Hall (1991) has stated that, "to become involved in service to others is thus a natural extension of Native Americans' traditional sense of communal responsibility" (pp. 754–755). Therefore, the NIYLP builds upon Native American traditions and integrates them into experiential teaching and learning strategies. Hall and colleagues began thinking of forming this organization when a group of people came together in Oklahoma to deal with rising drop-out rates by Cherokee students in 1981 (Hall, 1991). From 1981 to 1983, Hall was also director of the alternative high school of the Cherokee Nation. For two decades, Hall has been a critical player in the development of programs to assist Native American schools, including service-learning, drop-out prevention, and leadership development. Hall received the Kurt Hahn award in 1995 from the Association for Experiential Education for his contributions to the field. (Kurt Hahn was the founder of Outward Bound.) He has also authored numerous articles on his work regarding service and published articles in the *Journal of Experiential Education* and *Phi Delta Kappan*. More information on the NIYLP is available in the organizations chapter of this book.

IRA HARKAVY

Harkavy has been committed to community service and community building since his youth (Stanton et al., 1999). He first became interested in working with the community in 1963, when he attended camp in the Poconos in Pennsylvania and learned from his counselors about their experience with the civil rights movement. In addition, Harkavy has a strong civil rights tradition in his family. His parents were Jewish and deeply dedicated to civil rights and antiwar activism. Harkavy honors his family's civil rights tradition by advocating and creating community-campus connections (Stanton et al., 1999). He attended the University of Pennsylvania as an undergraduate and a graduate student. After working for several years in the community, Harkavy returned to the University of Pennsylvania to get his Ph.D. in history. While working in the surrounding community, he became interested in understanding how the university could engage with the community to promote effective service delivery to urban youth. After graduation, he stayed and worked in the community as a community worker. Harkavy developed the West Philadelphia Improvement Corps and is known for advocating university-assisted community schools and for university-community partnerships in general. He believes that the university is directly linked with change in the community, which could be developed through service-learning (Harkavy, 1996). Harkavy is the current director of the Center for Community Partnerships at the University of Pennsylvania since its founding in 1992. The center encourages initiatives that link the academic mission of the university to service the West Philadelphia community. The center was founded on the notion that the welfare and interests of the surrounding West Philadelphia community and the University of Pennsylvania are interconnected. The university can make significant contributions to the community. The center coordinates university-wide efforts in community service and creates collaborative initiatives to benefit the community. Although his focus has been on the University of Pennsylvania, he views changing all higher education establishments as both crucial and inevitable. Harkavy has written numerous articles and publications and has presented at conferences and governmental hearings on the topics service-learning and community-university partnerships.

EDWARD (TED) M. KENNEDY

Elected to the U.S. Senate in 1962, Senator Edward Kennedy is in his sixth term of service. As a Democratic Senator, Kennedy has long been a champion of such causes as education and health care. He serves on the Labor and Human Resources Committee, the Judiciary Committee, and on the Armed Services Committee. Kennedy was instrumental in the passage of the National and Community Service Act of 1990. He advocated for including service-learning as a means of education reform. Kennedy wrote an influential piece in the June 1991 issue of *Phi Delta Kappan* that promoted his position for national service for youth.

He is also a trustee of the John F. Kennedy Center for the Performing Arts in Washington, D.C. He graduated from Harvard University and received his law degree from the University of Virginia Law School. He served as an assistant district attorney for Suffolk County in Massachusetts. Kennedy is the youngest of nine children of Joseph P. Kennedy and Rose Fitzgerald Kennedy, and the brother of John F. Kennedy and Robert Kennedy.

JAMES C. KIELSMEIER

The founder, president, and CEO of the National Youth Leadership Council (NYLC), Jim Kielsmeier has extensive experience in experiential education, service-learning, and leadership development programs. The NYLC, which he founded in 1983, is a nonprofit organization located in St. Paul, Minnesota. The NYLC partners with schools, community and faith-based agencies, corporations, colleges, and the government in order to achieve the goals of building better communities through engaging youth in service. Since 1993, the NYLC has served as the primary national training agency for service-learning for the Corporation for National Service, which operates regional centers and a network of peer mentors. In addition, the NYLC sponsors the annual National Service-Learning Conference and was involved in the Presidents' Summit for America's Future and in the 2000 National Youth Summit held in Orlando, Florida. Kielsmeier also founded the Center for Experiential Education and Service-Learning at the University of Minnesota. In addition, he has been instrumental in developing and implementing state and federal service-learning and youth service models and has worked with both state and federal government. For example, he worked with the Clinton administration on the implementation of AmeriCorps and cochairs the service-learning committee of the Minnesota Commission on National and Community Service implemented by Governor Jesse Ventura. He also consults, gives speeches, and teaches courses at the University of Minnesota. Furthermore, he is a member of the Learning In Deed National Leadership Network Steering Committee of the W. K. Kellogg Foundation. He has authored many publications on service-learning and youth leadership, including an important piece in the recent special issue of *Phi Delta Kappan* (2000). Kielsmeier received his bachelor's degree from Wheaton College in Wheaton, Illinois, a master's degree in international relations from American University in Washington, D.C., and his Ph.D. in education from the University of Colorado. He was an Outward Bound instructor, junior and high school teacher, and served in the U.S. Army. He also received numerous awards, including the Kurt Hahn Award of the Association for Experiential Education, the National Indian Youth Leadership Project's Lifetime Achievement Award, and the Rotary Club's Paul Harris Award.

FRANK NEWMAN

Frank Newman was the former president of the Education Commission of the States from 1985 to 1999, where he played a key role in the founding of Campus Compact. The Education Commission of the States brings together governors, legislators, and state education leaders to improve education. Currently, Newman is a visiting professor of public policy and sociology at Brown University. At Brown, he also directs The Futures Project: Policy for Higher Education in a Changing World, which attempts to develop policies and address the role of higher education in a changing, global society. He is also visiting professor at Teachers College, Columbia University, in New York City. Newman also served as the president of the University of Rhode Island from 1974 to 1983. At Stanford University, he served as director of university relations. He was also a presidential fellow at the Carnegie Foundation for the Advancement of Teaching. Currently, he is also a member of the National Commission on Service-Learning of the Learning In Deed initiative of the W.K. Kellogg Foundation. Newman received a B.A. in engineering, naval sciences and economics from Brown University, an M.S. in business from Columbia University, and Ph.D. in history from Stanford University. More information on Campus Compact and the Education Commission of the States is available in the organizations chapter of this book.

COLIN L. POWELL

Born in New York City in 1937, Retired General Colin Powell was raised in the South Bronx, New York. He attended City College of New York where he received his bachelor's degree in geology and he later earned a master's degree in business administration from George Washington University in Washington, D.C. While at City College, General Powell participated in the ROTC program, where he began his career in the military. He is the recipient of numerous medals and honors from the military in addition to many civilian awards. General Powell served as a soldier for thirty-five years, during which time he held high positions such as the chairman of the Joint Chiefs of Staff of the Department of Defense during the Desert Storm War in the early 1990s.

Since 1997 and the Presidents' Summit for America's Future, General Powell served as the founding chairman of America's Promise—The Alliance for Youth (America's Promise, 2000). This organization strives to strengthen and build character in today's youth through the acceptance of the Five Promises that guide children to successful adulthoods. These promises are as follows: maintain ongoing relationships with a caring adult; safe places with structured activities during nonschool hours; a healthy start; marketable skills through effective education; and opportunities to give back through community service. The organization encourages young people to give back to their communities as a whole, as well as to help their peers. Youth participate by volunteering in such organizations as the Boy Scouts, Girl Scouts, Boys and Girls Clubs, and Catholic Campus Ministry Associations in addition to national days of service. America's Promise works with the youth to help them realize their potential and help them find significance in giving to their communities. General Powell also serves on the board of governors of the Boys and Girls Clubs of America. He has authored a best-selling book, *My American Journey—An Autobiography* (1995), chronicling the amazing story of his life. In January 2001, General Powell was sworn in as the 65th U.S. Secretary of State, but continues his involvement in America's Promise and with the youth of America. More information on America's Promise is available in the organizations chapter of this book.

LYNDA JOHNSON ROBB

As the daughter of President Lyndon Baines Johnson and Lady Bird Johnson and wife of former Senator Charles Robb of Virginia, Lynda Johnson Robb has spent most of her life concerned with community issues. More than thirty years ago, Robb began to volunteer reading to children in hospitals, which led to her interest in children's literature. This experience led her to become involved with Reading Is Fundamental (RIF). When Robb joined RIF, it was a small group that encouraged literacy among children. Currently, Reading Is Fundamental is the nation's largest children's literacy organization. Robb has been the chairperson of the RIF board of directors since May 1996. Her responsibilities in this role include traveling around the country encouraging support for the organization and meeting with teachers, parents, and local volunteers who run the RIF programs. Lynda Johnson Robb is also the president of the National Home Library Foundation and the former vice chair of America's Promise. She is a graduate of the University of Texas.

JOAN SCHINE

Joan Schine first volunteered when she was a student in the 1930s (Stanton et al., 1999). She attended a demonstration school at Columbia University's Teacher's College, which was modeled after John Dewey's educational philosophy and advocated service. She noted that the learning component was a missing piece of this experience. She was then a parent school volunteer and was committed to issues of poverty and civil rights. She then became a pioneer in the service-learning field by working with middle and high school youth in 1967 with the National Commission of Resources for Youth (NCRY). Schine's passion was combating racism by working with minority youth who were poor to become productive and active citizens. NCRY advocated youth participation and offered programs to give youth an active role in their lives by encouraging preparation, reflection, and responsibility. The NCRY promoted youth participation, an important service-learning feature. In 1982, she founded the Early Adolescent Helper Program, part of the Graduate School and University Center of the City University of New York. The program expanded and was renamed the National Center for Service-Learning in Early Adolescence to promote service-learning in middle schools across the nation. This program is currently the National Helper Network, and more information on it is available in the organizations chapter of this book. Schine is author of many publications on service-learning, including serving as the editor of a book on service-learning for the National Society of Experiential Education (1997).

ROBERT SHUMER

In 1992, Robert Shumer was appointed the director of the National Service-Learning Clearinghouse housed at the University of Minnesota. The National Service-Learning Clearinghouse is a resource for information, research, and technical assistance on service-learning. He has also codirected the Center for Experiential Education and Service-Learning at the University of Minnesota and has been responsible for directing a number of research studies on service-learning and experiential learning. Shumer also has extensive experience in program evaluation of service programs, including Learn and Serve programs in Minnesota and Wisconsin, and developed a self-assessment survey for service program coordinators to monitor and evaluate their programs (Shumer et al., 2000). At the University of Minnesota, he has taught courses in the theory and practice of experiential education and evaluation. In addition to the clearinghouse, Shumer has extensive program development experience. For example, he has been working on developing technology applications of service-learning to bridge the digital divide in schools and communities with a grant from the AOL Foundation. Shumer's experience in the Key Club was a formative experience that led to his commitment to service (Stanton et al., 1999). Shumer has been a high school teacher, has helped to develop a community school, and was the director of the Field Studies Department at UCLA. He has been dedicated to giving youth opportunities for civic engagement and service to their communities. He received his bachelor's degree in history from the University of California at Santa Barbara, a master's in educational psychology from California State University at Northridge, and a Ph.D. in education from UCLA. Shumer has published numerous articles and writings in the area of service-learning (e.g., Shumer, 1994; Shumer & Belbas, 1996), as well as many presentations at professional conferences. More information on the National Service-Learning Clearinghouse is available in the selected resources chapter of this book and can be accessed at http://www.nicsl.coled.umn.edu.

TED SIZER

Ted Sizer was instrumental in the school-reform movement in the 1980s. Sizer received his bachelor's degree in English literature from Yale University, his M.A.T. in social studies from Harvard University, and his Ph.D. in education and American history from Lawrence University. He also received a Guggenheim Fellowship in 1971. Sizer has an extensive background as an educator, including teaching math and English at Boston's Roxbury Latin School and teaching history and serving as headmaster at Phillips Academy in Andover, Massachusetts. In addition, he was a professor of education and dean of the Graduate School of Education at Harvard University. Sizer then became a professor of education and was the chairman of Brown University's education department. He founded and was chairman of the Coalition of Essential Schools at Brown from 1984 until 1997. The Coalition of Essential Schools (CES) is an educational reform movement that grew out of a five-year study of American high schools. The coalition originally started with 12 schools and grew to over 230 schools by 1997. The schools are very diverse, but have the common goal of structuring themselves according to the Nine Common Principles that Sizer derived from his research. The coalition is funded by local private companies, state governments, the Education Commission of the States, the Annenberg Foundation, and other gifts. In 1993, as a part of former Ambassador Walter Annenberg's $500 million pledge to improve public education in the United States, Sizer became the director of Brown's Annenberg Institute of School Reform. He has also been awarded honorary degrees from Brown, Williams, Dartmouth, and Connecticut College.

Sizer has written many books and contributed many articles to education journals. His book, *Horace's Compromise: The Dilemma of the American High School* (1984), presents his findings from a five-year study of American high schools, from which the Nine Common Principles of the Coalition of Essentials Schools were developed. In *Horace's School: Redesigning the American High School* (1992), Sizer presents a hypothetical high school that illustrates the restructuring process based upon the nine principles outlined in *Horace's Compromise.* His vision of education in America is to give the management of the schools back to the teachers, students, and parents who are the most invested in improving children's education. Students should also become active learners with teachers serving as coaches.

GRAHAM B. SPANIER

Graham Spanier has been president of the Pennsylvania State University, one of the nation's largest and most comprehensive universities with 80,000 students spanning twenty-four campuses, since 1995. Prior to becoming president of Penn State, Spanier served as chancellor of the University of Nebraska, provost and vice president for academic affairs at Oregon State University, provost for undergraduate studies at the State University of New York, and as a member of the faculty and administration at Penn State's College of Health and Human Development.

As a leader in higher education, Spanier is well known for his commitment to university engagement with the local and global community and has initiated major efforts to connect Penn State with the community. Spanier reorganized the university campuses to have increased flexibility in meeting local community needs and expanded community outreach through Penn State Cooperative Extension to better meet the needs of Pennsylvania citizens. Among other initiatives, Spanier increased the internationalization of the university, created the Penn State World Campus, and developed the Consortium in Children, Youth, and Families. Beyond his accomplishments at Penn State, Spanier is chair of the board of directors of the National Association of State Universities and Land-Grant Colleges and deputy chair of the Worldwide Universities Network. He has also served as chair of the Kellogg Commission on the Future of State and Land-Grant Universities, which prepared the influential report "Returning to Our Roots: The Engaged Institution," which described how and why land-grant colleges are responsible for the betterment of the community. Spanier also served on the board of trustees of the National 4-H Council. In addition, Spanier was a founding member of the board of directors of the University Corporation for Internet Development, was president of the National Council on Family Relations, and chairman of the board of directors of the Christian Children's Fund.

As a scholar, Spanier is a professor of human development and family studies, sociology, demography, and family and community medicine. He has authored more than 100 scholarly publications, including 10 books. He completed his bachelor's and master's degrees at Iowa State University and his Ph.D. in sociology at Northwestern University.

TIMOTHY STANTON

Timothy Stanton is a national leader in the field of service-learning and has documented his legacy as well as that of other pioneers of the field in a recent book, *Service-Learning: A Movement's Pioneers Reflect on Its Origins, Practice, and Future* (1999). Stanton was first involved in service to community when he was invited to participate in a civil rights march in 1964, as a high school student in Hartford, Connecticut. At Stanford in the late 1960s, Stanton discovered that he was moving from civil rights to antiwar work and learning more from his experiences than in the classroom. Stanton received his Ph.D. from the Field Institute in Human and Organizational Systems. In 1971, Stanton was invited to develop and direct a youth community service program in Marin County, California, where he formalized his commitment to service. In the 1970s, he was also involved with the National Student Volunteer Program and the Society for Field Experience Education.

At Cornell, Stanton was involved in setting up Cornell University's Human Ecology Field Study Program in 1977. He advocated for the intensive field studies approach, which he employed at Cornell. He worked to design and implement an experience-based, interdisciplinary curriculum in human ecology with a focus on working with communities. The program was founded on the belief that experiential learning was not just combining education with action. The program at Cornell was crafted after visiting a program in China and was based on a reflective curriculum, where students were given opportunities to combine intellect with action in an organized and systemic manner. The key to the program is student empowerment.

As a result of the expressed dedication and support of President Donald Kennedy, Stanton moved to Stanford in 1985 to help establish the Haas Center for Public Service. At Stanford, Stanton moved away from using terms such as *service-learning* and *experiential learning* for the first several years as a way to connect with and gain support from other faculty members. The Haas Center helps to organize and support public service in the Stanford community. In addition, students are able to respond to community needs (as identified by community members) and are able to connect these needs with academic knowledge and skills. Stanton became the director of the Haas Center in 1991.

Stanton further advocated service-learning by completing a national survey and report in 1990 asking presidents of universities to be involved in an organization called Campus Compact to support service-study connections, which link academic material with reflection activities. He has advocated for developing the best practices in service-learning training, and determining the best ways to connect learning and service. Stanton believes that campus-community partnerships for service-learning and community development are necessary steps toward change in institutions. In other words, he believes that service-learning is a way to move universities toward changing their beliefs about how and where students learn. When universities change the beliefs about how and where students learn, the resulting actions of the universities will change as well. He has authored numerous publications on service-learning. Stanton left the position as director of the Haas Center and became the center's first senior fellow. He continues to be committed to community service and development work in California and in South Africa.

HARRIS WOFFORD

Throughout his life, Harris Wofford has been an important leader in the national service movement in the United States, striving to give

Americans the opportunity to participate in service. As a teenager, he was an activist when he formed the group called the Student Federalists. He also served as a private in the U.S. Army. Wofford was also an activist in the civil rights movement working with Dr. Martin Luther King Jr. and serving as a special assistant to former president John F. Kennedy; he was chairman of the White House Sub-Cabinet group on Civil Rights from 1961 to 1962. In 1961, Wofford played an instrumental role in establishing the Peace Corps. He served as the Peace Corps's special representative to Africa between 1963 and 64 and served as director of the Ethiopia program. He was the associate director of the Peace Corps during President Johnson's administration.

During the 1970s, Wofford turned his attention to national service and formed a panel to examine this issue. In 1979, this panel generated the report "Youth and the Needs of the Nation." He was actively involved in establishing a service movement in the state of Pennsylvania, including school-based service-learning and youth corps. He became involved in working with the National Governors Association and a group of senators to help develop the National and Community Service Act of 1990. Wofford served as a U.S. Senator from Pennsylvania from 1991 to 1994. He was also instrumental in creating and working to pass federal legislation (the National Civilian Community Corps and the National and Community Service Trust Act) that established the Corporation for National Service and AmeriCorps. From October 1995 through January 2001, Wofford served as the CEO of the Corporation for National Service. In addition, Wofford was involved in the Presidents' Summit for America's Future, which established America's Promise. Wofford remains actively committed to national service and is involved with the National Commission on Service-Learning chaired by former senator John Glenn and sponsored by the W.K. Kellogg Foundation. He also serves on the board of directors of the Points of Light Foundation and Youth Service America. In March 2001, he was appointed to the board of directors of America's Promise.

During his career, Wofford has also been a professor of law and president of the State University of New York at Old Westbury and of Bryn Mawr College. He received his bachelor's degree from the University of Chicago and his law degree from Yale Law School. He has practiced law and authored books and numerous articles.

JAMES YOUNISS

James Youniss has a long commitment to studying the impact of community service on youth development, including moral, political, and social dimensions. He is a professor of psychology and member of the Center for the Study of Youth Development/Life Cycle Institute at the Catholic University of America, in Washington, D.C., where he conducts research and teaches. Youniss was Director of the Life Cycle Institute at the Catholic University of America from 1988 to 1999. Youniss and colleagues' research has been critical in revealing that the type of program matters regarding the impact of service experiences. Youniss is also examining the impact of mandatory community service and investigating what service programs are most effective in promoting positive youth development. He received his B.S. from Marquette University, his M.A. from Hollins College, and his Ph.D. from the Catholic University of America. He has written many books and articles on adolescent development and community service. With Miranda Yates, he is the coauthor of the books *Community Service and Social Responsibility in Youth* (1997) and *Roots of Civic Identity: International Perspectives on Community Service and Activism in Youth* (1998).

EDWARD ZLOTKOWSKI

Zlotkowski received his bachelor's degree in English and his Ph.D. in comparative literature from Yale University. He is currently a professor of English at Bentley College in Waltham, Massachusetts. He is also a senior faculty fellow at the National Campus Compact and senior associate at the American Association for Higher Education. In 1990, Zlotkowski founded the Bentley Service-Learning Project, a program that includes all of Bentley College's undergraduate departments. In addition, he has authored an eighteen-volume series of books for the American Association of Higher Education that examines service-learning and individual academic disciplines. He is also the author of the book *Successful Service-Learning Programs: New Models of Excellence in Higher Education* (1998).

Zlotkowski has focused his teaching on integrating service-learning into his courses at Bentley. In addition, he consults with many colleges and universities on how to integrate service and learning. Currently, Zlotkowski is engaged in a number of national and state Campus Compact projects. Furthermore, he has partnered with many national associations on service-learning, including the American Sociological Association, National Council of Teachers of English, the Academy of Management, the National Communication Association, and the American Accounting Association. His primary research interests include contemporary American poetry and German and English romanticism and his teaching interests including English, Latin, and German.

REFERENCES

America's Promise. General Powell's corner: biography. Retrieved October 19, 2000, from http://www.americaspromise.org/GenPowellCorner/biography.cfm.

Barber, B. (1984). *Strong democracy.* Berkeley: University of California Press.

Barber, B. (1988). *The conquest of politics.* Princeton, NJ: Princeton University Press.

Barber, B. (1992). *An aristocracy of everyone: The politics of education and the future of America.* New York: Oxford University Press.

Barber, B. (1998). *A place for us: How to make society civil and democracy strong.* New York: Hill and Wang.

Benson, P. L. (1997). *All kids are our kids: What communities must do to raise caring and responsible children and adolescents.* San Francisco: Jossey-Bass.

Benson, P. L. (1998). *What kids need to succeed: Proven, practical ways to raise good kids.* Minneapolis, MN: Free Spirit.

Benson, P. L. (1998). *What teens need to succeed: Proven, practical ways to shape your own future.* Minneapolis, MN: Free Spirit.

Benson, P. L. (1999). *Fragile foundation: The state of development assets among American youth.* Minneapolis, MN: Free Spirit.

Benson, P., & Roehlkepartain, E. (1993). *Beyond leaf raking: Learning to serve, serving to learn.* Nashville, TN: Abingdon Press.

Blyth, D. A., Saito, R., & Berkas, T. (1997). A quantitative study of the impact of service-learning programs. In A. S. Waterman (Ed.), *Service-learning: Applications from the research* (pp. 39–56). Mahwah, NJ: Lawrence Erlbaum.

Boyer, E. L. (1983). *High school: A report on secondary education in America.* New York: Harper & Row.

Boyer, E. L. (1987). *College: The undergraduate experience in America.* New York: Harper & Row.

Boyer, E. L. (1990). *Scholarship reconsidered: Priorities of the professorate.* Princeton, NJ: The Carnegie Foundation for the Advancement of Teaching.

Boyer, E. L. (1991). *Ready to learn: A mandate for the nation.* Princeton, NJ: The Carnegie Foundation for the Advancement of Teaching.

Boyer, E. L. (1996). *The basic school: A community for learning.* The Carnegie Foundation for the Advancement of Teaching.

Boyte, H. C. (1980). *The backyard revolution: Understanding the new citizen movement.* Philadelphia, PA: Temple University Press.

Boyte, H. C. (1989). *CommonWealth: A return to citizen politics.* New York: Free Press.

Boyte, H. C. (1991). Community service and civic education. *Phi Delta Kappan, 72,* 765–767.

Boyte, H. C., & Kari, N. N. (1996). *Building America: The democratic promise of public work.* Philadelphia, PA: Temple University Press.

Carnegie Foundation for the Advancement of Teaching. (1996). Ernest L. Boyer: A leader of educators, an educator of leaders. In *Ninety-first annual report of the Carnegie Foundation for the Advancement of Teaching.* Princeton, NJ: Author.

Coles, R. (1986). *The moral life of children.* Boston: Atlantic Monthly Press.

Coles, R. (1986). *The political life of children.* Boston: Atlantic Monthly Press.

Coles, R. (1989). *The call of stories: Teaching and moral imagination.* Boston: Houghton Mifflin.

Coles, R. (1990). *The spiritual life of children.* Boston: Houghton Mifflin.

Coles, R. (1993). *The call of service: A witness to idealism.* Boston: Houghton Mifflin.

Corporation for National Service. Letter from Harris Wofford. Retrieved June 11, 2001, from http://www.cns.gov/news/pr/011901.html.

Dewey, J. (1900/80). *The school and society.* Carbondale: Southern Illinois University Press.

Dewey, J. (1916). *Democracy and education: An introduction to the philosophy of education.* New York: The Macmillan Company.

Dewey, J. (1938/74). *Experience and education.* New York: Collier Books.

Eberly, D. J. (1988). *National service: A promise to keep.* Rochester, NY: J. Alden Books.

Eberly, D. J. (1990). *The moral equivalent of war: A study of non-military service in nine nations.* New York: Greenwood Press.

Eberly, D. J. (Ed.). (1991). *National youth service: A democratic institution for the 21st century.* Washington, DC: National Service Secretariat.

Eberly, D. J. (Ed.). (1994). *Building a community of citizens: Civil society in the 21st century.* Lanham, MD: University Press of America.

Eberly, D. J. (Ed.). (1998). *America's promise: Civil society and the renewal of American culture.* Lanham, MD: Rowman & Littlefield Publishers, Inc.

Ehrlich, T. (2000). *Civic responsibility and higher education.* Phoenix, AZ: American Council on Education/Oryx Press Series on Higher Education.

Eyler, J., & Giles, D. E., Jr. (1997). The importance of program quality in service-learning. In A. S. Waterman (Ed.), *Service-learning: Applications from the research* (pp. 57–76). Mahwah, NJ: Lawrence Erlbaum.

Eyler, J., & Giles, D. E., Jr. (1999). *Where's the learning in service-learning?* San Francisco: Jossey-Bass.

Hall, M. (1991). Gadugi: A model of service-learning for Native American communities. *Phi Delta Kappan, 72,* 754–757.

Harkavy, I. (1996, August). *Service learning as a vehicle for revitalization of education institutions and urban communities.* Paper presented to the Education Directorate Miniconvention on Urban Initiatives: In Partnership with Education at the American Psychological Association Annual Meeting, Toronto.

Kennedy, E. M. (1991). National service and education for citizenship. *Phi Delta Kappan, 72,* 771–773.

Kielsmeier, J. C. (2000). A time to serve, a time to learn: Service-learning and the promise of democracy. *Phi Delta Kappan, 81,* 652–657.

Penn State University. Penn State President Graham B. Spanier. Retrieved June 27, 2002, from http://www.psu.edu/ur/GSpanier/biography.html.

Powell, C., & Persico, J. E. (1995). *My American journey: An autobiography.* Random House.

Schine, J. (Ed.). (1997). *Service-learning. Ninety-sixth yearbook of the National Society for the Study of Education. Part I.* Chicago: University of Chicago Press.

Shumer, R. (1994). Community-based learning: Humanizing education. *Journal of Adolescence, 17,* 357–367.

Shumer, R., & Belbas, B. (1996). What we know about service-learning. *Education and Urban Society, 28,* 208–223.

Shumer, R., et al. (2000). *Shumer's Self Assessment for Service-Learning (instrument).* St. Paul, MN: Center for Experiential Education and Service-Learning, Department of Work, Community, and Family Education, University of Minnesota.

Sizer, T. (1984). *Horace's compromise: The dilemma of the American high school.* Boston: Houghton Mifflin.

Sizer, T. (1992). *Horace's school: Redesigning the American high school.* Boston: Houghton Mifflin.

Stanton, T. K., Giles, D. E., Jr., & Cruz, N. I. (1999). *Service-learning: A movement's pioneers reflect on its origins, practice, and future.* San Francisco, CA: Jossey-Bass.

Tufts E-News. President John DiBiaggio. Retrieved June 27, 2002, from http: www.tufts.edu/communications/stories.

Yates, M., & Youniss, J. (1998). *Roots of civic identity: International perspectives on community service and activism in youth.* New York: Cambridge University Press.

Youniss, J., & Yates, M. (1997). *Community service and social responsibility in youth.* Chicago: University of Chicago Press.

Zlotkowski, E. (1998). *Successful service-learning programs: New models of excellence in higher education.* Bolton, MA: Anker Publishing.

4

Facts and Data

with Jennifer M. Grossman and Molly Jilek

COMMUNITY SERVICE

Community service and volunteerism have been common practices among teenagers and adults in our country for a long period of time. Hundreds of thousands of teenagers and college students, for example, give their time to provide service in activities and organizations such as blood drives, clothing collections, cooking and serving meals, day care, environmental cleanup, charitable fundraisers, crisis hotlines, Meals on Wheels, planting trees, recycling, recreation programs, Special Olympics, tutoring, youth agencies, and coaching youth sports (Cairn & Kielsmeier, 1991), to name just a few. Community service and volunteerism have received much attention in recent years as a result of developments in the field of service-learning.

This chapter provides facts and data from recent major reports and documents on community service and service-learning, including information on levels of participation in service, standards for service-learning, evaluations of service programs, and public and professional attitudes toward service activities. The data presented in this chapter provide valuable information for understanding trends in service participation and for understanding the factors that contribute to successful service programs.

COMMUNITY SERVICE AND SERVICE-LEARNING

Legislation, such as the National and Community Service Act of 1990 and the National and Community Service Trust Act of 1993, has provided strong nationwide administrative and financial support for school and community involvement in service activities. Learn and Serve America, for example, was created as part of the National and Community Service Trust Act of 1993. In 1994–1995, the first year of the program, Learn and Serve America contributed $30 million to support school and community service-learning programs involving more than 750,000 youth (Melchior et al., 1999). Between 1995 and 1997, the higher education branch of Learn and Serve America, called Learn and Serve Higher Education (LSAHE), awarded more than $35 million to 500 colleges/universities and community organizations (Gray, Ondaatje, & Zakaras, 1999). Although many schools offered community service programs for their students prior to this federal funding, the number of schools incorporating service-learning into the curriculum has vastly increased in recent years. According to a report released by the Bureau of Labor Statistics in December 2002, 26.9 percent of teenagers had engaged in volunteer services in the period from September 2001 to September 2002. The authors interpreted this relatively high rate of volunteerism among teens as reflecting volunteer activities available through their schools. The shift in connecting service with the academic curriculum is a major distinction between community service and service-learning programs.

In defining the Standards of Quality for School-Based and Community-Based Service-Learning, the Alliance for Service-Learning in Education Reform (1993) sought to distinguish between community service and service-learning. In comparison with community service, service-learning requires two essential elements. These are: (1) a deliberate connection between the service experience and learning goals and (2) opportunities designed to foster conscious reflection on the service experience and the learning that has occurred. Although service-learning is often associated with school settings because of its link with learning objectives, service-learning programs can be developed through other organizations. Faith-based institutions and youth organizations may organize service-learning programs that have somewhat different objectives than school programs. For example, a school may engage older youth in tutoring younger children for the primary purpose of developing academic skills. A youth organization may view the same activity as ideal for the development of social skills, whereas a faith-based organization may emphasize the development of caring and patience (Search Institute, 2000).

Service-learning does not mean the same thing to everyone. Several definitions follow to provide you with a better understanding of how the concept is used.

DEFINITIONS OF SERVICE-LEARNING

According to the Commission on National and Community Service (CNCS), National and Community Trust Act of 1993, service-learning:

- "is a method whereby students learn and develop through active participation in thoughtfully organized service that is conducted in and meets the needs of communities;
- is coordinated with an elementary school, secondary school, institution of higher education, or community service program and the community;
- helps foster civic responsibility;
- is integrated into and enhances the students' academic curriculum, or the education components of the community service program in which the participants are enrolled;
- and provides structured time for students or participants to reflect on the service experience." (National Service-Learning Clearinghouse, 1999)

According to the *Research Agenda for Combining Service and Learning in the 1990s* "...service-learning is both a program type and a philosophy of education. As a program type, service-learning includes myriad ways that students can perform meaningful service to their communities and to society while engaging in some form of reflection or study that is related to the service. As a philosophy of education, service-learning reflects the belief that education must be linked to social responsibility and that the most effective learning is active and connected to experience in some meaningful way" (Giles, Honnet, & Migliore, 1991 p. 7).

According to the Alliance for Service-Learning in Education Reform (1993), "service learning is a method by which young people learn and develop through active participation in thoughtfully-organized service experiences...

- that meet actual community needs;
- that are coordinated in collaboration with the school and community;
- that are integrated into each young person's academic curriculum;

- that provide the structured time for a young person to think, talk, and write about what he/she did and saw during the actual service activity.

- that provide young people with opportunities to use newly acquired academic skills and knowledge in real life situations in their own communities.

- that are a practical application of what is taught in school.

- that help to foster the development of a sense of caring for others" (Alliance for Service-Learning in Education Reform, 1993; Close Up Foundation, 2000).

PARTICIPATION IN COMMUNITY SERVICE AND SERVICE-LEARNING

Several national surveys completed in recent years (Maloy & Wohlleb, 1997; Nolin, Chaney, & Chapman, 1997; Skinner & Chapman, 1999) shed light on the number of schools offering community service and service-learning programs and the types of service opportunities available. Comparisons between these surveys and earlier research also provide information about how participation in community service and service-learning has changed over time. Since community service opportunities have increased within schools, schools are now a primary setting through which youth become involved in community service. Thus, when considering participation of teenagers in community service, it is important to consider the number and types of service programs offered through school settings.

Schools Offering Community Service

A survey completed by the National Center for Education Statistics (NCES) in 1999 assessed the extent to which community service programs were offered in K–12 public schools (Skinner & Chapman, 1999). The National Student Service-Learning and Community Service Survey was used to measure the degree to which community service was offered across all grade levels. Community service was defined as activities that are "non-curriculum-based," but are recognized by the school. Community service can either be voluntary or mandatory and typically does not incorporate learning objectives or critical thinking. Service activities can take place off school grounds as well as within the school building.

The NCES 1999 survey indicated that 64 percent of all public schools offered community service activities that are recognized or arranged by the school. More high schools offered community service opportunities for students than did either elementary or middle schools. Fifty-seven percent of high schools organized the community service activities for students.

The NCES survey also looked at the characteristics of schools offering community service opportunities for students. For example, they assessed the prevalence of community service programs in schools based upon the economic background of students (measured by percentage eligible for free or reduced lunch), urban or rural locale, geographic region, and minority enrollment (Table 4.1). In brief, schools where less than 50 percent of students were eligible for free or reduced lunches were more likely to offer community service than schools in which 50 percent or more qualified for free or reduced lunch. Schools in city or town locations were slightly more likely to offer community service activities than rural or urban schools. In addition, schools located in the northeast and central areas of the country were more likely to participate than schools in the southeast or west. Schools where 21 to 49 percent of students identify as ethnic minorities were most likely to be involved with community service, whereas schools with 50 percent or more minority enrollment were the least likely to offer community service opportunities.

Schools Offering Service-Learning

The NCES 1999 survey also assessed the extent to which service-learning programs were offered in K–12 public schools. Service-learning is curriculum-based and integrates classroom teaching and community activities.

Although service-learning is becoming more common within K–12 schools, the percentage of public schools nationwide offering service-learning was 32 percent, still considerably less than those offering community service (64 percent). With regard to student grade level, high schools were most likely to offer service-learning (46 percent), followed by middle schools (38 percent) and then elementary schools (25 percent) (Table 4.1). Findings pertaining to economic status were similar to those found for community service. Schools with less than 50 percent of students eligible for free or reduced lunch were more likely to offer service-learning activities than schools with more students on free or

Table 4.1
Percent of Public Schools That Have Students Participating in Community
Service, Arrange Community Service Opportunities for Students, and Have
Students Participating in Service-Learning, by School Characteristics: Aca-
demic Year 1998–1999

School characteristic	weighted N	% with community service	% organizing community activities	% with service-learning
All public schools	79,750	64	57	32
Instructional level				
Elementary	49,350	55	49	25
Middle	14,398	77	71	38
High	16,002	83	71	46
Type of locale				
City	20,742	66	61	36
Urban Fringe	26,579	63	57	27
Town	11,614	65	59	43
Rural	20,814	64	53	27
Geographic region				
Northeast	16,121	67	64	30
Southeast	15,927	63	56	35
Central	22,442	67	58	32
West	25,259	61	53	30
Percent minority enrollment				
Less than 6 percent	25,925	67	58	31
6 to 20 percent	16,965	65	56	31
21 to 49 percent	18,208	72	67	36
50 percent or more	17,798	54	50	29
Percent of students eligible for free or reduced lunch				
Less than 50 percent	50,975	69	63	36
50 percent or more	15,409	50	43	23

Source: U.S. Department of Education, National Center for Education Statistics, Fast
Response Survey System (FRSS), National Student Service-Learning and Community
Service Survey, FRSS 71, 1999. As cited in Skinner and Chapman (1999).

reduced lunch programs. Also, schools located in cities and towns were more likely to offer service-learning than were rural or urban fringe schools. Schools in the southeastern United States were more likely to have students participating in service-learning than any other geographic region (Table 4.1).

Service-learning can be implemented in several different ways (Skinner & Chapman, 1999). Service-learning activities can be associated with a single course, such as government or health education, or there may be a program for all students in a particular grade at school. "School-wide" service-learning involves the entire student body, "grade-wide" service-learning involves students in a particular grade, and "course-involved" service-learning pertains only to students in a particular class. The NCES survey indicated that 79 percent of the schools implemented service-learning in two or more ways. The most popular practice was "grade-wide" which was prevalent in 70 percent of the schools. Approximately 62 percent of the schools implemented service-learning through individual courses and 33 percent reported having "school-wide" service-learning (Table 4.2). Elementary schools were

Table 4.2
Of Public Schools with Service-Learning, Percent Implementing Service-Learning in Various Ways

	Percent participation	
	All schools	Middle/high
Grade-wide service learning	70	53
Service-learning in individual academic courses that are not part of a broader grade-or school-wide initiative	62	70
Discipline-wide service-learning	53	44
Service-learning as part of a special education program	34	33
School-wide service-learning	33	28
Service-learning as a separate elective or advisory period	29	38
Service-learning as part of a dropout prevention course or program	14	16

Source: U.S. Department of Education, National Center for Education Statistics, Fast Response Survey System (FRSS), National Student Service-Learning and Community Service Survey, FRSS 71, 1999. As cited in Skinner and Chapman (1999).

Table 4.3
Of Public Schools Receiving Special Funding for Service Activities, Percent
Receiving Various Sources of Funding: Academic Year 1998–1999

Source of funding	% of schools receiving funding
Learn and Serve America	10%
AmeriCorps	11%
Other federal/state grants	38%
Foundation grants	37%
Corporate/business grants	43%
Other	29%

Source: U.S. Department of Education, National Center for Education Statistics, Fast
Response Survey System (FRSS), National Student Service-Learning and Community
Service Survey, FRSS 71, 1999. As cited in Skinner and Chapman (1999).

more likely to have "grade-wide" service-learning than middle or high
schools. On the other hand, middle and high schools were more likely
than elementary schools to offer service-learning as part of a particular
class that was not part of a grade or school-wide program (Table 4.2).

Federal, state, foundation, and corporate grants have been important
in supplementing school district funds that support school-based service
programs. Sources of funding for school service programs are presented
in Table 4.3.

TRENDS IN COMMUNITY SERVICE AND SERVICE-LEARNING IN HIGH SCHOOLS FROM 1984 TO 1997

Shumer and Cook (1999) provide a comparison regarding the prevalence of community service and service-learning programs offered by
high schools in 1984 and 1997. Shumer and Cook obtained the 1984
data from a study that had been completed by Newman and Rutter
(1985). The 1984 study surveyed 204 high schools and found that 27 percent of those schools offered opportunities in community service, with
900,000 students actually participating in community service programs.
At that time, only 9 percent of the schools offered service-learning
opportunities and only 81,000 students were enrolled in courses that
included service-learning. Newman and Rutter also examined the characteristics of students most likely to participate in service-learning activ-

ities. Interestingly, 60 percent of all participants were female, with just 40 percent being male. Eighty-two percent were White, 16 percent were African American, and 2 percent were members of other racial and ethnic groups. Furthermore, private schools were more likely to offer service opportunities than were public schools. Among students involved in community service, 51 percent of the students performed service for two hours or less per week during the year. In conclusion, the 1984 survey indicates that more than one-fourth of high schools offered some type of community service program and that the vast majority of students participating in service were Caucasian. Out of the high schools offering service opportunities, less than 10 percent offered service-learning that linked community service with the academic curriculum.

To evaluate more recent levels of service involvement, Shumer and Cook (1999) report data from two recent studies; one done regionally in the eastern United States (Maloy & Wohlleb, 1997) and the other completed nationally for the U.S. Department of Education (Nolin et al., 1997). According to the U.S. Department of Education (USDE) report, 84 percent of U.S. school districts offered community service programs and 56 percent offered service-learning. In the eastern United States, 96 percent of school districts offered community service programs, with 88 percent providing service-learning opportunities (Maloy & Wohlleb, 1997). The characteristics of students who participated in community service programs were also assessed in the USDE report. Approximately 53 percent of student service participants were female and 45 percent were male. Seventy-two percent were White, 14 percent were African American, 10 percent were Hispanic, and 2 percent were from other racial and ethnic backgrounds. Among White students, approximately 53 percent reported involvement in community service. Among Black and Hispanic students, 38 to 43 percent reported community service involvement. Eighty percent of the participants received "A" and "B" grades and 21 percent received "C" grades or lower. Out of 12,605,740 students who participated in service programs, 5,068,699 were from public middle schools, 732,600 were from private middle schools, 6,181,797 were from public high schools, and 831,600 were from private high schools. Sixty-six percent of private school students reported participation in community service in comparison with 47 percent of public school students. Students attending church-related schools were most likely (69 percent) to have participated in community service. The USDE study also reported that 51 percent of students had completed no community service during the year, 23 percent had participated in one or two service activities, 7 percent of students completed 10 hours or less, 7 percent completed 11 to 30 hours, 7 percent completed 31 to 80 hours, and 5 percent had completed more than 80 hours of community service over the course of the year.

Shumer and Cook (1999) compare the 1984 study's findings with the 1997 studies, noting some significant differences. The number of high school students involved in community service programs increased, with the student participation in community service programs increasing 686 percent and the number of students in service-learning increasing dramatically by 3,663 percent. Shumer and Cook (1999) attribute the overall expansion of student involvement in service-learning to the increased support by school systems for educators to incorporate service programs into the curriculum (Shumer & Cook, 1999). Other aspects of community service have been more stable. In both 1984 and 1997, more girls than boys participated in community service. The percentage of student volunteers who were White declined somewhat, as the percentage of student volunteers who are Hispanic increased. In general, however, the ethnic/racial representation of students involved in service was relatively stable. Students continue to work about the same number of hours (51 percent perform less than two hours of service per week, but 49 percent perform some service each year), and high-achieving students continue to be more likely to participate in volunteer service than low-achieving students (over 50 percent of students involved in service are in college preparatory courses).

A Comparison of Youth Service-Learning and Community Service among Students from Sixth to Twelfth Grade between 1996 and 1999

Kleiner and Chapman (2000) present data from the National Household Education Surveys of 1999 (Skinner & Chapman, 1999) and 1996 (Nolin et al., 1997) to compare community service and service-learning opportunities offered in grades six through twelve (see Tables 4.4, 4.5, and 4.6). Both surveys were conducted through telephone interviews. Students were asked whether their schools offer or require community service activities. In both 1996 and 1999, students were more likely to attend schools that offered but did not require community service. Only 19 percent of students in 1999 and 16 percent in 1996 stated that their schools both required and organized community service activities.

According to the NHES surveys, overall student participation in community service was 52 percent in 1999, which was an increase of 46 per-

Table 4.4
Sixth through Twelfth Grade Students' Reports of School Practices to Promote Student Community Service: 1999

Characteristics	Number of students (thousands)	School requires and arranges community service (percent)	School only requires community service (percent)	School only arranges community service (percent)	School does not require or arrange community service (percent)
Total	26,990	19	2	67	12
Student's grade					
6 – 8	11,713	16	2	67	15
9 – 10	7,933	24	2	65	10
11 – 12	7,322	20	1	69	10
Student's sex					
Male	13,599	20	2	66	13
Female	13,392	19	2	68	12
Student's race/ethnicity					
White, non-Hispanic	17,354	16	1	70	12
Black, non-Hispanic	4,206	22	3	62	13
Hispanic	4,067	28	3	58	11
Other race/ethnicity	1,363	24	1	65	11
School type					
Public	24,550	17	2	69	12
Private church-related	1,786	42	2	48	7
Private not church-related	655	41	3	45	11

Source: U.S. Department of Education, National Center for Education Statistics, National Household Education Survey (NHES), Youth Interview, 1999. As cited in Kleiner and Chapman (2000).

Table 4.5

Student, Household, and School Characteristics of Students in Grades 6 through 12 Who Participated in Community Service: 1996 and 1999

Characteristics	Participation in community service (percent)	
	1996	1999
Total	49	52
Student's grade		
6 – 8	47	48
9 – 10	45	50
11 – 12	56	61
Student's sex		
Male	45	47
Female	53	57
Student's race/ethnicity		
White, non-Hispanic	53	56
Black, non-Hispanic	43	47
Hispanic	38	39
Other	50	53
Language spoken most at home by student		
English	50	54
Other	32	34
Parents' highest level of education		
Less than high school	34	37
High school graduate or equivalent	42	45
Voc/tech education after high school or some college	48	50
College graduate	58	62
Graduate or professional school	64	65
School type		
Public	47	50
Private Church-related	69	72
Private Not church-related	57	68

Source: U.S. Department of Education, National Center for Education Statistics, National Household Education Survey (NHES), Youth Civic Involvement Interview, 1996, and Youth Interview, 1999. As cited in Kleiner and Chapman (2000).

Table 4.6
Community Service and Service-Learning Program Activities Reported by Students in Grades 6 through 12 Who Engaged in Community Service: 1999

Characteristics	Number of students participating in community service (thousands)	Participation in service-learning among students who did service (percent)	Talked about service activity in class (percent)	Required to keep a journal or write an essay for class (percent)	Service activity contributed to a grade (percent)
Total	14,063	57	45	19	24
Student's grade					
6–8	5,610	62	50	22	27
9–10	3,955	52	40	15	23
11–12	4,486	56	45	19	22

Source: U.S. Department of Education, National Center for Education Statistics, National Household Education Survey (NHES), Youth Interview, 1999. As cited in Kleiner and Chapman (2000).

cent from 1996. In 1999, 30 percent of students were engaged in service-learning, which was only slightly higher than in 1996 (27 percent). Many students who participated in community service were also involved in service-learning. Fifty-six percent of the students in 1996 and 57 percent of the students in 1999 who were part of community service programs were also involved in service-learning activities. Also shown in Table 4.6 is the percentage of students who reported involvement in each of three service-learning activities: discussion of service experiences in the classroom, journal writing, and service participation contributing for a course grade. Overall, students were more likely to discuss their service participation in class than to keep a journal or to have service participation count towards a grade.

The surveys revealed similarities and changes between 1996 and 1999 regarding the students and schools who participated in community service and service-learning. In both 1996 and 1999, students in grades six through eight were less likely than students in grades nine and ten to report that their school required and organized community service, suggesting that high schools provide more incentives than middle schools for their students' service involvement. Church-related and private schools were more likely to require and arrange community service than public schools, although the gap between the number of public and private schools requiring and organizing community service narrowed significantly. The percentage of White students participating in community service was higher in both 1996 and 1999 than the percentage of Black and Hispanic youth involved in community service. However, the percentage of Black (22 percent) and Hispanic (28 percent) students who attended schools that both arranged and required community service was greater than the percentage of White students (16 percent) attending such schools in 1999. These findings suggest that students are more likely to participate in community service when schools both require and arrange service activities.

TYPES OF COMMUNITY SERVICE PROGRAMS

Community service programs differ in their goals, structures, and implementation. Programs may focus primarily on promoting student growth, or they may seek to change the ways in which the school interacts with the local community. Programs can be voluntary or required for all students. Finally, programs can be conducted across a variety of community contexts, such as soup kitchens, neighborhood clean-ups, or hospitals, for different lengths of time and intensity, and with different levels of integration with academic courses.

Program Goals

Service-learning programs may be organized to achieve a variety of individual, school, and community goals. Research by the Search Institute (1991) indicated that students who were involved in service differed from students who were not involved in community service. Those involved in community service were more likely in comparison with non-volunteers to value sexual restraint (47 percent vs. 24 percent), to be involved in the community (62 percent vs. 20 percent), to express motivation to succeed in school (82 percent vs. 60 percent), and to value people's feelings (95 percent vs. 79 percent). Advocates of community service suggest that involvement in service may promote personal, social, and civic development among youth.

A report of Community Service Programs in High Schools (Raskoff & Sundeen, 2000) described three goals for service-learning programs: youth reform, educational reform, and citizenship. Youth reform focuses on reducing youth risk behaviors, increasing student sense of social responsibility, and increasing rates of student school attendance. Youth reform is the most commonly identified goal for service-learning programs and is associated with efforts to promote student growth in self-esteem and moral development. Educational reform seeks to increase student motivation for learning and school achievement by providing students with "life-relevant learning" and opportunities to apply what they learn in school to real-life situations. Some programs aim to increase the ability to learn concepts and gain knowledge in academic subjects, improve grades, and increase school engagement. Another program focus is on citizenship, including the development of social responsibility and civic engagement. These programs attempt to get students involved in community life and to increase their sense of responsibility to other people and to society.

Many programs hope to achieve multiple goals. The NCES national survey of public schools (Skinner & Chapman, 1999) lists ten reasons given by school representatives for encouraging student involvement in community service (see Table 4.7). School representatives reported most often that they wanted to help students to better understand, care for, and be more involved in their community, as well as to help address real community needs. Schools, thus, expect that service-learning will

Table 4.7
Public School Reports of Most Important Reasons for Encouraging Student
Involvement in Service-Learning: Academic Year 1998–1999

Reason for encouraging service	Percent (%) of schools supporting this statement
Help students become actively involved in their community	53%
Increase student knowledge and understanding of communities	51%
Meet real community needs/foster school-community connections	48%
Encourage student caring for others	46%
Enhance student personal and social development	26%
Teach critical thinking and problem solving	19%
Increase career knowledge and opportunities	18%
Increase student school engagement and support positive attitudes toward school	16%
Enhance student academic performance	12%
Reduce student risk behaviors	10%

Source: U.S. Department of Education, National Center for Education Statistics, Fast
Response Survey System (FRSS), National Student Service-Learning and Community
Service Survey, FRSS 71, 1999. As cited in Skinner and Chapman (1999).

promote positive change among students, as well as benefit their communities.

Characteristics of Effective Programs

Although the research on community service has revealed many positive effects, a number of findings are inconclusive or contradictory. The
preponderance of findings do indicate that service-learning is effective
in achieving varied positive effects (see chapter 1 of this volume).
Service-learning researchers have come to understand that the critical
question is not whether service-learning works, but what kind of service-
learning works. Research suggests that there are some essential compo-

nents and considerations for all service programs if efficacy is to be achieved. Additional elements must be attended to in order to produce specific desired outcomes. We will first discuss some of the general components for effectiveness and then will discuss program activities relative to specific goals.

Service programs are generally perceived by youth as meaningful, fun, and interesting when they meet an authentic community need, involve thoughtful planning, include reflection, and celebrate service accomplishments (Billig, 2001). Although these elements serve to increase youth interest in learning, they do not automatically result in a range of positive student outcomes.

Billig (2001) and Stukas, Clary, and Snyder (1999) have identified elements that are common among many successful programs. The first relates to student autonomy and responsibility. Programs are more successful when students have opportunities to work independently, to be active in making decisions and solving problems, and to be responsible and accountable for their involvement in community service projects. The second element is the matching of goals and outcomes to student interests and needs. Students need to be able to decide how they want to participate and what they hope to accomplish from service-learning. They should have a choice in the activities that they want to participate in and a choice in how they design and evaluate the effects of their service. A third element is the presence of positive relationships among students and teachers. Teachers need to offer not only support, but need to actively participate with students in thinking about their service project. Teachers ask questions and help students to understand the meaning of their service experience. A fourth element relates to providing opportunities for reflection, during which students can think, talk, and write about their experiences, alone, or with other students and teachers. Good quality reflection goes beyond summarizing or describing the experience and involves in-depth thought and analysis. Effective service experiences also provide substantial contact with service recipients that is ongoing over a period of time. Brief and superficial experiences will have little impact. In addition, students who have training to prepare them for their service work have more positive service-learning experiences (Kleiner & Chapman, 2000). Student interest in course content has also been related to positive student outcomes in service-learning courses (Astin, Vogelgesang, Ikeda, & Yee, 2000).

According to Billig (2001), the program characteristics listed above contribute positively to a range of personal development outcomes, such as self-esteem, social competence, and reduction of negative behaviors. Additional specific elements are needed to strengthen academic, civic, and career outcomes. To enhance academic outcomes, for example, specific attention must be paid to linking the subject matter and service. Making connections between service experience and academic material (such as reading about local government in class and then spending time volunteering at the local town hall) helps students to integrate learning in school and community settings (Kleiner & Chapman, 2000). The specific content of the service experience will influence the content of student learning. Volunteering at town hall, for example, may contribute to gains in civics understanding but should not be expected to impact interest or engagement in mathematics. For students to develop greater civic responsibility, the teacher must help the students to make connections between the service experience and political, social, and cultural concerns. Connections between service experience and career pathways, workplace skills, and knowledge of the world of work need to be emphasized for career-related outcomes to be realized. Billig's model of "Learning Mediators and Student Outcomes" can be accessed through the Internet at http://www. LearningInDeed.org/research/slresearch/model.html.

Overall, research suggests that students who are involved in selecting, planning, and implementing their service-learning activities, and who are able to understand the relationship between their service and academic experiences, have the most positive responses to service-learning. A more thorough discussion of service-learning program goals and outcomes can be found in chapter 1 of this book. In addition, several recent reports are advancing knowledge and ideas about how to involve youth in community service and how to sustain their interest and involvement over time. We will first review the 1999 report and guide issued by Do Something, and then describe the 2000 Learning In Deed Issue Paper on "Integrating Youth Voice in Service-Learning" and the National 4-H "Youth in Decision-Making" report. Finally, we present a brief overview of the Learning In Deed National Commission on Service-Learning 2002 report, "The Power of Service-Learning for American Schools."

The Do Something Community Connections Campaign

Do Something, a national, nonprofit youth leadership organization with the purpose of encouraging youth to make a difference in the world, initiated a Community Connections Campaign to connect youth with civic organizations. A guide was issued by Do Something (1999), with support from the Pew Charitable Trusts, to provide community organizations with the necessary information to recruit and develop young leaders. The guide includes the findings of an extensive study completed by Do Something to learn about why youth become involved in community organizations, the roles that they fill, and the benefits of youth involvement. The research findings inform recommendations on how to get youth more involved in serving their communities and how to sustain their interest over time.

The study used several strategies to obtain information from young people and from volunteer organizations. Eight groups of young people, ranging from the ages of fifteen to thirty, were interviewed nationwide. Group participants were asked to comment on their experiences in community organizations. A Young People's Involvement Survey (YPIS), which asked about volunteer experiences in community-based organizations, was also distributed to 1,000 young people ages fifteen to twenty-nine. A second survey, the Community Organizations Survey (COS), was sent to 250 volunteer coordinators from community-based organizations to obtain information on their experiences in working with youth. Case studies were completed of ten organizations, representing varied geographic regions of the United States and known for their success in involving youth in their work.

Organizations identified a number of reasons for involving youth in leadership roles. First of all, organizations whose missions concerned young people felt that it was important to involve youth in their operations. Some organizations felt that youth helped to expand their membership and size of their volunteer workforce. Other organizations felt that youth should be included because they are an essential part of the community. Finally, young people were believed to bring energy and necessary skills that adults often lack. They have enormous "assets" to offer and bring vitality to organizations, while also developing skills and habits of civic participation.

The Do Something study also revealed that young people are ready and willing to participate in their communities but need encouragement from adults. The study found that the best way to get teens and young adults involved is to ask them directly. Youth typically find out about opportunities for community participation through coaches, friends, family, or teachers. Almost 60 percent of youth had heard of opportunities for involvement through a friend or family member.

Fifty-four percent of students in schools and colleges learned of local organizations through a teacher, with 49 percent having learned of service opportunities through a poster or flyer at school. Forty-two percent of those surveyed became aware of opportunities through their place of worship, and 30 percent heard through related organizations. The Community Organization Survey revealed that 78 percent of organizations recruit youth volunteers through family and friends; 61 percent through local schools, teachers, and administrators; 45 percent through posters or flyers; and surprisingly, 63 percent of community organizations recruit through places of worship. Furthermore, many community organizations stated that they rely on other organizations as a way of networking to recruit volunteers. For example, the Cross-Organizational Collaboration in Oakland, California works closely with four other area organizations that all share a focus on building youth leadership.

The Young People's Involvement Survey also revealed that youth are twice as likely to participate in community organizations when they play an active role in the decision-making. In addition, the Community Organizations Survey found that organizations that provide their young participants with meaningful responsibilities are more likely to retain members. The findings also revealed that teens and young adults were more likely to get involved when flexibility in hours and days is offered for volunteer service. Furthermore, organizations need to devise innovative ways to challenge and hold the interest of youth. Finally, organizations that have open communication, sufficient staff, and provide training to support young people are more likely to achieve their overall goals and retain participants.

Integrating Youth Voice in Service-Learning

A number of organizations have paid close attention to the Do Something research. Following from the Do Something findings that youth are more likely to remain interested in service if they believe they are actively contributing, the Education Commission of the States, the Compact for Learning and Citizenship, and Learning In Deed produced an Issue Paper entitled "Integrating Youth Voice into Service-Learning" (Fredericks, Kaplan, & Zeisler, 2001). The paper defines youth voice as "the inclusion of young people as a meaningful part of the creation and implementation of service opportunities" (p. 1). The paper maintains that when youth are given active roles for participating in their communities, they develop valuable skills to be lifelong citizens. At the same time, organizations gain the energy, skills, and creativity of young people.

Furthermore, the paper states that it is important for youth to be given significant responsibility, to be allowed to consider problem resolutions, and to make decisions concerning issues of importance. When this happens, youth feel that they are viable resources and are making a difference, which encourages their involvement. Youth participation is also sustained when youth understand the social and political issues that the community faces. Educators and adult leaders of youth organizations can play key roles in providing such information. With this knowledge, teens and young adults are motivated to address significant problems.

An organization called Fresh Youth Initiatives, located in New York City, creates new initiatives based upon the ideas of youth. The program is structured on the premise that young people are the best ones to address community needs and offer solutions. Some of the initiatives begun by Fresh Youth include a traveling clothing and food pantry, antidrug workshops, and a program that constructs sleeping bags for the homeless and fills them with necessities. The program participants who are "older" by experience in the organization (rather than by age) provide training for newcomers.

High school students in Madison, Wisconsin, developed a project in which they spent a day in wheelchairs to investigate handicap accessibility in their town. The youth found that more than half of the area businesses had obstacles to wheelchair access. After reading the Americans with Disabilities Act in class, youth participants educated local business owners, who in return were responsive in making changes.

Active youth involvement is a relatively new idea, however, which brings forth skepticism and fear by both youth and adults. The following is a list of five challenges and strategies suggested in the Issue paper.

1. Since many young people and adults may have different understandings of what is meant by "youth voice," it may be helpful to hold a meeting among youth, parents, and other adults to define "youth voice" and develop a common understanding. The group might try to identify examples that already exist in the community where young people have an active voice in decision-making.

2. Adults and young people may have different levels of trust and confidence in one another. Thus, it is important to establish guidelines for open-minded and respectful communication. Adults and youth should be helped to identify the assets that

each brings to the organization. Meaningful roles for all ages should be established based upon their needs and assets.

3. Since some adults may be reluctant to give youth an active voice in the organization, changes should be introduced and implemented gradually. Support and training need to be provided for both youth and adults.

4. Young people should be offered meaningful roles. Youth need to be listened to and their ideas need to be given real consideration.

5. Since adults may have difficulty in giving up decision-making responsibilities, they may be helped to identify those areas where they are most willing to include youth. As the adults gain more trust and confidence in the young people, the scope of youth responsibility can be expanded. Adults who are working with youth as decision-makers should be provided with ongoing support and peer-mentoring in the process.

The above challenges and strategies were put to test by a group of high school students in Maine when adults and teens served together on the Learning Results Team. This is a state policy panel that facilitates service-learning in school districts across the state. At the beginning, only adults served on the panel; however, after one adult member advocated for the participation of younger members, youth were added to the panel. Both the students and the adults agreed that the rules of the organizations should apply to adults and young people alike. Mentoring relationships were developed between the adults and young participants. Finally, after every meeting, all members gave written feedback to the panel leader so every "voice" was heard.

Adults need to remember several things when integrating "youth voice" into service-learning programs. Clear guidelines need to be established regarding what is expected of both young people and adults. Adults need to be open and flexible and be willing to takes risks and admit to mistakes when they occur. In return, youth learn that adults do not have all the answers and that they need to rely more on their own knowledge, as well.

The paper also offers recommendations for young people as they seek to take on important roles in service-learning and society as a whole. Youth need to be assertive and know that by doing so they can make a difference. Young people should ask questions about policies that they do not understand and should seek out support and training. It is also important that young people be responsible in following through with assignments and documenting their involvement through writing and pictures. These can be shared with other young people as both education and inspiration tools.

Youth in Decision-Making: A Study on the Impacts of Youth on Adults and Organizations

The National 4-H Council also has a long-standing interest in the development of leadership among young people. Like Do Something, a division of 4-H called the Innovation Center for Community and Youth Development has focused attention in recent years on ways to increase youth involvement in decision-making roles.

The Innovation Center sponsored a study (Zeldin, McDaniel, Topitzes, & Calvert, 2001) to determine whether involving youth in the decision-making of organizations changed adults' attitudes toward youth and whether organizations benefited from youth involvement. The findings of this study are also helpful for service organizations that wish to give youth more responsibility. The study interviewed nineteen youth and twenty-nine adults from fifteen organizations across the country. The findings revealed that young people often have strong effects on adults and the organizations of which they are a part. Adult attitudes toward youth changed as adults gained the opportunity to observe the skills and competence of the youth. As adults interacted with youth in positive ways, negative stereotypes of adolescents diminished.

Findings also suggest that youth involvement benefits organizations and that the contributions of both adults and young people contribute to effective decision-making. For example, youth bring to the table an "honest" and "fresh" voice. Youth bring new ideas, creativity, and high energy to the group and are often relentless in finding the answers that they seek. Many adults commented that meetings would be "boring" without the presence of youth. Furthermore, youth have first-hand knowledge of the interests and concerns of other youth, which provides the organization with a closer connection to the ideas of young people. At the same time, adults bring years of experience, knowledge, and skill. Youth spoke positively of the advice, direction, and lessons they learned from adults.

Including youth in decision-making requires organizational change, which is not easy to achieve. The report highlights conditions that are needed to create organizational change. First, the board members of the organization need to be committed to youth decision-making and "governance." In addition, adult leaders within the organization should also strongly advocate for including youth. Youth need to do their part in advocating for their position. Organizations need to provide support and training that will help youth to excel and make effective decisions. Older adolescents should be given responsibility first, and then younger adolescents can be gradually given more responsibility as adults gain confidence in the youth. Finally, involving young people at the highest levels of the organization is risky and goes against strong societal norms. Therefore, leaders in the organization need to be very selective when choosing youth to take on such roles. If such conditions are closely followed, organizations should benefit from the help of youth decision-making.

The Power of Service-Learning for American Schools

The National Commission on Service-Learning was formed in 2001, chaired by former Senator John Glenn and cosponsored by the W.K. Kellogg Foundation and the John Glenn Institute for Public Service and Public Policy at the Ohio State University. After almost one year of study and discussion, including the review of research data, visits to schools, and interviews with students, teachers, and administrators, the commission released a report in 2002 identifying the benefits of service-learning for promoting student learning, academic engagement, and citizenship. The report describes feelings of alienation from school and traditional forms of civic activity prevalent among youth and discussed how service-learning can simultaneously increase school engagement and inspire active citizenship. In consideration of the benefits of service-learning, the report maintains that every school child in the United States should participate in service-learning each year. In order to accomplish this, program support must be significantly expanded. The report emphasizes, however, that standards of good practice must be established and maintained for service-learning to achieve its desired impact.

The recommendations of the report include the importance of providing "meaningful leadership roles for youth in all aspects of service-learning" (p. 17). More specifically, the recommendations include providing support for adults to develop meaningful roles for youth, expanding a national network of youth leaders in service-learning, and increasing mechanisms for publicizing and rewarding the accomplishments of youth. Educators need increased training and support to develop and implement quality service-learning programs. Service-learning should be part of the training of teachers and administrators being offered or required by accredited professional preparation programs. In addition, ongoing professional development is recommended through in-service training and access to web-based resources.

PRINCIPLES OF GOOD PRACTICE FOR COMBINING SERVICE AND LEARNING

Over the years, several organizations have identified standards that remain consistent with current research findings for the development of effective service-learning programs. The Principles of Good Practice for Combining Service and Learning were formulated at the Wingspread Conference at the Johnson Foundation in Racine, Wisconsin, in October 1989 (Honnet & Poulsen, 1989). More than seventy organizations developed the principles in consultation with the National Society for Internships and Experiential Education (now known as the National Society for Experiential Education). The principles emphasize the mutual needs of volunteers, the persons being served, and the organizations using volunteers and are relevant for programs across a variety of settings, including community organizations, K–12 schools, colleges and universities, government agencies, and policy and research institutions. The authors provide examples to illustrate the application of these principles across all of these settings. According to the principles, an effective program

1. "engages people in responsible and challenging actions for the common good
2. provides structured opportunities for people to reflect critically on their service experience
3. articulates clear service and learning goals for everyone involved
4. allows for those with needs to define those needs
5. clarifies the responsibilities of each person and organization involved
6. matches service providers and service needs through a process that recognizes changing circumstances
7. expects genuine, active, and sustained organizational commitment
8. includes training, supervision, monitoring, support, recognition, and evaluation to meet service and learning goals

9. insures that the time commitment for service and learning are flexible, appropriate and in the best interests of all involved

10. is committed to program participation by and with diverse populations (Honnet & Poulsen, 1989, pp. 2–3).

ALLIANCE FOR SERVICE-LEARNING IN EDUCATIONAL REFORM

The Alliance for Service-Learning in Educational Reform developed Standards of Quality for School-Based and Community-Based Service-Learning. These standards were built upon the Wingspread Principles of Good Practice for Combining Service and Learning described above and have been considered a primary benchmark in guiding service-learning program development since 1993.

The standards are consistent with other overviews of "best practices" for service-learning programs. According to these standards, service-learning programs should

1. support both service involvement and academic learning (there are opportunities to integrate service and academic learning for all age groups, which should be consistent with students' developmental levels)

2. provide concrete opportunities for youth skill development and role exploration, encouraging risk-taking and the development of competencies (students learn to function effectively in real-world settings)

3. include preparation of volunteers (participants learn about contexts and history that frame their service activities and learn skills necessary to perform service work)

4. include reflection (students integrate and process service experience and academic learning to gain increased understanding and insight into themselves and their environments through discussion and writing assignments)

5. recognize within the school and/or community the service accomplishments of volunteers

6. include youth in planning service programs (gain support and trust of involved youth and empower them to help understand community needs and their own roles in community service)

7. involve youth in service that makes a real difference to their communities (service should fill a recognized community need and also fit the developmental level of involved students)

8. include program evaluation (programs must be formally assessed to see if they meet their identified goals and to better understand their benefits to students, schools, and communities)

9. support school and community connections (break down barriers between the school and community and recognize and respect each other's service-learning goals)

10. be integrated as a critical part of school experience (need for institutional support of time, recognition, and expenses)

11. involve support and guidance from skilled adults (need for trained adults to support effective and consistent student learning)

12. include staff training and education on service-learning goals and process (prior to student involvement, staff must understand and support school service-learning initiatives)

In 1995, thirty states participated in a meeting called School Improvement: Strategies for Connecting Schools and Communities, which was sponsored by the U.S. Department of Education and the Corporation of National Service. The meeting identified six principles that were supported by teachers, administrators, students, and community participants and were designed to link schools and communities through service. The principles are as follows:

Principle 1: All children can achieve higher levels of academic success while learning to serve if they are provided challenging standards and given the opportunity to reach them.

Principle 2: By solving real-life problems, students engaged in service-learning are challenged to exercise leadership and responsibility.

Principle 3: Teachers engaged in school improvement and service-learning require continuing professional development and training.

Principle 4: Improving our schools requires parent and community involvement.

Principle 5: Improving our schools requires the participation of the private sector and a full range of resources from every community.

Principle 6: School improvement and service-learning build on the realization that ours is a nation of diverse cultures. (Riley & Wofford, 2000, pp. 670–672)

These principles were endorsed in 1995 by Secretary of Education Richard Riley and Eli Segal, then chief executive officer of the Corporation for National Service, thereby demonstrating a national commitment to provide support for service-learning and community partnerships. Continued support for these goals was given by the reaffirmation of these principles in 2000 by Richard Riley and the current chief executive officer of the Corporation for National Service, Harris Wofford.

The above principles have been implemented in various ways across the country, as described by Riley and Wofford (2000). One high school in Virginia designed service projects that educated students on the dangers of drinking and driving, restored an American Indian burial ground, and repaired donated computers for community agencies. In a school in Wisconsin, students who were studying literature about domestic violence became inspired to write poems on this topic. The students read their poems in coffee houses in the community and donated the money that they raised to domestic violence shelters. The University of Pennsylvania's America Reads Partnership with Drew Elementary School exemplifies principle four, where schools, students, and community all get involved. They established a during and after-school program that provides activities that promote literacy. The program is staffed by work-study students from the university studying to be teachers, high school students involved in service-learning, and teachers. Regardless of the school and location, everyone can get involved in implementing the six principles.

The above six principles reflect some of the Essential Elements of Service Learning (National Service-Learning Cooperative, April 1998) developed by the Youth Leadership Council as criteria for quality service-learning programs. The "essential elements" include the necessity for professional training to support program development and implementation, the necessity for evaluating programs and using that data for program improvement, and the necessity for building program support among teachers and administrators.

EVALUATIONS OF SERVICE PROGRAMS

The Standards of Quality for School-Based and Community-Based Service-Learning include the necessity for program evaluation. A national evaluation of Learn and Serve service-learning programs in high schools and middle schools between 1995 and 1997 was completed by the Center for Human Resources at Brandeis University (Melchior et al., 1999) and contributes to current knowledge about the outcomes of service-learning and the characteristics of effective programs. The evaluation looks at both individual and community outcomes, as well as impact on the schools. The following is a summary of that report.

To better understand the potential effects of quality service-learning programs, programs were selected for evaluation that were comprehensive and well established. These programs devoted a significant time commitment to service (average students provided more than seventy hours of direct service), involved students in direct service work, provided opportunities for reflection, and gave students opportunities to contribute in substantive and meaningful ways. All programs were school-based and connected to academic course-work. The study included surveys of teachers and students, school records from seventeen high schools and middle schools, and telephone interviews and on-site school visits. Participants were diverse in terms of age, gender, ethnicity, social class, and prior service-learning experience.

Student Outcomes

Student outcomes were evaluated according to the three program goals:

1. help students become responsible citizens
2. increase academic skills
3. support student development through combined service and academic experience.

The following program effects were found for participating students immediately following participation:

1. positive civic development (attitudes toward service, understanding of community needs)
2. greater involvement in community service in the past six months
3. increased school engagement and improved math grades
4. slight reductions in risk behaviors (arrests in the last six months) for middle school students, but no change for high school students. Positive program impacts were evidenced across student

groups, with positive academic effects being greater for non-White than for White participants

5. student satisfaction with service-learning programs and beliefs that they learned from their experiences.

Researchers were also interested in determining whether the positive effects of service-learning were long-lasting. The positive effects that continued after one year were in areas of service leadership and science grades for high school students only. Students who continued to be involved in service work showed more positive long-term impacts than those who stopped after one year.

Community Evaluation

1. 99.5 percent of agencies reported positive experiences with students
2. 90 percent of agencies said that students helped to improve services
3. 75 percent of agencies said that students directly helped clients
4. 82 percent of agencies said that program helped to increase positive attitudes toward community youth.

Impact on the Schools

1. most programs continued running after the original grant funding had ended
2. more than half of the schools used grant funds to expand their service-learning programs
3. over 90 percent of teachers showed positive attitudes about service-learning in their schools
4. few schools made systemic changes to improve service-learning programs.

Was It Worth the Investment?

The researchers measured the cost of the services invested in this project compared to the positive impact on communities. They determined that the value of the services provided was worth more than four times the total cost of the program. Although this cannot be considered an exact comparison of costs and benefits, the researchers estimated that the overall benefits greatly outweighed the costs of the project.

PUBLIC ATTITUDES TOWARD COMMUNITY SERVICE AND SERVICE-LEARNING

In September 2000, the W. K. Kellogg Foundation and the Ewing Marion Kauffman Foundation sponsored a survey conducted by Roper Starch Worldwide to assess public attitudes toward K–12 education, citizenship, and service-learning. The researchers conducted a national telephone survey of more than 1,000 adults to find out how knowledgeable Americans were about service-learning programs, whether they support service-learning, and what they perceive as benefits of and concerns about service-learning.

More than 80 percent of Americans believe that a good education should include more than literacy and math skills. Skills to succeed in the workplace, leadership skills, citizenship, and the opportunity for students to apply what they learn in the classroom to real-world projects and work with people different from themselves were all endorsed by the majority of Americans as responsibilities of the public schools. Many of these goals are consistent with the intent of service-learning projects. The research revealed, however, that most Americans (about 61 percent) are not familiar with the term *service-learning*. Although they lack knowledge of the term, approximately 90 percent of adults support the presence of service-learning programs in their schools once the programs are explained. Typically parents, who have children under the age of eighteen and who have volunteered themselves are most likely to support such programs. Furthermore, Americans are most supportive of service-learning projects that involve opportunities for young people to enhance their academic skills through "real-world" situations. For example, 78 percent of the people surveyed stated that they were likely to endorse English students tutoring younger children to aid them in reading. Sixty-five percent supported service-learning activities that involved students applying their science skills to improve the community's water quality. In addition, approximately 63 percent of Americans supported the idea of students using their math skills to build a local playground. Table 4.8 presents the variety of service-learning activities that were most strongly supported by the survey respondents.

Americans believe that students can benefit from service-learning activities by acquiring skills that they will need once they graduate from

Table 4.8
Types of Public School Service-Learning Programs Supported by Adult
Americans: 2000

Type of service-learning	% of respondents supporting service-learning
English classes tutoring younger kids to help them read better	78%
Improving science skills by testing the water quality of a lake and reporting the findings	65%
Using geometry and math skills to design and lay out a playground	63%
Improving literacy skills by writing and publishing books for preschool children in their neighborhood	59%
Various age levels working together in teams to design and build a nature trail	58%
Prepare meals at a local soup kitchen	56%
Conducting research on their community and writing stories for display at the town hall	55%

Source: Prepared for the Academy for Educational Development and the Learning In
Deed Initiative. As cited in Academy for Educational Development and the Learning In
Deed Initiative (November 2000).

high school, by decreasing rates of destructive behavior, and by increasing their self-esteem. Overall, they found that women, more than men, supported service-learning programs for their emotional benefits, such as feelings of self-worth, confidence, and morale. Table 4.9 lists further perceived benefits of service-learning. Americans expressed concerns about whether schools have the time or money to support service programs. Fifty-three percent of adults surveyed felt that schools did not have the money, while 49 percent stated that they thought teachers would not have the time. Thirty-seven percent thought that service-learning sounded like a good idea, but might be difficult to do.

An overwhelming majority of Americans believe that schools are not fulfilling the needs of students in preparing them for life after graduation. They believe, however, that service-learning can have a positive impact in helping youth to develop the kinds of skills and qualities that they will need to succeed in work and throughout life.

A parent survey (Learning In Deed, 2000) conducted in 1998 and 1999 for Learning In Deed by Public Agenda, a nonprofit public opinion

Table 4.9

Potential Benefits of Service-Learning That Move People the Most

% who say each benefit makes them "much more" supportive of service-learning	
Helps students develop self-confidence	65%
Builds the skills students will need to succeed after graduating from school	64%
Helps reduce the likelihood of children getting involved in self-destructive behavior	63%
Helps students feel a sense of achievement	64%
Makes many students more interested in school and learning	62%
Helps create more orderly classrooms and reduces discipline problems	62%
Connects the basic skills students learn in the classroom to real life	61%
Encourages students to care about their community	61%
Activities improve students' grasp of academics	59%
Students involved are less likely to skip school	59%
Enables young people to understand their responsibility to their community	59%
Helps create a partnership between schools and their communities	58%
Helps students practice what they learn from books and lectures	57%
Different from mandatory service requirements, which are not linked to what students are studying in class	34%

Source: Prepared for the Academy for Educational Development and the Learning In Deed Initiative. As cited in Academy for Educational Development and the Learning In Deed Initiative (November 2000).

research group, identified some of the common misperceptions about service-learning. Many parents, for example, confuse service-learning and mandatory service and think that service-learning is a source of cheap help for community organizations that does not benefit young people. Other parents recognize that service-learning is intended to benefit students but do not understand that it also benefits the communities served. Many parents are not aware that service-learning is for all students, believing that it is only for certain students, such as the gifted or at-risk. Criticisms of service-learning are often based upon misperceptions. For example, parents who oppose service-learning sometimes believe that parents should be responsible for teaching values of responsibility and caring and not rely on the schools to teach values. Some parents fear that academics are being watered down and that students are wasting their time on mindless tasks. Another concern of some parents is that youth will be exposed to danger through interaction with people and places away from the school. Well-run service programs, however, enhance student academic learning, support student and parent autonomy and values, and take reasonable precautions to ensure the safety of participants.

Adult attitudes toward community service were also assessed through a nationwide survey commissioned by the Prudential Insurance Company. With financial support from Prudential, 500 adults were surveyed in May 1995 by The Wirthlin Group, a well-known opinion research firm, to assess adult attitudes about their communities, volunteerism, and community service.

The 1995 survey found that most adults (71 percent) believed that their communities were good places to live. Most adults (67 percent) said that it was important for people to volunteer their time in their communities, with 58 percent of adults reporting that they did give some of their time to community service. Twelve percent reported that they were actively involved as community volunteers, 29 percent were moderately involved, and 59 percent were less actively involved. Family and work commitments were identified as major obstacles to being more involved in community service. Adults felt that community service involvement would increase if schools encouraged students to volunteer. More than half of adults (58 percent) felt that community service should be a requirement for high school graduation.

YOUTH ATTITUDES ABOUT VOLUNTEERISM AND COMMUNITY SERVICE

Prudential also commissioned The Wirthlin Group to assess the attitudes of high school students about their communities and volunteerism (Wirthlin Group, 1995b). Like their parents, most teens (62 percent) felt that their communities were good places to live. More than 70 percent of teens felt, however, that their communities would be better if more teens and more adults participated in volunteer service. Ninety-five percent of teens reported that it was important for people to be involved in their communities and 62 percent felt that it was very important. Most teens, however, felt that adults and students were not as involved as they should be. Sixty-seven percent of students said that they did do some volunteer service, but only 20 percent said they volunteered at a meaningful level. Teens reported that more encouragement from parents and teachers would increase their involvement in service, but only 40 percent felt that they received this encouragement at their schools and only 30 percent felt that they received this encouragement at home. Less than 50 percent of teens could identify an adult that they admired for community service participation. Teens who do volunteer were compared with teens that do not volunteer. Teens who volunteer reported more encouragement from their schools and parents than nonvolunteers did. More volunteers were also able to name a specific role model for community service than were nonvolunteers. Commitments with school, jobs, and homework were a major reason cited by 91 percent of teens as obstacles to volunteerism. A preference for other activities, such as vacation, TV, and music, was another obstacle identified by 71 percent of teens. Not knowing how to get involved (74 percent) and not being asked to volunteer (60 percent) were also believed to limit volunteer involvement.

Teens identified a number of reasons why they participate in community service, including feeling good about oneself (89 percent), being able to list volunteer activities on their college applications (81 percent), learning new skills (81 percent), feeling that they have roots in the community (78 percent), giving something back to their communities (75 percent), and because it is fun or to participate with friends (75 percent). Teens reported that they liked volunteering the most (88 percent) for charitable organizations that provide services to the needy, youth, and elderly. Service in education, such as tutoring, peer counseling, coaching, and student government, was also a popular choice (83 percent) among teens as a type of service involvement, as were environmental activities, such as improving and cleaning up parks (82 percent). Cultural activities, such as working with music, art, and theater, ranked fourth (69 percent).

MANDATORY SERVICE-LEARNING

One service-learning issue that is hotly debated relates to whether service should be required for all students. One question in this debate is how effective are programs that are required? Are they more or less effective than programs that are voluntary? A second question is whether mandatory service is a violation of students' constitutional rights. The first issue of program effectiveness relates to potential negative outcomes when students feel they have been forced to participate in service-learning. Research findings indicate that student perceptions of autonomy and responsibility are critical to program success. That is, the more students feel that they are making their own choices and are taking responsibility for their own actions, the more they are likely to benefit from a program. It is, thus, possible that if students feel that service-learning has been imposed upon them, positive outcomes of service-learning programs may be diminished. In their review of research on this issue, Raskoff and Sundeen (2000) reported mixed findings as to the effects of required participation. They found some negative responses from students (particularly boys) who felt they were being controlled by mandatory participation. For many students, however, there was no negative response to mandatory participation. The possible negative reactions of students to mandatory service-learning must be weighed against the possible good that could come from student participation in these activities. The impact of mandatory community service is discussed further in chapter 1.

The second issue relates to whether it is constitutional to require students to participate in service-learning. In a discussion of this issue, Smith (1999) argues that mandatory service-learning is constitutional. He asserts that public schooling is a privilege, rather than a right, which means that students in public school do not have all of the same constitutional rights that they have in other situations. A related issue raised by critics is whether students are free to choose where they perform their service. However, as schools often provide many service options, this issue has been less volatile than questions about service-learning requirements.

THREE CRITICAL COURT CASES

While there have been voluntary community service programs in secondary schools for decades, it is only recently that public school districts have begun to require community service work for high school graduation. These three federal court cases represent the central legal challenges directed at mandatory school-community service in the 1990s. Each case was filed in a different geographical area, although many of the constitutional issues raised in these three cases are the same. Next, summaries are provided of each of these three cases, emphasizing the central issues argued in each case, as well as the rulings of the Supreme Court (Hyman, 1999).

Steirer v. Bethlehem Area School District (1990)

The first major court challenge to mandatory service programs in school took place in Bethlehem, Pennsylvania. The Bethlehem high school requires sixty hours of public service as a graduation requirement. Two families sued the school district, school board members, and the superintendent. They argued that mandatory community service violated the students' Thirteenth Amendment Rights, requiring involuntary servitude. This amendment was written as a protection against "slavery and involuntary servitude," so the critical question was whether mandatory community service could be understood in relation to laws prohibiting slavery. The courts stated that mandatory school service could not be compared to slavery and that unpaid work does not necessarily constitute involuntary servitude as defined in the Thirteenth Amendment. The plaintiffs also claimed that mandatory service violated their First Amendment Rights to express or to not express certain beliefs (such as altruism, as demonstrated by community service). The court rejected this claim as service activity was not considered to be a direct expression of beliefs.

Immediato v. Rye Neck School District (1996)

This second major court case took place in Mamaroneck, New York, in Westchester County. The Rye Neck School District public high school requires forty hours of public service in order to receive a high school diploma. The Immediato family and their representatives sued the local school district and district officials challenging the constitutionality of mandatory school community service. They argued that the service requirement violated the student's Thirteenth and Fourteenth Amendment Rights, as well as the Fourteenth Amendment Rights of his parents. The most important constitutional issue in this case relates to the parents' Fourteenth Amendment Right to direct the education of their children. The district court decided that this mandatory service program did not violate the constitutional rights of either students or their parents. The Immediato family appealed this decision, but the court once again decided in favor of the district's mandatory service policy, stating that it did not violate the family's constitutional rights.

Herndan v. Chapel Hill-Carrboro City Board of Education (1997)

A third major court case took place in Chapel Hill, North Carolina. The city schools in this area require fifty hours of community service in

Table 4.10

Percent of Public Schools with Service-Learning That Have Mandatory or Volunteer Student Participation: Academic Year 1998–1999

School Context	% with Mandatory Student Participation	% with Voluntary Student Participation
Elementary	56%	67%
Middle/High School	49%	79%
Total	53%	73%

Source: U.S. Department of Education, National Center for Education Statistics, Fast Response Survey System (FRSS), National Student Service-Learning and Community Service Survey, FRSS 71, 1999. As cited in Skinner and Chapman (1999).

order to receive a high school diploma. A suit was filed by two high school students and their parents against the city board of education, school board members, and the superintendent. They argued that this mandatory service requirement was unconstitutional as it violated student rights of freedom from involuntary servitude, personal liberty, and privacy, as well as parental rights to raise their children as they see fit. The issues here were very similar to those discussed in the two earlier court cases. The district court determined that this mandatory service program did not violate the constitutional rights of either students or parents.

While the debate around this issue continues, statistics from national surveys indicate that most school-based programs do not require service-learning participation. Results from the student-based National Household Education Survey (2000) suggest that there has been a slight increase in mandatory student participation over the past three years. This increase, however, shows only a 3 percent rise over three years (a rise from 16 percent to 19 percent from 1996 to 1999). The highest percentage of students (67 percent in 1999) reported that their schools support, but do not require service-learning. Another national survey shows similar findings. Middle schools and high schools are more likely to have voluntary rather than mandatory service-learning programs, while elementary schools have a less clear distinction between these categories (Skinner & Chapman, 1999) (see Table 4.10).

COLLEGE STUDENTS AND COMMUNITY SERVICE

Because the focus of this book is on teenagers and community service, we concentrate primarily on middle school and high school students. It is important to recognize, however, that many students are still in their teenage years during the first two years of college. College-level community service and service-learning have also experienced tremendous growth during the last decade (Kenny, Simon, Kiley-Brabeck, & Lerner, 2002). Developments in programs for college students have had a large influence on programs for early and middle adolescents, and developments in programs at the high school level have had a large influence on college-level service programs. The growth in service-learning opportunities at the elementary and secondary levels has contributed to an increase in volunteerism among incoming college students. Many students enter college with community service experience and wish to continue to engage in service at the college level. Because of the importance of college programs for late adolescents and the interrelationship of service programs at the high school and college levels, we provide a brief overview of college-level service programs. This section covers many of the same issues that were discussed for secondary school programs, so you can see the similarities, as well as the differences, between high school and college community service-learning.

Participation in service among college students continues to increase. Statistics reveal large numbers of students participating in community service and an increase in college-level participation over the one-year period from 1998 to 2000 at colleges belonging to Campus Compact (Table 4.11). Campus Compact is a national organization that supports

Table 4.11

Overview of Service on Campus Compact Member College Campuses (Includes 703 Member Campuses): Academic Years 1998–2000

College-level service participation	1998	1999	2000
Total number of students involved in service work	610,000	688,000	712,000
Number of students participating In one-time community service	316,000	314,872	382,449
Number of service-learning courses available	11,800	11,876	13,661

Source: Campus Compact (2001), *Annual Service Statistics 2000.*

service-learning in higher education. The organization began in 1985 with four member colleges and had a membership of 703 two- and four-year colleges and universities in 2000 (Campus Compact, 2001). (More information on Campus Compact is available in the organizations chapters of this book.) As discussed earlier in this book, studies show that numbers of secondary students participating in community service have increased exponentially in the last fifteen years (Shumer & Cook, 1999). Growth in the numbers of students participating in community service is thus documented in both college and secondary school settings.

Goals of College Service Programs

As at the secondary level, college service programs include a focus on students and on the community (Kenny et al., 2002). A major national study of the impact of service-learning in higher education (Gray, Ondaatje, & Zakaras, 1999) identified primary service-learning goals as helping students to understand community needs, increasing student learning and development, and increasing opportunities for student service.

Table 4.12 presents goals of college-level service-learning programs as reported by college faculty. These goals are similar in many ways to the

Table 4.12
Goals and Benefits for College-Level Service-Learning as Reported by Faculty Members: Academic Year 1998–1999

Goal for Supporting Service	Percent (%) of Faculty Reporting this Goal
Promoting active/engaged learning	77%
Developing civic skills/responsibilities	76%
Addressing campus responsibility to communities	72%
Developing critical thinking skills	71%
Taking social action	70%
Providing opportunities for career exploration	66%
Exposing students to diversity	57%
Promoting moral development	51%
Religious	24%

Source: Data from 1999 Campus Compact Faculty Survey. http://www.compact.org/news/stats/2-student-service.html.

goals expressed by high school teachers as reported in Table 4.2. University faculty identified student engagement in learning and the development of civic skills as primary. The third most frequently endorsed goal, supported by 72 percent of college faculty and by 48 percent of secondary teachers, involves student and institutional responsibility to make a difference in their local communities. Both college faculty and secondary school teachers endorse community involvement. Other similarities in service-learning goals in secondary and higher education include support of student development, the enhancement of critical thinking skills, and career exploration and planning. One notable difference is the emphasis among college programs on social action, which was not explicitly stated as a goal for younger students. College-level programs focus on a number of pertinent social issues as described in Table 4.13. Reducing risk behaviors of participating students, which was a goal at the secondary level, was not mentioned by college faculty.

Table 4.13
Percentage of Responding University-Level Programs Which Address the Following Issues in Their Service-Learning Programs (Top 14 Issue Areas Listed): Academic Year 1999–2000

Issue area	Percent (%) of schools addressing this issue
Housing/Homelessness	79%
Reading/Writing Tutoring	77%
Environment	77%
Mentoring (Big Brother/Sister, etc.)	73%
Hunger	72%
Health	65%
Women's Issues	65%
Math Tutoring	61%
Multicultural Issues	59%
Parenting/Child care	56%
HIV/AIDS	54%
Mental Health	48%
Urban Environment	47%
Sexual Assault	47%

Source: Campus Compact (2001), *Annual Service Statistics 2000.*

Outcomes of Service Programs in Higher Education

Service-learning programs in higher education appear to have positive effects according to two recent major reports. The Learn and Serve America Higher Education report (Gray et al., 1999) found that service-learning programs had positive effects on students by fostering an understanding of their communities, increasing learning and development, and enhancing a sense of civic responsibility. Research by the Higher Education Research Institute (Astin et al., 2000) found positive effects for academic and personal development, including improved grades, leadership and personal efficacy, increases in service-related career interests, and gains in personal engagement and responsibility. A summary of each of these reports can be found in this chapter.

The outcomes for college students are in many ways similar to outcomes identified for secondary school students. Similar to college students, secondary students demonstrated growth in personal and academic development and community engagement. At the secondary level, increased levels of community service involvement and school engagement, as well as slightly decreased levels of risk behaviors, have been documented (Melchior et al., 1999). Stukas and colleagues (1999) reported student growth in self-confidence, understanding, values (such as commitment to communities), and academic work. While these broad effects are consistent across high school and college-level programs, effects vary depending on the goals and structure of service programs. Also, despite these similarities, developmental differences between high school and college students impact the ways in which students are influenced by community service involvement. For example, the ways in which college students are able to understand the problems of the communities in which they are performing service may be more complex than the understanding achieved by the typical high school student.

The Corporation for National Service authorized evaluations of programs for which it had provided financial support. The summary report by Gray et al. (1999) provides findings from the evaluation of Learn and Serve America, Higher Education (LSAHE). The research was supported by the Corporation for National and Community Service and was completed by RAND Education, an independent nonprofit research organization. The impact of the programs on students, universities, and recipients of services was assessed.

This evaluation focused on college programs that were funded by LSAHE between 1995 and 1997. The main goal of this funding was to increase connections between community service and academic work. Of the financial resources received by colleges and universities, a large portion of the funds were spent to develop structures to provide and to sustain service-learning rather than to pay for direct services to the community. In terms of the type of service provided by students, the most frequent type of service provided to the community was education, with more than 75 percent of college students involved in offering educational services.

This study gathered information through surveys distributed to program directors, students, and community organizations. More than 1,300 students from twenty-eight institutions completed the survey. Researchers also visited programs and interviewed students and staff. Telephone interviews were conducted with representatives of eighteen institutions within the two years after the site visit to assess how programs had developed over that time.

Goals of Learn and Serve Higher Education

1. help students understand the needs of communities
2. increase student academic learning, civic commitment, and social responsibility
3. increase quality and quantity of student service opportunities.

What LSAHE Provided

1. contributed more than 10 million dollars in grants for each of the three years from 1995 to 1997
2. supported direct student service involvement through courses and extracurricular work
3. focused on helping organizations to develop strong service-learning programs
4. supported student volunteering in education settings (75–80 percent of college volunteers).

Program Effects for Students

1. helped students understand the needs of communities
2. increased quality and quantity of student service opportunities
3. increased student academic learning, civic commitment, and social responsibility.

Community Responses to Student Service

1. student volunteers helped to improve community services (served as role models and helped to reach more people)
2. communities were very pleased with student involvement
3. scheduling and transportation were the two central difficulties.

Program Effects on Institutions

1. increased integration of service-learning into class content (helped to develop service-learning courses and content)
2. supported mutual and positive relationships between college institutions and communities
3. provided increased service-learning opportunities for students.

It is unclear whether service-learning programs will be able to continue after federal funding has ended. Findings show that the following factors increase the chances that programs will survive over time:

1. long-term service commitment of schools/organizations
2. strong, individual leadership at the university
3. support from faculty
4. service centers available to bring service-learning activities together.

Was the Financial Investment Worthwhile?

The researchers measured the value of the services invested in higher education programs compared to the positive impact on communities. Over three years, there was a gradual shift toward more gains than losses. If these programs continue, the value of the community services should be greater than the investment, making service-learning a good investment choice.

The following report (Sax, Astin, Korn, & Mahoney, 1999) was prepared by the Higher Education Research Institute (HERI) at the University of California, Los Angeles (UCLA) Graduate School of Education and Information Studies. The Learn and Serve America Service-Learning Clearinghouse Project is also located at UCLA. HERI has conducted studies of college students every year since 1973. In their 1999 survey of first-year college students, HERI found that 73.5 percent of freshmen reported they had done volunteer work during their senior year of high school. Student attitudes toward social activism had declined from previous years, however, with fewer students endorsing the importance of becoming a community leader and participating in community action programs. In 1999, the percentage of students who responded that it is very important or essential to "influence social values" was just 35.8, the lowest percent since 1986. UCLA education professor Alexander Astin, who started the survey in 1973, believes that this data indicate the desirability of expanding college-level service-learning programs.

Dr. Astin is also first author of a study on how service-learning affects students (Astin, Vogelgesang, Ikeda, & Yee, 2000). This study had two major goals. The first was to assess the effects that service-learning and community service involvement had on college student development. The second was to explore the ways in which service-learning works to positively affect college students. The researchers studied over 22,000 college students across the country. The study was begun in 1994, and follow-up data from college students was collected in 1998. This study used both quantitative (test scores, school grades, self-efficacy, etc.) and qualitative (case studies, interviews of teachers and students, and class observations) data. While this study focused on college-aged students, the findings may be usefully applied to younger students, as well.

Positive Effects of Service-Learning

1. positive impact was measured on many developmental and academic outcomes (grades, writing skills, self-efficacy, leadership, choice of a service career). Outcomes were strongest for academic skills, especially writing

2. admissions test scores were not related to impact

3. the strongest impact was observed on students' decisions to follow service-related careers

4. students benefited most when service was connected to the academic curriculum. The benefits were particularly evident for academic learning

5. most students felt that their service work "made a difference." Increased personal efficacy, awareness of the world, knowledge of personal values, and engagement in class were demonstrated

6. increased civic responsibility was documented for both teachers and students.

Important Factors in Service-Learning Success

1. student interest in subject matter is important to positive outcomes
2. class discussion of service work contributes to positive effects
3. professors need to relate service work with course material
4. students need substantial training before beginning service work
5. reflection, including discussion, journals, and papers, is important in helping students relate the service experience to their course work.

The 1999 Service-Learning Needs Assessment

Between December 1998 and March 1999, the UCLA Higher Education Research Institute Service-Learning Clearinghouse Project conducted the 1999 Service-Learning Needs Assessment. The UCLA Higher Education Research Institute Service-Learning Clearinghouse Project works in conjunction with the Learn and Serve America National Service-Learning Clearinghouse. The goal of this study was to increase understanding of the needs of service-learning practitioners in higher education. To accomplish this, survey information was gathered via the Internet from service-learning program directors and from faculty involved with service-learning. This study specifically focused on areas of training, technical assistance, research, and program needs.

This survey included fourteen sections, which addressed multiple service-learning issues. One area focused on respondents' perceptions of the greatest faculty needs in order to improve or support service-learning efforts. An additional section assessed current status and components of service-learning programs. Finally, respondents were asked to share comments and ideas on their experiences with service-learning. Overall, the survey included issues of relevance to student, faculty and community concerns, program resources and development, and research issues.

Surveys were completed by seventy respondents. The majority of respondents were affiliated with public universities and were members of Campus Compact. Respondents' work settings included two-year colleges and four-year colleges and universities.

The survey asked respondents to evaluate the areas of greatest need in their service-learning work. Increased research and evaluation of

service-learning programs and greater faculty involvement were identified by faculty as the two greatest needs. Each of these needs was
endorsed by 70 percent of respondents as moderately high or high. Also
rated as moderately high or high need were more student involvement
(endorsed by 59 percent of faculty), more information on integrating
service into the curriculum (42 percent), more staff development (41
percent), and stronger partnerships with the community (41 percent).

In the area of research and evaluation, respondents rated the need for
research and evaluation in nine research categories. Respondents indicated
a need for more research concerning the impact of service-learning on students (16 percent), impact on faculty (15 percent), longitudinal studies (14
percent), curriculum integration and outcomes (11 percent), program
impact on service recipients (10 percent), and the impact of program
design on outcomes (10 percent). Respondents also indicated a need for
more research concerning program impact on community agencies (9 percent), including qualitative (8 percent) and quantitative studies (7 percent).
These ratings reflect the scarcity of longitudinal studies as compared with a
greater number of short-term qualitative and quantitative studies.

With respect to faculty needs, the top two identified needs relate to
institutional awareness and support for faculty service-learning efforts.
These include the availability of faculty time for service-learning work
(endorsed by 62 percent) and the clarification of faculty roles in university service-learning programs (57 percent). The need to increase awareness of service-learning programs across the campus was endorsed by 56
percent of respondents. Other highly ranked faculty needs included
departmental and administrative support (54 percent), technical assistance in assessment (53 percent), more discipline-based resources (53
percent), promotional advancement (52 percent) and financial incentives (46 percent) for involvement, training on reflection activities (49
percent), support for a "service-learning coordinator" staff position (44
percent), and a higher level of administrative support (42 percent). The
Campus Compact Annual Service Statistics 2000 (Campus Compact,
2001), an annual survey of member institutions, also assessed obstacles
to the institutionalization and advancement of service-learning. According to this survey, the three greatest obstacles are faculty time and pressure, faculty teaching load (endorsed by 84 percent), insufficient funds
to support programs (58 percent), and lack of common understanding of
service-learning (54 percent). It is clear that significant resources and
institutional commitment are needed to support faculty involvement in
service-learning within institutions of higher education.

REFERENCES

Academy for Educational Development and the Learning In Deed Initiative. (2000, November). *Public attitudes toward education and service-learning.* New York: Roper Starch Worldwide Inc.

Alliance for Service-Learning in Education Reform. (1993). *Standards of quality for school-based and community-based service learning.* Washington, DC: Author.

Astin, A. W., Vogelgesang, L. J., Ikeda, E. K., & Yee, J. A. (2000). *How service-learning affects students.* Los Angeles: Higher Education Research Institute, University of California, Los Angeles.

Belbas, B., Gorak, K., & Shumer, R. (October 1993). Commonly used definitions of service-learning: A discussion piece. Retrieved February 24, 2000, from http://www.nicsl.coled.umn.edu/res/mono/def.html.

Billig, S. (2000). A model of school-based K–12 service-learning mediators and student outcomes. Retrieved February 8, 2001, from http://www.Learning InDeed.org/research/slresearch/model.html.

Bureau of Labor Statistics. (2002). *Volunteering in the United States.* Washington, DC: United States Department of Labor.

Cairn, R. W., & Kielsmeier, J. C. (Eds.). (1991). *Growing hope: A sourcebook on integrating youth service into the school curriculum.* Minneapolis, MN: National Youth Leadership Council.

Campus Compact. (1999). Highlights and trends in student service and service-learning: Statistics from the 1999 campus compact member and faculty surveys. Retrieved January 31, 2001, from http://www.compact.org/stats.

Campus Compact. (2000). *Introduction to service-learning toolkit: Readings and resources for faculty.* Providence, RI: Brown University.

Campus Compact. (2001). *Annual service statistics 2000.* Providence, RI: Brown University.

Close Up Foundation. Service-Learning Quarterly: ASLER Standards. Retrieved June 28, 2000, from http://www.closeup.org.servlern/sl_asler.htm.

Commission on National and Community Service. (1993). *What you can do for your country.* Washington, DC: U.S. Government Printing Office.

Do Something, Inc. (1999). *Community connections campaign: Do Something's how-to guide.* New York: Author.

Fredericks, L., Kaplan, E., & Zeisler, J. (2001). *Integrating youth voice in service-learning.* Denver, CO: Education Commission of the States.

Giles, D., Honnet, E. P., & Migliore, S. (Eds.). (1991). *Research agenda for combining service and learning in the 1990s.* Raleigh, NC: National Society for Internships and Experiential Education.

Gray, M. J., Ondaatje, E. H., & Zakaras, L. (1999). *Combining service and learning in higher education: Summary report.* Santa Monica, CA: RAND.

Honnet, E. P., & Poulsen, S. J. (1989). *Principles of good practice for combining service and learning: A Wingspread report.* Racine, WI: Johnson Foundation.

Hyman, R. T. (1999). *Mandatory community service in high school: The legal dimension.* Dayton, OH: Education Law Association.

Kenny, M. E., Simon, L. A. K., Kiley-Brabeck, K., & Lerner, R. M. (Eds). (2002). Promoting civil society through service learning: A view of the issues. In M. E. Kenny, L. A. Simon, K. Kiley-Brabeck, & R. M. Lerner (Eds.), *Learning to serve: Promoting civil society through service learning* (pp. 1–14). Norwell, MA: Kluwer.

Kinsley, C. W., & McPherson, K. (Eds.). (1995). *Enriching the curriculum through service-learning.* Reston, VA: The Association for Supervision and Curriculum Development.

Kleiner, B., & Chapman, C. (2000). Youth service-learning and community service among 6th through 12th grade students in the United States: 1996 and 1999. *Education Statistics Quarterly, 2,* 34–52.

Learning In Deed (2000). *Perceptions: Understanding and responding to what people think about service-learning.* Battle Creek, MI: W. K. Kellogg Foundation.

Maloy, R., & Wohlleb, B. (1997). *Implementing community service in K–12 schools: A report on policies and practices in the eastern region.* Amherst, MA: University of Massachusetts School of Education.

Melchior, A., et al. (1999). *Summary report: National evaluation of Learn and Serve America.* Waltham, MA: Center for Human Resources, Brandeis University.

National Commission on Service Learning. (2002). *Learning In Deed: The power of service-learning for American schools.* Battle Creek, MI: W.K. Kellogg Foundation.

National Service-Learning Clearinghouse. (1999). What is service-learning? Retrieved June 7, 2001, from http://www.nicsl.coled.umn.edu/navbar2.htm.

National Service-Learning Cooperative. (April, 1998). *Essential elements of service-learning.* St. Paul, MN: National Youth Leadership Council.

Newman, F., & Rutter, R. (1985). A profile of high school community service programs. *Educational Leadership, 43,* 65–71.

Nolin, M. J., Chaney, B., & Chapman, C. (1997). *Student participation in community service activity* (NCES 97–331). U.S. Department of Education. National Center for Education Statistics. Washington, DC: U.S. Government Printing Office.

Raskoff, S. A., & Sundeen, R. A. (2000). Community service programs in high schools. *Law and Contemporary Problems, 62,* 74–106.

Riley, R., & Wofford, H. (2000). The reaffirmation of the Declaration of Principles. *Phi Delta Kappan, 81* (9), 670–672.

Sax, L. J., Astin, A. W., Korn, W. S., & Mahoney, K. M. (1999). *The American freshman: National norms for fall 1999.* Los Angeles: Higher Education Research Institute, UCLA Graduate School of Education and Information Studies.

Search Institute. (1991). Kids who care. *Source: A Quarterly Newsletter on Issues Facing Children, Adolescents, and Families, 7,* 1–3.

Shumer, R., & Cook, C. (June, 1999). *The status of service-learning in the United States: Some facts and figures.* Minneapolis: The National Service-Learning Clearinghouse, University of Minnesota.

Skinner, R., & Chapman, C. (1999). *Service-learning and community service in K–12 public schools* (NCES 1999–043). U.S. Department of Education. Washington, DC: U.S. Government Printing Office.

Smith, R. S. (1999). Volunteering and community service. *Law and Contemporary Problems, 62,* 169–176.

Smolla, R. A. (1999). The constitutionality of mandatory public school community service programs. *Law and Contemporary Problems, 62,* 113–140.

Stukas, A. A., Clary, G. E., & Snyder, M. (1999). Service learning: Who benefits and why? *Social Policy Report: Society for Research in Child Development, 13,* 1–19.

UCLA Service-Learning Clearinghouse Project. 1999 service-learning needs assessment. Retrieved March 21, 2001, from http://www.gseis.ucla.edu/slc/slcp.html.

Wirthlin Group (1995a). *The Prudential spirit of community adult survey on community involvement.* Newark, NJ: Prudential Insurance.

Wirthlin Group. (1995b). *The Prudential spirit of community youth survey.* Newark, NJ: Prudential Insurance.

Yates, M., & Youniss, J. (1996). A developmental perspective on community service in adolescence. *Social Development, 5,* 85–111.

Yates, M., & Youniss, J. (1998). Community service and political identity development in adolescence. *Journal of Social Issues, 54,* 495–512.

Zeldin, S., McDaniel, A. K., Topitzes, D., & Calvert, M. (2001). *Youth in decision-making: A study on the impacts of youth on adults and organizations.* Madison: University of Wisconsin-Madison.

5

Directory of Organizations, Associations, and Government and International Agencies

This chapter presents an extensive compilation of organizations that support community service and service-learning for youth. Each organization is listed with contact information and a brief summary about the purpose, mission, and programs available through the organization. The majority of organizations selected in this chapter are nonprofit organizations through which teens can find opportunities to participate in service to their communities. These organizations range from local or regional agencies that provide necessary services to the community to national organizations that often partner with local community agencies to involve youth in service. We have included profiles of youth organizations, such as the Girl Scouts, Boy Scouts, and 4-H, that have a long-standing commitment to promoting positive development of youth in the United States, as well as promoting community service among youth. In addition, we have included organizations, including the National Youth Leadership Council, National Indian Youth Leadership Project, Do Something, City Year, and AmeriCorps, that are dedicated to giving youth opportunities to serve their communities and to build civic responsibility and leadership skills. These organizations provide youth with a variety of service opportunities, such as helping to clean-up and preserve the environment, tutoring children, and caring for the elderly. Although these organizations have diverse program goals, many provide youth with necessary life skills, promote activism and citizenship, and increase school engagement and academic skills. Although the majority of organizations profiled in this chapter are located and based in the United States, we have also included organizations that support service programs internationally. For example, Global Volunteers, Cross-Cultural Solutions, and the International Partnership for Service-Learning offer opportunities for individuals to complete service programs abroad, through which they provide essential services, but also learn about diverse cultures and important global issues.

In addition, many organizations were formed to support the development, implementation, evaluation, and improvement of service programs. Thus, we have chosen to highlight organizations that community agency staff, faculty and teachers, and other professionals can contact to receive technical assistance, resources, or support for their community service or service-learning programs. Furthermore, we have included organizations such as the American Youth Policy Forum and the Search Institute that are engaged in research and involved in developing policies and issuing reports that support community service and positive youth development. We have also included profiles of some key foundations and organizations, including the W. K. Kellogg Foundation, that have supported initiatives in community service and service-learning for youth.

Adopt-A-Watershed
P.O. Box 1850
Hayfork, CA 96041
Telephone: (530) 628-5334
Fax: (530) 628-4212
Internet: http://www.adopt-a-watershed.org

Adopt-A-Watershed is a service-learning program geared towards students in kindergarten to twelfth grade. Adopt-A-Watershed uses a local watershed (i.e., an area of land that drains water into a river system or other body of water) in the school's community and all of the watershed's natural resources to engage students in hands-on activities making science applicable to their lives. Combining education with helping the local environment, Adopt-A-Watershed develops collaborative partnerships with schools, communities, government agencies, and public and private agencies to promote learning through community service. Enhancing and improving science education in grades K–12 and supporting watershed stewardship are the goals of Adopt-A-Watershed. Adopt-A-Watershed utilizes the following approach to meet the goal of combining community service, preserving the environment, and improving science education. Students apply science concepts by monitoring local watersheds through experiential learning. Students also help to restore watersheds through community-needs based projects. For example, kindergartners learn what a watershed is and plant trees; they can visit and monitor the trees' changes and growth throughout the rest of their school career. Community action projects also help to educate the public about the need to restore the local watersheds. Finally, students are encouraged to reflect upon the ideas and concepts they learned and the benefits they make to the community and environment. This strategy becomes integral to the science curriculum and at each grade level, students gain increased exposure to the watershed ecology and science concepts. On the Adopt-A-Watershed website, students can share their findings with other Adopt-A-Watershed school projects. A detailed curriculum is also available for each grade on the website. Adopt-A-Watershed schools are currently in Alabama, Arizona, California, Colorado, Florida, Illinois, Indiana, Maine, New Jersey, New York, Texas, Virginia, Washington, and Wyoming.

America Reads
U.S. Department of Education
400 Maryland Avenue SW
Washington, DC 20202-0107
Telephone: (202) 401-8888
Email: americareads@ed.gov
Internet: http://www.ed.gov/inits/americareads

America Reads is a national service program that was established after the results of a number of research studies revealed that American students who cannot read well by the fourth grade have higher drop-out rates and more difficulty achieving success in their lives. The goal of America Reads is to make certain that every child in the United States can read well by the end of the third grade. The Corporation for National Service has collaborated with the U.S. Department of Education to recruit colleges and universities to sign up for the America Reads Challenge Federal Work-Study program, to create and distribute materials to recruit tutors and to provide training for directors of literacy programs. America Reads trains volunteers as reading tutors. Volunteers can be parents, teachers, students, senior citizens, and other professionals. These volunteers help individual children, families, support classroom activities, and organize community reading initiatives.

America Reads tutors can be involved in classrooms, after-school programs, Head Start programs, early childhood programs, and reading with children at home. In addition, America Reads supports nondirect service programs that support and benefit literacy activities, including book drives, coordinating parental involvement projects, and fixing up school libraries.

American Association of School Administrators
1801 North Moore Street
Arlington, VA 22209-1813
Telephone: (703) 528-0700
Fax: (703) 841-1543
Internet: http://www.aasa.org

Founded in 1865, the American Association of School Administrators (AASA) is a professional membership organization that consists of school leaders. The mission of the AASA is to develop the abilities and talents of educational leaders with the aim to improve the public educational system. Some of the activities of the AASA include publishing resources, an annual conference on educational issues, professional development opportunities, and awards and scholarship programs. The AASA is committed to improving the lives of children and connecting communities and schools. The AASA operates the *Opening the School House Doors* program, a service-learning initiative in cooperation with the National Youth Leadership Council and local schools. This initiative, which is supported by the Corporation for National Service, aims to develop the best practices for establishing volunteer programs in schools. Available on the AASA website is a checklist of successful practices that school administrators and educators can use to assess their volunteer programs.

American Institute for Public Service
100 West 10th Street, Suite 215
Wilmington, DE 19801
Telephone: (302) 622-9101
Fax: (302) 622-9106 or (302) 622-9108
E-mail: info@aips.org
Internet: http://www.aips.org

President's Student Service Challenge
P.O. Box 189
Wilmington, DE 19899-0189
Telephone: (302) 622-9107
Fax: (302) 622-9106
Email: pssainfo@dca.net
Internet: http://www.student-service-awards.org/default.asp

President's Student Service Scholarships
1505 Riverview Road
P.O. Box 68
St. Peter, MN 56082
Telephone: (888) 275-5018
Fax: (507) 931-9168
Email: RDCSFA@aol.com
Internet: http://www.student-service-awards.org/default.asp

The American Institute for Public Service was founded to encourage young people in America to become engaged in community and public service. The American Institute for Public Service was created in 1972 with support from Jacqueline Kennedy Onassis, Senator Robert Taft Jr., and Sam Beard. The Jefferson Awards are given on the local and national level to people who make significant contributions to their communities without expectation of a reward. The American Institute for Public Service also began National Youth Service Day with the support of U.S. Senator John Heinz. National Youth Service Day, which takes place each April, involves thousands of youth in making their communities a better place. The institute also helps sponsor the *Weekly Reader Magazine*, which is geared toward youth service. In addition, the institute also supports the President's Student Service Challenge, which consists of two programs: President's Student Service Awards and President's Student Service Scholarships. Kindergarten through college students may receive a President's Student Service Award for a minimum of 100 hours of service to their community. The President's Student Service Awards are modeled after the Presidential Physical Fitness Awards and help to recognize and encourage youth to serve their communities. Through the President's Student Service Scholarship program, two exceptional juniors or seniors in each high school may receive scholarships for their service, with awards matched by the Corporation for National Service funds from the community.

American Red Cross
17th and D Streets NW
Washington, DC 20006
Telephone: (202) 737-8300
Internet: http://www.redcross.org

Founded in 1881 by Clara Barton, the American Red Cross is committed to helping those in need due to disasters or emergencies. In 1917, the Junior Red Cross was established to involve youth in Red Cross activities, including volunteering, education, and training. There are 2,675 local chapters throughout the United States. Activities and opportunities for youth include leadership development, community service, health promotion, and awareness of international issues. Classes and opportunities vary by local chapter and there are fees for some of the programs.

American Youth Policy Forum
1836 Jefferson Place NW
Washington, DC 20036
Telephone: (202) 775-9731
Fax: (202) 775-9733
Email: aypf@aypf.org
Internet: http://www.aypf.org

The mission of the American Youth Policy Forum is to inform decision-makers in Washington, DC, about relevant issues that are facing youth today. The main vehicle for meeting its mission is to bring together key decision-makers and legislators with researchers and practitioners who have expertise in the youth-development field. For example, the American Youth Policy Forum offers in-service trainings, workshops, site visits to youth organizations, and issues reports. One key activity of the American Youth Policy Forum is the lunchtime forums held on Capitol Hill in Washington, DC, throughout the year. These forums provide legislators and staff, government workers, and other interested individuals with opportunities to learn about youth issues from researchers and practitioners. Topics of these lunchtime forums include improving education, youth and community development, and career development and preparation. The American Youth Policy Forum then publishes briefs based on these forums that are available on its website. The American Youth Policy Forum is nonpartisan and does not take a position on these issues but hopes to develop improved communication that informs the decisions made regarding youth policy.

America's Promise—The Alliance for Youth
909 North Washington Street, Suite 400
Alexandria, VA 22314-1556
Telephone: (703) 684-4500
Email: local@americaspromise.org
Internet: http://www.americaspromise.org

America's Promise—The Alliance for Youth was founded in 1997 at the Presidents' Summit for America's Future by Presidents Ford, Carter, Bush, Reagan, and Clinton, Nancy Reagan, and 1,700 delegates from across the nation. America's Promise is a nonprofit organization dedicated to changing the lives of at-risk youth in the United States. America's Promise has successfully pooled the talents of hundreds of corporations, service providers, state and local governments, and not-for-profit organizations to form a cohesive alliance aimed at providing essential resources to children in need. Services provided include youth volunteers to serve as tutors and mentors, creating safe places for youth to go after school, access to health services, job training, career guidance, and after-school jobs. With the help of the America's Promise staff, these organizations work to fulfill five specific promises to America's youth. The five promises or resources include: a consistent relationship with an adult mentor or tutor; the establishment and maintenance of structured activities and safe places during nonschool hours; a healthy start for youth by access to medical care; marketable skills learned through education that prepares youth for the future; and the opportunity for youth to serve or give back to the community. America's Promise believes that with these five tools or resources, every at-risk young person will both create and improve opportunities for success.

Supporters of America's Promise include high-profile organizations such as Lens Crafters, Fannie Mae, and the NBA, which contribute the full spectrum of business services, products, business plans, marketing and public relations, and overall business philosophy. Retired General and former chairman of the Joint Chiefs of Staff Colin Powell was appointed as Chairman of America's Promise. As both the chairman and spokesperson for America's Promise, Powell has traveled the country to marshal support for improving the lives of children. Although President George W. Bush has recently appointed him secretary of state, Powell has declared that he remains committed to youth in the United States and will continue to remain involved in America's Promise.

ASPIRA Association, Inc.
1112 16th Street NW, Suite 340
Washington, DC 20036
Telephone: (202) 835-3600
Internet: http://www.aspira.org

Founded in 1961, ASPIRA is a national organization committed to encouraging leadership development and education for Puerto Rican and Latino/a youth. Although the organization began in New York City, its national office is now located in Washington, DC. There are now affiliates in Illinois, New Jersey, Florida, Connecticut, Pennsylvania, and Puerto Rico. ASPIRA's programs aim to have Puerto Rican and Latino/a youth learn important life skills, including academic and leadership skills, community service, and career-development activities. This organization also sponsors research on the needs of Latino/a youth, as well as advocates for policy development.

Association for Experiential Education
2305 Canyon Boulevard, Suite 100
Boulder, CO 80302
Telephone: (303) 440-8844
Fax: (303) 440-9581
Internet: http://www.aee.org

The Association for Experiential Education is a nonprofit membership organization that promotes the use of experiential education in order to make education more relevant and useful in the United States and around the world. Members can be individuals or organizations that are involved in a variety of settings, such as schools, youth service, mental health, outdoor/recreation, and environmental education. To promote experiential education, the Association for Experiential Education supports professional development, research and evaluation, and theoretical development. The association sponsors an annual international conference and regional conferences for members and parties interested in experiential education. In addition, this organization has an accreditation program for adventure-based education programs. The Association for Experiential Education has a professional journal entitled *Journal of Experiential Education,* which includes many relevant articles on outdoor education, service-learning, arts, environmental education, research, and theoretical writings. The association also offers publications on a variety of topics relevant to experiential education. Individuals can also subscribe to a listserv with other members and interested parties.

Best Buddies International
100 Southeast Second Street, Suite 1990
Miami, FL 33131
Telephone: (305) 374-2233
Fax: (305) 374-5305
Email: info@bestbuddies.org
Internet: http://www.bestbuddies.org

Founded in 1989 by Anthony Kennedy Shriver, Best Buddies International is a nonprofit organization that helps bring together individuals with mental retardation with volunteers across the United States and internationally, including Canada, Greece, and Egypt. Volunteers provide social, recreational, and employment opportunities for individuals with mental retardation. There are currently six Best Buddies programs, including Best Buddies Middle Schools, Best Buddies High Schools, Best Buddies Colleges, Best Buddies Citizens, Best Buddies Jobs, and e-buddies. Best Buddies sponsors leadership conferences for the training of individuals to be student leaders at college campuses. In 1999, there were 298 college chapters and 186 high school chapters according to the Best Buddies website.

Big Brothers Big Sisters of America
National Headquarters
230 N. 13th Street
Philadelphia, PA 19107
Telephone: (215) 567-7000
Email: national@bbbsa.org
Internet: http://www.bbbsa.org

Founded in 1904, Big Brothers Big Sisters of America organization is a youth mentoring program. Big Brothers Big Sisters of America has local chapters in all fifty United States, which pair adult volunteers with children from single-parent, low-income homes. Adult volunteers serve as mentors or role models to youth in order to create nurturing and supportive one-on-one relationships. Volunteers usually spend approximately three to six hours per week for at least one year as a Big Brother or Big Sister. Big Brothers Big Sisters of America are also teamed up with numerous large corporations in order to benefit youth in need. The goals of the programs are to promote self-esteem, school achievement, and leadership skills in youth through positive relationships and examples in their lives.

Boy Scouts of America
National Council
P.O. Box 152079
Irving, TX 75015-2079
Internet: http://www.scouting.org

The Boy Scouts of America has been one of the largest youth organizations in the United States since it was founded in 1910. Today, there are more than 300 local councils. The Boy Scouts' mission is to educate youth through physical activity and community involvement with the aim to strengthen character and promote responsible citizenship. Boys between the ages of seven and twenty can join one of the scouting programs—Tiger Cubs, Cub Scouting, Boy Scouting, Varsity Scouting, Venturing, and Eagle Scouting. Youth can participate in many activities and programs through scouting including summer camps, national jamborees and conferences, and high adventure and sports activities. Since 1912, the Boy Scouts of America has been promoting Good Turns or acts of goodwill and kindness. Since that time, the Boy Scouts has encouraged doing such good deeds by campaigning nationally for important causes, including food drives, participation in the national census, and advocacy of the importance of organ donation and environmental conservation.

Boys and Girls Clubs of America
771 First Avenue
New York, NY 10017
Telephone: (212) 351-5900
Internet: http://www.bgca.org

The Boys and Girls Clubs of America has approximately 2,600 local clubs throughout the United States, as well as in the Virgin Islands and on military bases, that provide supportive and caring places for youth to spend their out-of-school time. Programs at the Boys and Girls Clubs promote positive development and build competence and character for young people through relationships with adult professionals. The clubs are open every day after school and on weekends. Due to their commitment to serving children and families that are less advantaged, the dues for the programs remain low (averaging $5 to $10/year). The staff at each club is trained in youth development and serve as role models for the youth. In addition, the Boys and Girls Clubs of America has national programs that focus on important issues for young people, including education and career, character and leadership development, sports and athletics, and the arts. The Character and Leadership Program aims to help build responsible citizenship in young people. For example, the TEENSupreme Keystone Clubs are groups of teens (ages fourteen to eighteen) who provide leadership and are involved in developing and carrying out community service activities.

Break Away
2121 W. Pensacola Street, Suite E-543
Tallahassee, FL 32304
Telephone: (850) 644-0986
Fax: (850) 644-1435
Internet: http://www.alternativebreaks.com

Founded in 1991 at Vanderbilt University, Break Away is a nonprofit organization that serves as a resource for information on alternative spring break programs for college or high school students. Currently based at Florida State University, Break Away provides key information on planning and running quality alternative break programs to schools and community organizations that are affiliated with Break Away. The goal of alternative spring breaks for college students is to give them opportunities to engage in service in communities during students' fall, winter, spring, or summer breaks. Students have completed service projects throughout the United States (e.g., Appalachian communities, California, Florida, Mississippi, and Washington, DC), as well as in international locations (e.g., Australia, Brazil, and Mexico). Through service to these communities, students have the opportunities to increase their awareness of social problems and issues, including homelessness, illiteracy, rural and urban poverty, domestic violence, gang violence, and education. Students are involved in such diverse opportunities as working with the environment, children and youth, and the elderly and participating in low-income housing renovation. Students also have the opportunity to gain invaluable experience working with culturally different individuals that they may otherwise not receive. Break Away aspires to have every college student in the United States participate in an alternative break program during college. Break Away's program includes training, retreats, and networking opportunities for students. On their website, individuals can access publications and a directory of organizations in the United States and internationally that host alternative break programs in their communities.

Campfire Boys and Girls
4601 Madison Avenue
Kansas City, MO 64112-1278
Telephone: (816) 756-1950
Fax: (816) 756-0258
E-mail: info@campfire.org
Internet: http://www.campfire.org

Founded in 1910, the Campfire Boys and Girls is a nonprofit organization that provides a comfortable environment in which boys and girls can learn to interact and develop in a healthy manner. Youth in kindergarten through grade twelve participate in either a day or resident camp that is designed to teach basic skills such as planning and decision-making, teamwork, conflict resolution, and friendship skills. In addition, the Campfire Boys and Girls sponsors programs and courses based on a national curriculum that encourage self-responsibility, youth leadership, and service to the community. These small group activities lead to important aspects of development. Local information, links to teen topics, and news releases relevant to the organization are available on the website.

Campus Compact
P.O. Box 1975
Brown University
Providence, RI 02912
Telephone: (401) 863-2876
Internet: http://www.compact.org

Established in 1985, Campus Compact is an organization of approximately 600 college and university presidents with a dedication to assisting college students develop into productive citizens by engaging in community and public service. Campus Compact promotes and supports community service on college campuses and communities across the United States. A range of programs is available for students' participation, such as programs to reduce racial tension, clean up the environment, work with the hungry and homeless, and teach children to read. The majority of this work is completed through service-learning, and students receive critical experiential learning.

Campus Compact is committed to working with lawmakers to support service programs sponsored by the federal government. Since 1990, Campus Compact has assisted in establishing critical federal legislation that promotes public and community service, including the National and Community Service Trust Act of 1993, the Student Literacy and Mentoring Corps, the America Reads initiative, and the use of new Federal Work-Study funds for community service to name a few examples. Campus Compact also forms partnerships with business, community, and government leaders in order to discuss issues such as community building, improving education, increasing citizen participation, increasing access to economic opportunities, and linking higher education to communities. Campus Compact provides funding through grants to member campuses and state compacts to aid faculty in creating a supportive atmosphere on their campus that promotes service-learning and in developing curricula for service-learning in their courses and to assist state affiliates in promoting Campus Compact's goals. Campus Compact grants awards for exceptional service work to faculty and students (the Howard R. Swearer Student Humanitarian Award and the Thomas Ehrlich Faculty Award for Service-Learning). Campus Compact also organizes conferences, workshops, and forums to exchange ideas and information on service-learning models and disseminates information about service-learning models, statistics and research, and best practices to its members.

Campus Compact National Center for Community Colleges (CCNC)

145 North Centennial Way, Suite 108
Mesa, AZ 85201
Telephone: (480) 461-6280
Fax: (480) 461-6218
Internet: http://www.mc.maricopa.edu/other/compact/

An affiliate of the National Campus Compact, the Campus Compact National Center for Community Colleges (CCNCC) was established in 1990 as a technical assistance center for community colleges throughout the country to support service-learning. The organization's goals are to sustain service-learning in community colleges as a national movement and to promote community service as a means of improving teaching and learning to benefit students and the community. The CCNCC provides technical assistance and support in the following areas: how to integrate service into the curriculum, program development, grant writing, and assistance with developing partnerships with community members to recruit and place participants. In addition, the CCNCC conducts presentations and workshops at higher education conferences, houses a clearinghouse with valuable information on exemplary programs, provides assistance on locating funding for programs, publishes a newsletter, partners with policymakers to promote service-learning, and supports research on service-learning programs. The CCNCC also sponsors annual awards to recognize excellent community college service-learning programs that are partnered with businesses, social service agencies, and the schools.

Campus Outreach Opportunity League (COOL)
National Office
37 Temple Place, Suite 401
Boston, MA 02111
Telephone: (617) 695-2665
Email: inquiry@cool2serve.org
Internet: http://www.cool2serve.org

The Campus Outreach Opportunity League (COOL) is a national, nonprofit organization that aims to educate and empower college students by involvement in community service. COOL connects diverse students to increase activism and civic engagement in order to build a stronger nation. Since 1984, COOL has partnered with more than 1,800 colleges and universities and more than 200 nonprofit organizations to tackle community problems, including caring for the elderly and homeless, addressing illiteracy, and improving the environment. In addition, COOL sponsors a national annual conference of workshops and national speakers to increase community service involvement and participation among college students. COOL also offers resources for individuals to help students initiate and expand community service programs on their campus.

Center for Democracy and Citizenship
301 19th Avenue South
Minneapolis, MN 55455
Telephone: (612) 625-0142
Fax: (612) 625-3513
Internet: http://www.publicwork.org/home.html

The Center for Democracy and Citizenship is a research center located at the Hubert H. Humphrey Institute of Public Affairs at the University of Minnesota. The center aims to engage people to become contributors to public life in order to strengthen democracy in the United States. The Center's work has three sections: Civic Laboratories, Civic Missions and Dissemination, and Communications Networks. The center supports projects to involve individuals, organizations, and communities as partners to renew citizenship. Examples of projects led by the center include Public Achievement, Jane Addams School for Democracy, Value of Citizen Work, the Mapping Project, and many more programs. The overall goal of this organization is to reach every citizen and help them understand the importance of democracy and citizenship and to promote its belief that everyone can contribute their talents to America.

Center for Global Environmental Education (CGEE)
Hamline University Graduate School of Education
1536 Hewitt Avenue
St. Paul, MN 55104-1284
Telephone: (651) 523-2480
Fax: (651) 523-2987
Internet: http://cgee.hamline.edu/index.html

The Center for Global Environmental Educators (CGEE) promotes environmental literacy in the United States. To accomplish this mission, CGEE combines environmental education and distance learning methods. This combination integrates practical learning to build a community among students and teachers. There are many learning programs for K–12 students that are multidisciplinary and use up-to-date technology to engage students in classroom learning and field experiences to learn about the environment (e.g., learning about rivers, the seasons, and frogs). CGEE provides community education programs that connect community partners who are dedicated to environmental causes. CGEE also provides program development for teachers through graduate level courses to incorporate these teaching methodologies in environmental education into their curriculum. In addition, CGEE also provides curriculum, publications, CD-ROM, videos, audiotapes, and interactive websites.

Center for School Change

Humphrey Institute
34 Humphrey Center
303 19th Avenue South
Minneapolis, MN 55455
Telephone: (612) 625-3506
Internet: http://www.hhh.umn.edu

The Center for School Change is a research and policy center at the University of Minnesota that supports school change, service-learning, and charter schools. The "changes" the center are striving for include improvements in students' achievement and attitudes toward school and learning, increases in graduation rates, and strengthened partnerships among students, parents, teachers, school administrators, and community members. The Center for School Change has many projects and models to make these changes. In addition, the Center for School Change supports conferences to increase support and raise awareness for change in schools, including improving student achievement and community-based learning. The center is also involved with local, state, and federal institutions. The center's publications, projects, grants, and goals are listed on their website.

Center for Youth as Resources (YAR)

National Headquarters
1000 Connecticut Ave. NW, 12th Floor
Washington, DC 20036
Telephone: (202) 261-4131

Indianapolis Office
3901 North Meridian Street, Suite 345
Indianapolis, IN 46208-0409
Email: yar@ncpc.org
Internet: http://www.yar.org

The Center for Youth as Resources (YAR) was created in 1987 by the National Crime Prevention Council with funding from the Lilly Endowment. YAR has community-based programs in the United States, Canada, Poland, and New Zealand. With support from YAR, young people ages five to twenty-one design and carry out volunteer projects with the assistance of adults, local board of directors composed of youth and adults, and a sponsoring group or organization in their community (e.g., churches, schools, environmental groups, police departments, and parks departments). These programs help youth to address social problems and contribute to community change. Some examples of projects completed include: helping to restore parks and nature trails; building affordable housing and restoring homes and apartments; providing assistance to the elderly, children, and homeless; and setting up study centers in urban neighborhoods.

Christian Appalachian Project

322 Crab Orchard Street
Lancaster, KY 40446-0001
Telephone: (859) 792-3051
Fax: (859) 792-6560
Internet: http://www.christianity.com/cap

Incorporated in 1964, the Christian Appalachian Project sends volunteers to the Appalachian Mountain region to help the people living in poverty. The project strongly emphasizes adult education and literacy to help individuals get out of poverty. Volunteer opportunities are available in educational and recreational activities, child and youth development programs, caring for the elderly, constructing and restoring housing, and respite care.

City Cares

1605 Peachtree Street, Suite 100
Atlanta, GA 30309
Telephone: (404) 875-7334
Fax: (404) 253-1020
Email: info@citycares.org
Internet: http://www.citycares.org

Founded in 1992, City Cares is an organization that networks volunteers in major cities across the United States and in the United Kingdom. For example, City Cares can help individuals locate local volunteer opportunities at community agencies in their cities that meet their needs and schedule. City Cares recruits and organizes teams of volunteers to carry out various volunteer projects that meet the needs of the community. In addition, City Cares also identifies special service events, such as serve-a-thons in City Cares cities. Volunteers can give any amount of time that they have available. City Cares also has a City Cares Ameri-Corps Promise Fellows program, in which selected individuals can learn about volunteerism and community service, recruit volunteers, develop and carry out projects, and establish partnerships in City Cares communities. Furthermore, corporations can partner with City Cares local organizations to give their employees opportunities to engage in community service.

City Year

National Headquarters
285 Columbus Avenue, 5th Floor
Boston, MA 02116
Telephone: (617) 927-2500
Fax: (617) 927-2510
Internet: http://www.cityyear.org

Founded in 1988, City Year is a national service organization that provides young people with opportunities to provide service to communities and promotes civic engagement and personal growth among young volunteers. There are 1,000 positions available each year in thirteen cities across the United States. City Year offices are located in the following communities: Boston; Chicago; Columbia, South Carolina; Columbus, Ohio; Detroit; Stratham, New Hampshire; Philadelphia; Providence, Rhode Island; San Antonio, Texas; Washington, D.C.; Seattle; and San Jose, California. City Year corps members work as teachers' aids, run camps, direct after-school programs, and deliver workshops. They also engage in cleaning up and preserving the environment, working with the elderly, and constructing and restoring buildings in the community. Members are expected to keep high standards of conduct, because their major role is mentoring. City Year volunteers are provided with intensive training to promote active citizenship. City Year's program is highly successful in retaining youth volunteers. According to the City Year website, over 85 percent of the corps members graduate from the City Year program.

Close Up Foundation

44 Canal Center Plaza

Alexandria, VA 22314-1592
Telephone: (703) 706-3300
Fax: (703) 706-0001
Internet: http://www.closeup.org

Established in 1970, the Close Up Foundation is one of the largest nonprofit, nonpartisan organizations that promotes civic participation in the democratic process. To achieve this goal, the Close Up Foundation encourages experiential learning so students can observe how democracy works. Through hands-on experience with the government, students will become more aware of issues that face their country and consider future involvement in civic affairs. Students can participate in the Close Up Foundation's programs in Washington, D.C., or in their local and state governments. The Close Up Foundation also supports service-learning through technical assistance, training materials and resources, and the publication of the *Service-Learning Quarterly*, an online magazine for service-learning information. The Close Up Foundation is a National Service-Learning Clearinghouse Consortium Member.

Compact for Learning and Citizenship (CLC)

c/o Education Commission of the States
707 17th Street, Suite 2700
Denver, CO 80202-3427
Telephone: (303) 299-3600
Fax: (303) 296-8332
email: ecs@ecs.org
Internet: http://www.ecs.org

Founded and operated by the Education Commission of the States, the Compact for Learning and Citizenship (CLC) is a national organization that supports service-learning. CLC consists of a group of school leaders, including chief state school officers and superintendents, and service-learning advocates who are dedicated to involving students in service-learning. CLC serves as a resource to organizations, school districts, and states regarding effective implementation of service-learning in K–12 schools. CLC provides publications on research and best practices, leadership, and networking. CLC also sponsors workshops and conferences, disseminates information, and advocates policies regarding service-learning.

Constitutional Rights Foundation (CRF)
601 South Kingsley Drive
Los Angeles, CA 90005
Telephone: (213) 487-5590
Internet: http://www.crf-usa.org

Constitutional Rights Foundation (CRF) is a national, nonprofit organization that encourages civic participation of youth and educates youth about citizenship, politics, law, and government. CRF provides training and technical assistance to teachers, coordinates civic participation programs in schools and communities, creates publications on law and government and civic participation programs, and coordinates student conferences and competitions. CRF also supports a number of youth programs.

Corporation for National Service
1201 New York Avenue NW
Washington, DC 20525
Telephone: (202) 606-5000
Email: webmaster@cns.gov
Internet: http://www.cns.gov

Established in 1993, the Corporation for National Service works with a number of key individuals and agencies, including state commissions, nonprofits, schools, and faith-based and community organizations, to offer opportunities for young people and adults to provide service to their communities. The corporation has three major service initiatives: AmeriCorps, Learn and Serve America, and the National Senior Service Corps. These programs address needs in the areas of health and human services, education, the environment, and community building by increasing leadership and civic participation. The corporation also provides training and program support for service programs and funds service-learning initiatives.

Council of Chief State School Officers
One Massachusetts Avenue NW, Suite 700
Washington, DC 20001-1431
Telephone: (202) 408-5505
Fax: (202) 408-8072
Internet: http://www.ccsso.org

The Council of Chief State School Officers is a national nonprofit organization that consists of leaders who represent the departments of education of each state in the United States and territories. This organization aims to improve the educational system in the United States by promoting higher standards and achievement for public schools (including pre-kindergarten students). The Council of Chief State School Officers is a key player in school reform efforts, such as improving state assessment systems, curriculum development, and efforts to improve the achievement of students who are faced with educational challenges. The council has taken an active position on integrating service-learning in the schools by partnering with the National Service-Learning Clearinghouse and the National Service-Learning Cooperative. This initiative involves working with state agencies to develop a network of consultants to provide technical assistance to promote and improve service-learning in the schools. The network also includes youth consultants who encourage other youth to get involved in community service-learning. The council identifies and shares information about model programs and helps schools to connect their service-learning programs with the education reform networks. The council is also completing a study of the connections between service-learning and school-to-work.

Cross-Cultural Solutions

47 Potter Avenue
New Rochelle, NY 10801
Telephone: (914) 632-0022 or (800) 380-4777
Fax: (914) 632-0022
Email: info@crossculturalsolutions.org
Internet: http://www.crossculturalsolutions.org

Cross-Cultural Solutions is a nonprofit, international volunteer organization that helps to promote change in communities around the world by increasing awareness of important global issues. Cross-Cultural Solutions has two main programs that work with local organizations in countries around the world. Through the Volunteers Program, individuals travel abroad and provide assistance in health care, education, and community development. Volunteers provide humanitarian services to India, Ghana, Russia, China, and Peru. For example in Russia, volunteers might provide services to children in orphanages and teach English. Program lengths range from two weeks to several months. The Insight Program provides opportunities for in-depth experience of different cultures, in India, Peru, Cuba, and Ghana. Interested individuals must complete an application process and pay a program fee. Students may be able to receive academic credit for their participation.

Do Something
423 West 55th Street
8th Floor
New York, NY 10019
Telephone: (212) 523-1175
Fax: (212) 582-1307
Email: mail@dosomething.org
Internet: http://www.dosomething.org

Do Something is a national nonprofit youth leadership organization that seeks to encourage youth to make a difference in the world. Do Something is partnered with MTV, Fox Television Network, and Blockbuster Entertainment (among other corporations) to help empower youth to become involved leaders in their communities. Do Something supports several interesting programs, such as the Do Something Community Connections Campaign, which strives to connect youth with civic organizations to improve communities. A curriculum, training program, media campaign, and website have been developed, providing strategies and ideas to engage young people actively in community organizations. Do Something also supports training activities and conferences to assist community organizations to increase youth engagement.

Do Something offers the Brick Award, in which young community leaders who demonstrate community leadership can apply for a $100,000 grant. The annual award honors and financially supports America's best young community leaders under age thirty who are taking action that significantly strengthens their communities. A school-based character education program is also supported during the two weeks around the national observance of the birthday of Martin Luther King Jr. The Do Something Kindness & Justice Challenge encourages students to engage in acts of kindness and to stand up for people's rights in schools across the United States. A national leadership program, the Do Something League, encourages young people, with the help of adult coaches, to become actively involved in leadership in their schools and communities. Supported by The Pew Charitable Trusts, a research project was conducted by Do Something to investigate youth involvement in civic organizations.

Earth Force

1908 Mount Vernon, Second Floor
Alexandria, VA 22301
Telephone: (703) 299-9400
Fax: (703) 299-9485
Email: earthforce@earthforce.org
Internet: http://www.earthforce.org

Earth Force was created in 1994 by The Pew Charitable Trusts in response to the emerging trend for youth involvement in community service and the need to preserve and protect the environment. Earth Force helps youth to gain representation in local governments or committees, giving youth a voice for the environment. Some of Earth Force's programs include Get Out Spoke'n, which helps to make neighborhoods more bike-friendly, and the GREEN program, which helps youth learn how to protect a river. Youth can also apply to be on Earth Force's Youth Advisory Board.

Expeditionary Learning

Outward Bound
122 Mount Auburn Street
Cambridge, MA 02138
Telephone: (617) 576-1260
Internet: http://www.elob.org

Expeditionary Learning is a school reform effort that extends the experience of Outward Bound, an adventure and service-based education program, into the public school classroom at the elementary, middle, and high school levels. Currently implemented in ninety-nine schools in the United States, Expeditionary Learning helps youth work together in teams to meet challenges and use their knowledge in service to the community. Expeditionary Learning involves learning expeditions, which are long-term, standards-based projects that focus on specific topics, integrating investigation, fieldwork, and service. Students and adults go into the community to do fieldwork and service, and community members, including parents, are invited into the schools to share their knowledge and experiences with youth. Expeditionary Learning also provides professional development and technical assistance to teachers and school staff. Sample learning expeditions are available on the Expeditionary Learning website.

The Ford Foundation
Headquarters
320 East 43rd Street
New York, NY 10017
Telephone: (212) 573-5000
Fax: (212) 599-4584
Internet: http://www.fordfound.org

The Ford Foundation was founded in 1936 and became a national and international foundation in 1950. It is an independent, nonprofit, non-governmental organization that espouses four central goals: to strengthen democratic values, to reduce poverty and injustice, to promote international cooperation, and to advance human achievement. Grants or loans to programs that build knowledge or strengthen organizations or networks are given to achieve these goals. The foundation focuses upon initiatives that involve those who live and work closely with the problems at hand; encourages collaboration among the nonprofit, government, and business sectors; and involves men and women from diverse communities and all levels of society. In the Governance and Civil Society unit, the foundation supports initiatives around the globe to increase civic participation, including voting and service involvement.

Generations United
122 C Street NW, Suite 820
Washington, DC 20001
Telephone: (202) 638-1263
Email: gu@gu.org
Internet: http://www.gu.org

A partner of the Learn and Serve America National Service-Learning Clearinghouse, Generations United identifies and provides information about intergenerational programs in the United States. In addition, Generations United gives technical assistance to individuals interested in developing and implementing intergenerational programs, including service-learning and mentoring, and for the public and policymakers to coordinate information on over 130 national, state, and local organizations. Generations United has partnered with the Points of Light Foundation to offer a resource guide for intergenerational programming and a referral list of organizations specializing in intergenerational initiatives.

The Giraffe Project

197 2nd Street
P.O. Box 759
Langley, WA 98260
Telephone: (360) 221-7989
Email: office@giraffe.org
Internet: http://www.giraffe.org

The Giraffe Project, a nonprofit organization founded in 1982, identifies and recognizes people who are committed and have taken action to solve social problems, such as hunger and pollution, in the United States. These individuals (known as Giraffes) become speakers spreading their messages and stories to youth through the media and in schools by motivating and "inspiring others to stick their necks out." The Giraffe Project has developed the Giraffe Heroes Program, a story-based, service-learning curriculum that teaches concern, kindness, character, and citizenship to youth. The Giraffe Project includes training, networking, workshops, television programming, and media service. The founders of Habitat for Humanity, Millard and Linda Fuller, and Patch Adams are two examples of the Giraffe Project Awardees. The Giraffe Project website has information on the Giraffe Awardees, the Giraffe Heroes Program, Giraffe Heroes Trainings, and Giraffe Productions television programming, as well as links to related organizations and publications for youth, educators, and parents.

Girl Scouts of the USA

420 5th Avenue
New York, NY 10018-2798
Telephone: (800) GSUSA4U
Internet: http://www.girlscouts.org

Founded in 1912 with the mission to give girls an opportunity to get out of their home environments to serve their community as a collective, the Girl Scouts has grown into the world's largest organization for girls in the world with over 2.7 million girls between the ages of seven and seventeen as members. The Girl Scouts aim is to bring together girls to find the power of friendship and community and build necessary life skills through group activities. The Girl Scout program consists of a progression of levels—Daisy, Brownie, Junior, Cadette, and Senior Girl Scout. Each program is age-appropriate and encourages character development and builds decision-making skills. The Girl Scouts programs have four main goals: making a contribution to society, developing values and ethics, building positive relationships with others, and developing one's potential and self-worth. Girl Scouts participate in a variety of activities to meet these goals, including the arts, environmental activities and exploring the outdoors, building awareness of diversity and global issues, engaging in health and fitness activities, reading and literacy-building activities, mentoring, and learning about science and technology. Of course, Girl Scouts also are involved in the annual cookie sale to build necessary life and business skills, including planning, handling customers and money, goal-setting, and team-work.

Give Water A Hand
216 Agriculture Hall
1450 Linden Drive
Madison, WI 53706
Telephone: (800) 928-3720
Fax: (608) 265-9203
E-mail: erc@uwex.edu
Internet: http://www.uwex.edu/erc/gwah

Give Water A Hand is a national program that is intended to give young people an opportunity to get involved in local environmental service projects. A class or youth group learns about the importance of water resources and plans and completes a service project to help protect water resources, such as lakes, streams, or wetlands, in their local community. The Action Guide, which can be downloaded or obtained from the organization, gives youth the directions and plans to develop an environmental community service project. The Leader Guidebook provides direction to teachers and adults to help youth in their pursuit to improve local water resources. This program helps youth learn more about water and their environment.

Global Volunteers
375 E. Little Canada Road
St. Paul, MN 55117
Telephone: (800) 487-1074 or (651) 407-6100
Fax: (651) 482-0915
Email: info@globalvolunteers.org
Internet: http://www.globalvolunteers.org

Founded in 1984, Global Volunteers is a private nonprofit organization that engages individuals in short-term volunteer projects in international locations. Individual volunteers must apply for the program and pay fees (ranging from $450 to $2,400) to spend one to three weeks in one of sixty-nine locations internationally and domestically to engage in a service project (or "service vacation"). Work projects take place in Europe (e.g., Greece, Ireland, Italy, Poland, Romania, and Spain), Africa (e.g., Ghana and Tanzania), Asia (e.g., China, India, Indonesia, and Vietnam), the Caribbean (e.g., Jamaica), Latin America (e.g., Costa Rica, Ecuador, and Mexico), the United States (Hawaii and continental states), and the Cook Islands in the South Pacific. At the request of local leaders, teams are sent to live and work with local people in various countries. Examples of work projects include construction of community centers, improving classrooms, construction of water systems, building bridges, working on environmental tasks, working with the elderly, caring for babies and children in orphanages and day care centers, and teaching English. The organization not only helps various communities in many ways, but gives volunteers a chance to learn about different cultures and traditions.

Grantmaker Forum on National and Community Service
2560 Ninth Street, Suite 217
Berkeley, CA 94710
Telephone: (510) 665-6130
Email: gfcns@informingchange.com
Internet: http://www.gfcns.org

Founded in 1993, the Grantmaker Forum on National and Community Service consists of over 1,000 grantmakers, including private and family foundations and corporate giving programs. The purpose of the Grantmaker Forum is to increase awareness of the utility and benefits of volunteering and service as ways to solving problems in communities. The Grantmaker Forum achieves its mission through assembling funders, engaging in research, outreach task forces, and through communications and policy work. In addition, this organization arranges workshops and meetings to discuss and debate important issues relevant to community service and volunteering. Publications are also available from the Grantmaker Forum on service and volunteering.

Habitat for Humanity International
121 Habitat Street
Americus, GA 31709
Telephone: (912) 924-6935
Internet: http://www.habitat.org

Established in 1976, Habitat for Humanity is a nonprofit, nondenominational Christian housing organization. Habitat for Humanity builds houses in more than sixty countries around the world. Students and young people worldwide spend school breaks or weekends on Habitat construction sites. Through campus chapters and in partnership with affiliates, young people sponsor Habitat houses, mentor children of homeowners, and educate others about the need for affordable housing. Habitat's Campus Chapters and Youth Programs engage students and youth ages five and up.

Institute for Global Education and Service-Learning
c/o Philadelphia University
Henry Avenue and School House Lane
Philadelphia, PA 19144
Telephone: (215) 915-2269
Fax: (215) 951-2128
Email: institute@philau.edu
Internet: http://philau.edu/institute

The Institute for Global Education and Service-Learning was founded as a result of the National and Community Service Act of 1993 and is the Atlantic regional center of the National Service-Learning Exchange. It is divided into several separate projects, all of which operate out of Philadelphia University. In general, the mission of the institute is to provide service-learning programs that will initiate community service activity around the world. The Read and Lead Program or National Literacy Corps' mission is to empower youth through helping other students learn how to read using a cross-age tutoring model. The Intergenerational Program aims to bridge the gap between today's youth and the senior citizens of the community and to encourage the preservation of the community's oral history. The Community Development Youth Corps is a citizenship service-learning program that helps youth take action in their communities. The institute also provides technical assistance to individuals, schools, and organizations interested in developing and implementing service-learning programs and holds workshops and conferences.

International Partnership for Service-Learning
815 Second Avenue, Suite 315
New York, NY 10017
Telephone: (212) 986-0989
Fax (212) 986-5039
Email pslny@aol.com
Internet: http://www.ipsl.org/

Founded in 1982, the International Partnership for Service-Learning is a nonprofit organization that serves colleges, universities, and service organizations around the world by developing programs that link community service with academic coursework. The International Partnership for Service-Learning believes that service-learning programs help to develop cultural competence. Programs are administered in diverse places around the world including the Czech Republic, Ecuador, England, France, India, Israel, Jamaica, Mexico, the Philippines, Scotland, and South Dakota. A one-year British Master's Degree Program in International Service is available through the International Partnership for Service-Learning and affiliated universities in Britain, Mexico, and Jamaica. This organization also sponsors conferences on service-learning and publishes information related to service-learning.

Jesuit Volunteer Corps
P.O. Box 25478
Washington, DC 20007
Telephone: (202) 687-1132
Internet: http://www.JesuitVolunteers.org

Founded in 1956, Jesuit Volunteers is one of the largest Catholic volunteer program in the United States and serves hundreds of organizations that are dedicated to helping the poor. Jesuit Volunteers are committed to social justice and peace based on Jesuit principles and work either in the United States for one year or abroad in developing countries for two years. Jesuit Volunteers must go through an extensive application process and once accepted are then placed in a range of social service agencies and ministries. Jesuit Volunteers may work with individuals who are homeless, unemployed, elderly, disabled, or mentally ill. The volunteers live modestly on a small stipend and are placed in low-income areas. Through this work, volunteers examine injustices and search for solutions.

Jumpstart
93 Summer Street, 2nd Floor
Boston, MA 02110
Telephone: (617) 542-5867
Internet: http://www.jstart.org

Founded in 1993, Jumpstart is a nonprofit organization that provides AmeriCorps college student volunteers with opportunities to help pre-school-age children in early education programs such as Head Start. Jumpstart seeks to increase school readiness. Jumpstart has two additional programs targeted at family involvement and building future teachers. In efforts to involve parents, Jumpstart provides information to parents with young children to help them acquire knowledge about their children's development and ways to assist their children's learning. Jumpstart has begun to form partnerships with colleges and universities across the United States to increase services to children in their communities. The program provides intensive training for volunteers in areas of child development and education (e.g., language and literacy). College students involved in Jumpstart received awards from AmeriCorps, as well as federal work-study funds. College students interested in education and other human service professions can gain hands-on experience working with young children. Jumpstart currently has programs in eleven cities across the United States

JustAct: Youth Action for Global Justice
333 Valencia Street, Suite 101
San Francisco, CA 94130
Telephone: (415) 431-4204
Fax: (415) 431-5953
Email: info@justact.org
Internet: http://www.justact.org

JustAct is a nonprofit organization that strives to help youth address issues such as social inequality, human rights, and environmental problems through education and movement-building. The organization was founded in 1983 as the Overseas Development Network and has since turned into a national organization that promotes global justice through youth leadership. Through education, JustAct provides workshops for young people about important global economic, political, and social issues that need to be addressed. In addition, JustAct provides hands-on opportunities for youth to become involved in making positive changes in their communities through group events, exchanges, and internship opportunities. For example, Bike Aid is a bicycle tour that occurs across the United States that includes educational and service components. On the summer tour, youth meet with organizations and communities to share their experiences in community improvement efforts. This organization has also created a national youth network that brings together youth of diverse backgrounds around pressing issues of global justice, in efforts to seek positive solutions.

KaBOOM!

2213 M Street NW, Suite 300
Washington, DC 20037
Telephone: (202) 659-0215, ext. 225
Fax: (202) 659-0210
Internet: http://www.kaboom.org

Founded in 1996, KaBOOM! is a national nonprofit organization that provides healthy play opportunities for children. The organization is committed to building safe playgrounds across the United States and Canada in order to prevent accidents from unsafe and substandard facilities. Safe playgrounds are built by bringing together individuals, organizations, and businesses in the community to work together. KaBOOM! has focused on building playgrounds in cities, including Atlanta, Boston, Chicago, Dallas, Los Angeles, Miami, New York, Philadelphia, San Francisco, and Washington, DC KaBOOM! provides information, including technical assistance, guides, and training on how to build a safe playground in one's community.

Kids Care Clubs

382 Smith Ridge Road
South Salem, NY 10590
Telephone: (914) 533-1101
Fax: (914) 533-2949
Internet: http://www.kidscare.org

The purpose of Kids Care Clubs is to promote charity and compassion in children through service experiences that aim to improve their local communities. Over 400 Kids Care Clubs are located in the United States and Canada. Kids Care Clubs has developed curriculum and examples of service projects that can be integrated into schools, religious groups, or other youth and community organizations. Adults can also volunteer to develop a Kids Care Club in their community.

KIDS Consortium
215 Lisbon Street, Suite 12
Lewiston, ME 04240
Telephone: (207) 784-0956
Fax: (207) 784-6733
Internet: http://www.kidsconsortium.org

The KIDS (Kids Involved Doing Service) Consortium is an organization primarily focused on the New England, New Brunswick, and Nova Scotia areas that promotes service for youth. The KIDS Consortium works with school systems to integrate KIDS as Planners Projects, a program that helps to involve youth in planning service-learning opportunities. The KIDS Consortium model identifies three key ingredients for their program: apprentice citizenship, student ownership, and academic integrity. By taking a leading role, kids identify a need in their schools and/or communities and then identify ideas for implementing a service project that is integrated with school curriculum to solve the problem. Examples of projects include building teen centers, documenting town histories, and assessing the water quality of ponds.

Landmark Volunteers
P.O. Box 455
Sheffield, MA 01257
Telephone: (413) 229-0255
Fax: (413) 229-2050
Email: landmark@volunteers.com
Internet: http://www.volunteers.com

Landmark Volunteers is a nonprofit community service organization that offers high school students in grades ten to twelve an opportunity to volunteer during two weeks of the summer. Landmark Volunteers offers opportunities for work with a variety of cultural, environmental, or historical organizations throughout the United States to assist with service projects. Examples of student service work include construction or repairing buildings, painting, or clearing trails. Current locations for service projects include: Acadia National Park in Bar Harbor, Maine; Grand Teton Music Festival/Jackson Hole Land Trust in Teton Village, Wyoming; and Berkshire South Community Center in Great Barrington, Massachusetts. Student volunteers are supervised by Landmark Team Leaders, who have extensive experience working with youth. Interested individuals need to apply for a position and contribute a proportion of the total cost for the service trip. The minimum age requirement is fourteen and some scholarships are available.

Leadership, Education, and Athletics in Partnership, Inc. (LEAP)
31 Jefferson Street
New Haven, CT 06511
Telephone: (203) 773-0770
Fax: (203) 773-1695
Email: info@leapforkids.org
Internet: http://www.leapforkids.org

Founded in 1992, Leadership, Education, and Athletics in Partnership (LEAP) helps at-risk youth from low-income backgrounds in Connecticut's cities through community and school-based programs. LEAP is currently involved in Bridgeport, Hartford, New Haven, New London, and Waterbury. College students and high school students are paired together to work as counselors for children ages seven to fourteen. The goal of the program is to promote positive youth development including improving school achievement and social skills. Youth receive a literacy-based and culturally sensitive curriculum. The counselors receive training and monitor youth's progress through parent visits and communication with teachers. Youth are also involved in a number of recreational activities (e.g., art and athletics), computer-based activities, and experiential activities (e.g., day trips and camping). Benefits for high school students include mentoring, advice and counseling about college options, and assistance with their schoolwork. In addition, college students are immersed in the community during the summer in order to learn about the neighborhood and build relationships with youth and families.

Learn and Serve America
Department of Service-Learning
Corporation for National Service
1201 New York Avenue NW
Washington, DC 20525
Telephone: (202) 606-5000
Internet: http://www.cns.gov

Learn and Serve America supports service-learning programs for students in kindergarten through college to increase civic participation and academic achievement. These programs engage youth in schools and community organizations to address issues of education, health, public safety, and the environment, while simultaneously building academic skills. Learn and Serve grants may be used to develop new programs or duplicate already existing programs that have been found to be effective. In addition, Learn and Serve grants support training and development for staff and volunteers. Funding for programs comes through state education agencies and nonprofit organizations through the Corporation for National Service. Learn and Serve America's programs are required to match federal funds with funding and resources from the community.

Learn and Serve America Exchange
Telephone: (877) 572-3924

Through peer-based training and technical assistance, the Learn and Serve America Exchange assists service-learning programs in schools, community organizations, and colleges and universities throughout the United States. Led by the National Youth Leadership Council, the exchange has trained a network of volunteer mentors who provide information about how to improve service-learning programs. See below a list of the Exchange National and Regional Centers and National Partner Organizations.

Exchange Atlantic Regional Center
Institute for Global Education and Service-Learning
Henry Avenue and Schoolhouse Lane
Philadelphia, PA 19144
Telephone: (877) LSA-EXCHange or (877) 572-3924 ext. 2
Internet: http://www.lsaexchange.org

Exchange National Center
National Youth Leadership Council
1910 W. County Road B
St. Paul, MN 55113
Telephone: (877) LSA-EXCHange or (877) 572-3924 ext. 7
Email: exchange@nylc.org
Internet: http://www.nslexchange.org

Exchange North Central Regional Center
University of Wisconsin
RDI Building
410 S. Third Street
River Falls, WI 54022
Telephone: (877) LSA-EXCHange or (877) 572-3924 ext. 4
Internet: http://www.lsaexchange.org

Exchange Pacific Regional Center
Educational Service District 112
2500 NE 65th Avenue
Vancouver, WA 98661-6812
Telephone: (877) LSA-EXCHange or (877) 572-3924 ext. 5
Internet: http://www.lsaexchange.org

Exchange Southern Regional Center
National Dropout Prevention Center
209 Martin Street
Clemson, SC 29634-0726
Telephone: (877) LSA-EXCHange or (877) 572-3924 ext. 3
Internet: http://www.lsaexchange.org

Exchange Southwest Regional Center
Texas Center for Service-Learning
2613 Speedway, NSA1.202
Austin, TX 78712
Telephone: (877) LSA-EXCHange or (877) 572-3924 ext. 6
Internet: http://www.lsaexchange.org

**Learn and Serve America National Service-Learning Clearinghouse
    (NSLC)**
University of Minnesota

1954 Buford Avenue, Room R460
St. Paul, MN 55108
Telephone: (800) 808-SERV-(7378) TTY Accessible
Internet: http://www.servicelearning.org

Learning In Deed
W. K. Kellogg Foundation
One Michigan Avenue East
Battle Creek, MI 49017-4058
Telephone: (202) 778-1040
Internet: http://www.LearningInDeed.org

The Learn and Serve America National Service-Learning Clearinghouse (NSLC) is a comprehensive information system that compiles and distributes resources and information on school and community service-learning across all levels of education, from kindergarten through higher education. The NSLC is located at the University of Minnesota in the Department of Work, Community and Family Education, in addition to thirteen other organizations. The NSLC gathers and distributes information for Learn and Serve America programs, as well as other community service programs.

Sponsored by the W. K. Kellogg Foundation, the Learning In Deed: Making a Difference Through Service-Learning initiative attempts to increase the use of service-learning in schools throughout the United States. The W. K. Kellogg Foundation is committed to the notion that service to the community when integrated meaningfully into the curriculum can promote academic achievement, increase civic engagement, and enhance necessary career development and workplace skills. For the initiative, the foundation has enlisted the expertise of teachers, parents, students, administrators, community leaders, policymakers, and national leaders, to increase the use and improve the practice of service-learning. There are four components to the initiative. The Policy and Practice Demonstration Projects currently are underway in California, Maine, Minnesota, Oregon, and South Carolina. Selected schools in these states receive resources and technical assistance to facilitate the identification of policies and practices that are most effective in fostering service-learning. The second component is the National Commission on Service-Learning, a committee of leaders from education, government, and youth and community development who collaborate to develop service-learning directives for school districts, policymakers, and funders.

The third component is a steering committee representing various key constituencies in the K–12 service-learning community. Finally, a research network disseminates evidence that supports the practice of high-quality service-learning programs.

Learning to Give
630 Harvey Street
Muskegon, MI 49442-2398
Telephone: (231) 767-7205
Fax: (231) 773-0707
Email: kagard@remc4.K12.mi.us
Internet: http://www.learningtogive.org

Learning to Give, formerly known as the K–12 Education in Philanthropy Project, was created by the Council of Michigan Foundations and leaders in the education, service, and nonprofit sectors. Learning to Give has developed and is implementing a K–12 curriculum to educate children about service and philanthropy in the state of Michigan. After the development of the curriculum and pilot testing, the curriculum materials will be available and distributed across the United States and internationally via their website.

National Association of Service and Conservation Corps
666 11th Street NW, Suite 1000
Washington, DC 20001
Telephone: (202) 737-6272
Fax: (202) 737-6277
Internet: http://www.nascc.org

The mission of the National Association of Service and Conservation Corps is to promote the youth corps as a mean of enhancing youth development through community service and improving the environment. The National Association of Service and Conservation Corps has a number of initiatives and programs to meet this mission, including the Corps-to-Career Initiative, Welfare to Work, Environmental, and Training and Technical Assistance. Environmental project opportunities include Urban and Community Forestry, Indoor Air Quality program, and the Five-Star Restoration Program.

National Drop Out Prevention Center
Clemson University
209 Martin Street
Clemson, SC 29631-1555
Telephone: (864) 656-0136
Email: ndpc@clemson.edu
Internet: http://www.dropoutprevention.org

The National Drop Out Prevention Center provides youth with an appreciation for the resources and benefits of a quality education. This knowledge and appreciation is thought to prevent high school students from dropping out of school. The program outlines fifteen effective strategies to help students realize the importance of obtaining a high school diploma. These strategies have been implemented at high schools across the nation in order to reduce the dropout rate among teens. As the southern regional center for Learn and Serve America Exchange, the National Drop Out Prevention Center assists organizations with service-learning programs, including providing access to publications on effective strategies, resources, conference information, and research and statistics. The center views service-learning as an effective method for dropout prevention and publishes a Resource Catalogue for Service-Learning through which guidebooks, games, and videotapes related to service-learning can be ordered. Information on model programs, materials, and special programs that may be helpful in the prevention process and on important people who have made a difference in the area can be located on the website.

National 4-H
1400 Independence Avenue SW
Washington, DC 20250-2225
Telephone: (202) 720-8855
Fax: (202) 720-9366 or (202) 690-2469
Internet: http://www.4-h.org

Founded in the early 1900s, 4-H (which stands for head, heart, hands, and health) was established to provide local educational clubs for rural youth. 4-H assists young people to increase their social networks, learn life skills, build self-esteem and self-responsibility, and set and achieve goals. There are now numerous clubs in urban areas that participate in various activities, including computer programming and recycling. 4-H clubs also participate in volunteering. Across the United States, individuals in 4-H help improve their communities by cleaning up trash in the community, assisting in literacy projects, and delivering food to hospice patients. Youth learn by doing and receive awards for projects. Members can range from age five to age twenty-one. 4-H operates on a club level, as well as county, district, state, national, and international levels. 4-H is overseen by the Cooperative Extension Service of the U.S. Department of Agriculture, state land-grant universities, and county governments. The 4-H Innovation Center for Community and Youth Development has focused on ways to give youth meaningful, responsible, and challenging roles in organizations, so that they may be prepared for future roles as responsible and caring adults.

National Helpers Network, Inc. (NHN)
875 Sixth Avenue, Suite 206
New York, NY 10001
Telephone: (212) 679-2482
Internet: http://www.nationalhelpers.org

Established in 1982, the National Helpers Network, Inc. (NHN) has developed several "Helper" programs that facilitate young people to assume positive and productive roles in their communities. Rooted in a special curriculum developed by NHN, adolescents around the country have participated in community-based programs including Learning Helpers Promoting Literacy, Community Problem Solvers, Common Ground/Common Purpose, and EnviroHelpers. The foundation of the Learning Helpers model is service-learning. Through this model, young Helpers are trained in various aspects of child development, including behavior management and appropriate communication. Students or Helpers are, therefore, equipped with essential skills and training to promote positive interactions with young children. With these skills, the Helpers go into the community and serve as role models, guides, and simple friends for young children. This model has several values and goals. As mentors, the Helpers learn about various aspects of child development, including how children learn, acquire knowledge, and interact with one another. With the help of a skilled facilitator, the Helpers establish a measure through which to evaluate their services. Through these weekly meetings with the facilitator, the Helpers come to understand the basic working relationship between employee and employer. Moreover, Helpers have the opportunity to acquire basic job skills including good attendance and punctuality, how to dress appropriately, keeping timesheets, and working productively on a team.

National Indian Youth Leadership Project (NIYLP)
814 S. Boardman
Gallup, NM 87301
Telephone: (505) 722-9176
Email: niylp@cia-g.com
Internet: http://www.niylp.org

The National Indian Youth Leadership Project (NIYLP) is a nonprofit service organization headquartered in Gallup, New Mexico, which has developed a variety of national and local programs for Native American youth and communities. Project Venture is a drug and alcohol abuse prevention program, which integrates outdoor and adventure activities and has a strong emphasis on service-learning. The Youth Connect program is a mentoring program that incorporates community service activities for middle school students (sixth graders) in Gallup. Supported by Learn and Serve America, the Al Chini Ba program provides opportunities for youth to engage in service activities, as well as tutoring and mentoring. In 1995, NIYLP created Native AmeriCorps, which is now known as the Native Youth Corps, a program for fourteen- to twenty-five-year-olds to receive entrepreneurial training. Youth provide environmentally friendly construction services to the community. This program also encourages completion of the high school degree. NIYLP also sponsors camps and special events for native youth. The NIYLP is guided by an all-Native American board of directors and supported by both federal and private funding sources.

National Mentoring Partnership
1600 Duke Street, Suite 300
Alexandria, VA 22314
Telephone: (703) 224-2200
Internet: http://www.mentoring.org

The National Mentoring Partnership provides resources for organizations that mentor youth. The National Mentoring Partnership is actively working toward increasing mentoring opportunities for youth by working with states and communities, schools, businesses, faith-based organizations, and youth organizations. Some of the resources offered by the National Mentoring Partnership include standards for effective mentoring practice, support at the state and organizational level, training for mentors, a question-and-answer line for concerns about mentoring and initiating a mentoring program, and campaigns to increase public awareness. Individuals interested in mentoring youth can also contact the National Mentoring Partnership for information and resources.

National School and Community Corps

The Woodrow Wilson National Fellowship Foundation
P.O. Box 3513
Princeton, NJ 08543-3513
Telephone: (609) 452-7007 or (800) 852-0626
Fax: (609) 514-1669
Email: NSCC@woodrow.org
Internet: http://198.139.224.157/index.htm

An AmeriCorps national service program, the National School and Community Corps places individuals in inner city schools with the aim of engaging students in national service that improves their quality of life. The mission of the organization is to establish or enhance the school community and to strengthen local education reform.

National Service-Learning in Teacher Education Partnership

Cascade Educational Consultants
2622 Lakeridge Lane
Bellingham, WA 98226
Telephone: (360) 676-9570
Fax: (360) 676-2619
Email: pickeral@az.com
Internet: http://www.az.com/~pickeral/partnership.html

The National Service-Learning in Teacher Education Partnership is a membership of experienced education professionals that provides resources for teacher education faculty interested in integrating service-learning into teacher preparation programs. The goal is to advance service-learning in teacher education through faculty development. Through the website, individuals can stay in contact with other educational professionals and can access available references and resources needed to integrate service-learning into the curriculum.

National Service-Learning Partnership at the Academy for Educational Development
100 Fifth Avenue
New York, NY 10011
Telephone: (212) 367-4570
Email: nslp@aed.org
Internet: http://www.service-learningpartnership.org

Sponsored by the Academy for Educational Development, the National Service-Learning Partnership is an influential resource for more than 2,000 individuals and organizations committed to promoting civic engagement through service-learning programs. The partnership links teachers, community leaders, policymakers, researchers, parents, students, and others interested in effectively integrating community service into the academic curriculum. The National Service Learning Partnership, along with the National Commission on Service-Learning, grew out of the work of the Learning In Deed initiative, funded by the W. K. Kellogg Foundation.

National Society for Experiential Education (NSEE)
1703 North Beauregard Street, Suite 400
Alexandria, VA 22311-1714
Telephone: (703) 933-0017
Fax: (703) 933-1053
Email: info@nsee.org
Internet: http://www.nsee.org

Founded in 1971 and formerly the National Society for Internships and Experiential Education, the National Society for Experiential Education (NSEE) is a nonprofit membership organization of teachers and school administrators, community leaders, businesses, individuals involved in service-learning programs, counselors, school-to-work coordinators, college presidents, researchers, and policymakers. NSEE supports the development and implementation of experience-based approaches to teaching and learning. For over twenty-five years, NSEE has developed best practices for effectively integrating experience and service into educational programs. This organization provides information on best practices and creative experiential programs and provides a mechanism to keep program directors up-to-date on information through the *NSEE Quarterly*. In addition, the NSEE also provides consulting services and information on current research regarding experiential-based learning to program members. NSEE also has an annual national conference to disseminate best practices and new ideas.

National Youth Leadership Council (NYLC)
1667 Snelling Avenue North, Suite D300
St. Paul, MN 55108
Telephone: (651) 631-3672
Internet: http://www.nylc.org
Email: nylcinfo@nylc.org

Established in 1983 by James Kielsmeier, the National Youth Leadership Council (NYLC) aims to involve students in their schools and communities through service-learning and youth leadership. NYLC is also a strong supporter of education reform and public policy for youth and conducts research on youth issues. NYLC has several programs that train youth leaders to address and solve problems in their communities and to increase youth involvement in national and youth summits. In addition, NYLC supports model service-learning programs in schools across the country. Integrated with a specific classroom curriculum, students who participate in the various programs have the opportunity to work as peer advisors, participate in community clean-up teams, and attend student rights meetings. The members and founders of NYLC advocate that the activities and lessons learned from community service not only increase student academic interest, but also improve school achievement. Service-learning supports educational reform and gives students the opportunity to improve their communities. In addition to the youth programs, the NYLC sponsors a professional development program for adults, mentors, teachers, and school administrators. NYLC also sponsors a national annual conference on service-learning and publishes a journal, *The Generator*, on service-learning and youth issues. In addition, NYLC offers curriculum, publications, and videos related to service-learning through its website.

Northwest Regional Educational Laboratory
101 SW Main Street
Suite 500
Portland, OR 97204
Telephone: (503) 275-9500

Fax: (503) 275-9489
Email: info@nwrel.org
Internet: http://www.nwrel.org/index.html

The Northwest Regional Educational Laboratory is a nonprofit corporation that provides research and development assistance to education, government, community, agencies, and businesses. The goal of the organization is to improve educational opportunities and provide equal access of educational opportunities for children and adults; it primarily serves the northwest region of the United States. The Northwest Regional Educational Laboratory conducts twelve programs in research and development and in training and technical assistance. Programs in research and development include assessment; child and family; education, career and community; evaluation; rural education; and school improvement. Training and technical assistance is provided through the Equity Center, Comprehensive Center, Mathematics and Science Education Center, National Mentoring Center, National Resource Center for Safe Schools, and Technology in Education Center. Each of these programs provides comprehensive information and resources to teachers and administrators to help improve educational outcomes. For example, the rural education program provides research and development on rural education to promote rural community renewal, and resources for educators on service-learning in rural schools, after-school and summer school programs, and links to national resources in rural education.

Outward Bound USA
100 Mystery Point Road
Garrison, NY 10524-9757
Telephone: (888) 882-6863
Internet: http://www.outwardbound.org

Outward Bound USA is an organization that teaches people about wilderness skills. There are five wilderness schools and two urban centers in the United States. The schools are located in Denver, Colorado; Rockland, Maine; Asheville, North Carolina; Portland, Oregon; Ely, Minnesota; New York; and Boston. There is also Outward Bound International and Expeditionary Learning Outward Bound. Courses are available for teenagers, college students, adults, families, and programs for women only and educators, groups and organizations, and Outward Bound instructors. Examples of course offerings include mountaineering, whitewater rafting, backpacking, rock climbing, sailing, desert ka-yaking, desert/canyon, as well as semester-long courses. Leaders teach groups of Outward Bound students safety skills, environmental steward-ship, and instruction for the various technical skills (e.g., rafting, rock climbing, snowshoeing, and sailing), and then the students gain respon-sibility on their own and become leaders of their group at some point. Another important aspect is to teach people to respect nature and to teach the importance of service. The groups take on one of the many service projects available, and through these projects, character is devel-oped. Individuals must apply for Outward Bound courses as well as pay tuition for the courses. Financial aid is also available on a limited basis for a portion of the tuition fee. Some high schools and colleges/universities have offered college credit for individuals who have completed Outward Bound courses.

Points of Light Foundation

1400 I Street NW, Suite 800
Washington, DC 20005
Telephone: (202) 729-8000
Fax: (202) 729-8100
Email: info@pointsoflight.org
Internet: http://www.PointsofLight.org

The Points of Light Foundation, which was created in 1990, seeks to engage individuals and organizations in volunteer service to help solve social problems in their communities. The Points of Light Foundation works with more than 500 volunteer centers across the country and is the center for community-based service-learning initiatives. Through such initiatives as Connect America and Family Matters, the Points of Light Foundation facilitates opportunities for people of all ages to come together to perform volunteer services. In addition, the foundation seeks to assist employers to develop workplace volunteer programs, creates youth service programs and builds youth leaders, and provides develop-ment, training, products, and services for individuals organizing volunteer programs in the Volunteer Centers across the country. Fur-thermore, the foundation is dedicated to promoting volunteering in fam-ilies. The honorary chairman of the foundation is former president George H.W. Bush. The Points of Light Foundation is a National Service-Learning Clearinghouse Consortium Member, and was a cosponsor of the 1997 Presidents' Summit for America's Future.

Project America
1520 West Main Street, Suite 102
Richmond, VA 23220
Telephone: (804) 358-1605
Fax: (804) 359-8160
Internet: http://www.project.org

Founded in 1993, Project America aims to make connections between volunteers and organizations. Project America identifies communities that are in need of support and designs programs for corporations and organizations to involve their employees in volunteer service projects. The goal of Project America is to improve and build communities. In addition, Project America sponsors alternative spring break programs for college students to experience a week-long service experience in a community and to engage in leadership development activities. Project America also provides volunteer education, including educational resources for both individual volunteers and organizations involved in service projects. Since 1994, Project America has sponsored, in conjunction with the Points of Light Foundation and Make A Difference Day, an annual day of national service.

Project Learning Tree
1111 19th Street NW, Suite 780
Washington, DC 20036
Telephone: (202) 463-2462
Email: info@afffoundation.org
Internet: http://www.plt.org

Project Learning Tree is an environmental educational program for educators who teach pre-K through twelfth grade, which is administered by the American Forest Foundation and the Council of Environmental Education. The mission is to increase students' knowledge and respect for the environment, as well as to build academic skills. This program helps students learn about natural and built environments. This program has been implemented throughout the United States and abroad (including Canada, Mexico, Chile, Brazil, the Philippines, Sweden, Finland, and Japan). It is estimated that more than 25 million students have been involved in the program and more than 500,000 teachers have been trained. The curriculum of Project Learning Tree provides accessible and user-friendly lessons and activities that can be easily incorporated into classrooms. Project Learning Tree also takes action in helping the community become more responsible toward the environment through such projects as recycling programs and tree plantings. The GreenWorks! Program partners teachers and students to engage in service projects to clean up the environment in their community, including recycling, graffiti clean-up, and tree planting. The PLT in the City program is a project targeted toward the improvement of urban centers. The Project Learning Tree newsletter, *The Branch*, keeps individuals, volunteers, and educators up to date on news about the organization and curriculum.

The Prudential Spirit of Community Initiative
The Prudential Insurance Company of America
751 Broad Street
Newark, NJ 07102-3777
Telephone: (888) 450-9961
Internet: http://www.prudential.com/community/spirit

The Prudential Spirit of Community Initiative is a series of programs meant to strengthen community spirit across the country by encouraging youth to become actively involved in their communities. The Prudential sponsors the Spirit of Community awards to recognize those young people who have made significant contributions. Youth ages eleven to eighteen are eligible to apply for these awards. Annual awards are given to two young people from each state. In order to gain an understanding of what people think about their communities, the organization conducted a survey of youth and adults. The results of the survey are posted on the website. In addition, the Prudential Spirit of Community Initiative has a Youth Leadership Institute for high school students with an interest in community service.

Public Achievement
Center for Democracy and Citizenship
HHH Institute for Public Affairs
301 19th Avenue South
Minneapolis, MN 55455
Telephone: (612) 625-0142
Fax: (612) 625-3513
Internet: http://www.publicachievement.org

Sponsored by the Center for Democracy and Citizenship and the University of Minnesota, Public Achievement focuses on preparing youth for citizenship. In 1990, Public Achievement was created by Harry Boyte as a civic education program. Based on the Southern Christian Leadership Conference (SCLC) approach to citizenship, Public Achievement encourages youth to take action and make important changes in their communities. Public Achievement has programs in Kansas City, Missouri; Minneapolis–St. Paul; Southern Minnesota; and Northern Ireland.

Public/Private Ventures
122 East 42nd Street, 41st Floor
New York, NY 10168
Telephone: (212) 949-0439
Fax: (212) 949-0439
Internet: http://www.ppv.org

Public/Private Ventures is a national nonprofit organization that works with various organizations from the nonprofit, business, philanthropic, and public sectors in efforts to improve the effectiveness of social policies and programs and improve the lives of children, families, and adults. Public/Private Ventures focuses on several key areas: Youth Development, Mentoring, Faith-Based Initiatives, Youth Violence Reduction, Working Ventures, Workforce Development, and National Service. Public/Private Ventures issues reports on these topics to assist individuals and organizations in developing effective programs, practices, and policies. Using rigorous research methods, these reports also evaluate the program effectiveness. In addition, another important role of the organization is to help to communicate research findings to communities and policymakers and to help implement effective programs.

RMC Research Corporation
Writer Square, Suite 540
1512 Larimer Street
Denver, CO 80202
Telephone: (303) 825-3636 or (800) 922-3636
Fax: (303) 825-1626
Email: rmc@rmcdenver.com
Internet: http://www.rmcdenver.com

The RMC Research Corporation offers support, services, and products to assist local, national, and international organizations in developing and maintaining successful programs. In particular, the RMC Research Corporation is committed to promoting the growth and positive development of individuals, families, and communities. To achieve its goal, the RMC Research Corporation provides consultation, research, evaluation, and technical assistance to education and human service organizations and agencies. Service-learning is one key area of expertise of the RMC Corporation. In addition, the RMC Research Corporation was a cohost of the first annual National Conference on Service-Learning Research in October 2001 that brought together researchers, professionals, and students to share information on the state-of-the-art of service-learning research.

Search Institute
700 South Third Street, Suite 210
Minneapolis, MN 55415-1138
Telephone: (612) 376-8955 or (800) 888-7828
Fax: (612) 376-8956
E-mail: si@search-institute.org
Internet: http://www.search-institute.org

Established in 1958, the Search Institute is a nonprofit organization that is dedicated to the creation of knowledge that can be applied for the betterment of youth, families, and communities. The Search Institute is well known for devising the developmental assets framework. Through research, the Search Institute identified forty assets or characteristics that contribute to optimal and healthy youth development. Some examples of assets include family support, caring school climate, service to others, positive peer influence, constructive use of time in creative activities, active school engagement, value on equality and social justice, cultural competence, and having a sense of purpose. The Search Institute promotes positive development for youth through research; publications and other resources for parents, schools, and organizations; national conferences and regional networking meetings; consulting to community agencies and organizations; and training. In 1996, the Healthy Families–Healthy Communities initiative was initiated to involve communities in developing these assets for positive youth development. Peter L. Benson, Ph.D., is the current president of the Search Institute.

Service-Learning Research and Development Center
University of California–Berkeley
615 University Hall, #1040
Berkeley, CA 94720-1040
Telephone: (510) 642-3199
Fax: (510) 642-6105
Internet: http://gse.berkeley.edu/research/slc/services.html

The UC Berkeley Service-Learning Center aims to advance service-learning, and sponsors K–12 projects as well as higher education projects. Furthermore, the UC Berkeley Service-Learning Center helps schools developing, implementing, and evaluating service-learning programs. Schools can access instruments and protocols for evaluation of their programs, as well as resources and publications for the development and implementation of their service-learning programs. The UC Berkeley Service-Learning Center was the cohost of the First Annual National Conference on Service-Learning Research in October 2001.

Sierra Club
85 Second Street, Second Floor
San Francisco, CA 94105-3441
Telephone: (415) 977-5500
Fax: (415) 977-5799
Internet: http://www.sierraclub.org

The Sierra Club is an organization for individuals of all ages that aims to protect the environment through education and the promotion of responsibility. The organization also promotes exploration and enjoyment of the natural environment. The Sierra Club has grown vastly since its founding in 1892 and currently has more than 700,000 members, making it one of the largest environmental groups in the world. The Sierra Club provides education and advocacy to conserve and restore the environment. In addition, the Sierra Club sponsors a number of national, international, and local outings for individuals of all ages to experience the wilderness and the environment. The Sierra Club also sponsors Inner City Outings, which are community outreach programs that encourage young people from low-income urban areas to experience wilderness trips. In addition, there are service trips that involve conservation and preservation of the natural environment, such as building trails and trail maintenance, fencing, boundary marking, repairing bridges and boardwalks, and working with archeologists to help document rock art. The Youth in Wilderness program also targets education for low-income youth about environmental issues through a grant-making program to schools and community agencies and advocacy activities to promote environmental education for youth.

Students Helping Street Kids International (SHSKI)
2720 Fillmore Street
Eugene, OR 97405-1831
Telephone: (541) 686-1396 or (877) KID-POWR
Fax: (541) 344-6538
Internet: http://www.helpthekids.org/

Students Helping Street Kids International (SHSKI) is a nonprofit organization that provides service-learning opportunities to U.S. students. Created in 1997 in Oregon, SHSKI recruits students to raise money for scholarships given to street kids from Brazil, Tanzania, and other countries, so they can attend school in their own communities. Having students become involved in service-learning that helps disadvantaged children increases students' awareness of different cultures and experiences of children. Students Helping Street Kids International also funds other projects benefiting street kids from developing countries around the world.

USA Freedom Corps
1600 Pennsylvania Avenue NW
Washington, DC 20500
Telephone: (877) USA-CORPS
Email: info@USAFreedomcorps.gov
Internet: http://www.usafreedomcorps.gov

The USA Freedom Corps, created by President George W. Bush, encourages Americans to get involved in their communities through service opportunities. The president has challenged all Americans to strengthen their communities by dedicating at least two years over the course of their lives to service. The USA Freedom Corps operates the largest clearinghouse for volunteer service opportunities. Visit their website to get involved in one of the 60,000 organizations around the country and the world.

United Way of America
701 N. Fairfax Street
Alexandria, VA 22314-2045
Telephone: (703) 836-7100 or (800) 411-UWAY
Internet: http://national.unitedway.org

The United Way of America is the national organization that provides funding, support, and training for local chapters of United Way throughout the United States. The United Way is an organization that develops partnerships and addresses major needs of communities across the United States. This organization promotes national and local policies and services to enhance human services and build communities. The United Way supports its mission by developing partnerships with other national organizations and grant programs to address critical issues in communities. In addition, the United Way also provides support, consultation, and technical assistance to organizations and communities. One important initiative is the Mobilization for America's Children, which attempts to improve the lives of children and families through programs that improve early childhood education, promoting adaptive development, academic success, and a positive transition to the world of work.

VISTA (Volunteers In Service To America)
Corporation for National Service
1000 Wisconsin Avenue NW
Washington, DC 20007
Telephone: (800) 942-2677
Internet: http://www.friendsofvista.org

VISTA (Volunteers In Service To America), an AmeriCorps program, is a full-time, year-long national service program for individuals dedicated to serving low-income individuals. VISTA volunteers serve in both urban and rural areas throughout the United States, working with non-profit community agencies. Each community site is working to alleviate problems critical to their community. These agencies generally are committed to addressing issues such as homelessness, illiteracy, economic development, and neighborhood revitalization. VISTA volunteers receive a small monthly stipend for expenses and educational vouchers in exchange for a term of service. Individuals must be eighteen years old or older to apply to be a VISTA volunteer. Currently, 4,000 VISTA volunteers are serving communities throughout the United States, and more than 100,000 individuals are former VISTA participants.

Wilderness Volunteers
P.O. Box 22292
Flagstaff, AZ 86002-2292
Telephone: (520) 556-0038
Fax: (520) 556-9664
Internet: http://www.wildernessvolunteers.org

Wilderness Volunteers is a nonprofit organization that provides volunteer services to many of the wilderness areas in the United States, including national parks, wildlife refuges, state parks, and recreation areas. Wilderness Volunteers works in cooperation with U.S. public land agencies to offer volunteer trips to repair or reconstruct these land areas, including building trails, cleaning up existing trails, and cutting off trail short-cuts. Examples of different service trip locations include Hawaii Volcanoes National Park, Mt. Hood National Forest in Oregon, Boundary Waters Canoe Area Wilderness in Minnesota, and the Great Smoky Mountains National Park in Tennessee. Not only do volunteers give their time to a project, they also have a chance to explore the area. The minimum age to volunteer is sixteen and volunteers should be in good physical condition. Trips are offered in three trip grades (active, strenuous, and challenging), and last approximately one week. Volunteers must apply for the service trip, pay a trip fee of approximately $198, and provide for their own transportation. Personal camping gear is also required, but tools are provided.

YMCA of the USA
101 North Wacker Drive
Chicago, IL 60606
Telephone: (312) 977-0031
Internet: http://www.ymca.com

Founded in London, England, in 1844, the YMCA has become one of the largest nonprofit community service organizations in the United States. The YMCA mission is "to put Christian principles into practice through programs that build healthy spirit, mind and body for all." It has programs for children, teens, adults, and the elderly. The programs consist of aquatics, arts, fitness, camping, and much more. There are 971 member locations and 1,401 branches located all over the United States, as well as branches in 120 different countries. The YMCA tries to respond to communities' needs by providing programs that support the development of children, strengthen families, and make the community a safer place.

YMCA Earth Service Corps

National Resource Center
909 Fourth Avenue
Seattle, WA 98104
Telephone: (206) 382-5013 or (800) 733-YESC
Email: info@yesc.org
Internet: http://www.yesc.org/

The YMCA Earth Service Corps is a service-learning program for teens. Young people develop leadership skills and cross-cultural awareness when developing and implementing community service programs based on environmental education. There are 111 Earth Service Corps programs that operate in YMCAs across the country. Teachers can form partnerships with the YMCA to incorporate service-learning and experiential education into the curriculum. Youth can initiate an Earth Service Corps program in their community if one does not already exist. The YMCA Earth Service Corps has been evaluated by the Search Institute, and the program has been found to increase leadership skills and commitment to volunteering in the future.

Youth Action Network

67 Richmond Street West, Suite 410
Toronto, Ontario, Canada M5H 1Z5
Telephone: (416) 368-2277
Internet: http://www.teaching.com/act/

The Youth Action Network is a Canadian-based youth-led organization. This organization provides the opportunity for youth to learn about important issues, to express their opinions about these issues, and to learn how to start doing something about them. Youth from more than eighty different countries communicate with each other online. Youth have a chance to make a difference by taking action with petitions, creating and taking surveys, and contacting the media and their local government.

Youth on Board
58 Day Street, 3rd Floor
P.O. Box 440322
Somerville, MA 02144
Telephone: (617) 623-9900 ext. 1242
Fax: (617) 623-4359
Email: YouthonBoard@aol.com
Internet: http://www.youthonboard.org

Youth on Board is an organization that attempts to change the attitudes of youth and adults in order to improve their communities. The goal of Youth on Board is to build relationships between adults and youth and to strengthen relationships among youth. In addition, this organization helps youth to build leadership skills and advocates for policies and laws that support youth. Youth on Board provides trainings and services for young people and adults who work with youth. Some examples of projects that Youth on Board organizes and implements include involving youth on the board of directors of major organizations, working with school systems, and giving speeches and presentations on youth involvement.

Youth Service America
1101 15th Street NW, Suite 200
Washington, DC 20005
Telephone: (202) 296-2992
Internet: http://www.ysa.org

Youth Service America is a resource center of organizations that are dedicated to increasing opportunities for youth service on the local, national, or global levels by developing effective and lasting programs. Youth Service America proposes that youth service will promote citizenship in young people and the creation of strong communities. The Youth Service Information Network allows service organizations to access vital information and research on opportunities and best practices for service through the www.SERVEnet.org website and the National Service Affiliates Program. Youth Service America's Youth as Assets Campaign supports National Youth Service Day each April and the President's Student Service Awards for youth, ages five to twenty-five, for providing service to their communities.

Youth Volunteer Corps of America

4600 West 51st Street, Suite 300
Shawnee Mission, KS 66205
Telephone: (913) 432-9822
Fax: (913) 432-3313
Internet: http://www.yvca.org

Founded in 1986, the Youth Volunteer Corps of America aims to enhance the development of youth and to address community needs through increasing volunteer and service opportunities for youth ages eleven to eighteen in communities throughout the United States. Through youth service, the Youth Volunteer Corps of America hopes to instill a commitment of service throughout the individual's lifetime. Another important goal of this organization is to promote an appreciation for diversity. Programs are sponsored in local communities through organizations such as the YMCA, United Way, and through schools. Youth can volunteer during the summer and/or school-year. The summer program is more intensive with youth working in teams with a leader on a project full time for two to four weeks. The goals of the summer program are to enhance skills working in teams and increase civic responsibility and valuing diversity. The school-year program involves a classroom teacher to design and carry out service programs within schools that are integrated with the curriculum. Service usually takes place after school, weekends, and during vacations. Other examples of Youth Volunteer Corps projects include working with the elderly, tutoring children, cleaning up the neighborhood, working at child care programs, and serving food to the homeless. The Youth Volunteer Corps is also affiliated with Learn and Serve America, AmeriCorps, and the Points of Light Foundation.

6

Selected Resources

The resources that are available for guiding the design, development and evaluation of community service and service-learning programs have grown tremendously in recent years. Print resources are now supplemented by a large number of Internet sites and a growing number of videos. This chapter provides a selected overview of these resources. We have included a selection of books that are most likely to be of interest to parents and professionals who want to learn more about the history, philosophy, and effects of community service for teenagers, as well as the practicalities of organizing and evaluating service programs. We describe a number of books relevant to teenagers who are thinking about becoming involved in community service and are wondering about the opportunities, benefits, and requirements of service activity. We have also included abstracts of selected journal articles, written by leading scholars in the field, which provide more detail on the philosophy and effects of community service. We have cited a number of these books and articles throughout other chapters of this book as well. The summaries in this chapter provide an additional resource for readers who want to know more about these citations. The Internet sites that we have listed offer a wealth of information. We encourage you to explore the links that allow you to navigate each website. For additional websites, explore the Internet addresses that accompany many of the organizations listed in chapter 5 of this book. Finally, we have listed a number of videos that provide examples of community service and service-learning programs and related issues.

GENERAL REFERENCE BOOKS FOR PARENTS AND PROFESSIONALS

Bellah, R. N., Madsen, R., Sullivan, W. M., Swidler, A., & Tipton, S. M. (Eds.). (1985). 355 pages. *Habits of the heart: Individualism and commitment in American life.* Berkeley, CA: University of California Press.

Habits of the Heart describes the social significance of individualism and religion in American society. Initially published in 1985, it was reissued in 1996 with a new introduction describing the book's relevance for contemporary racial and social class divisions. The authors describe the importance of social organizations as vehicles for humanizing society. Service-learning is another means to promote citizenship and societal commitment. This book emphasizes some of the inherent tensions in American society between individualism and commitment and has inspired many to advocate increased involvement in community service.

Benson, P., & Roehlkepartain, E. (1993). 123 pages. *Beyond leaf raking.* Nashville, TN: Abingdon Press.

Although currently out of print, this guide provides practical suggestions for church organizations interested in involving youth in community service. The book includes guidelines for assessing community needs, preparing youth for service, and developing reflection activities to accompany service experiences. Worksheets, checklists, and other practical resources are also provided.

Cairn, R. W., & Kielsmeier, J. C. (Eds.). (1995). 260 pages. *Growing hope: A sourcebook on integrating youth service into the school curriculum.* Minneapolis, MN: National Youth Leadership Council.

A practical reference for educators wishing to implement service-learning programs in their school or district, this book is divided into three main parts. The first section outlines the background and philosophy of the youth service movement in America. The second section offers practical advice for project implementation and overviews research on service-learning. The final section of the book provides samples of program materials and a list of service-learning resources.

Campus Compact. (2000). 200 pages. *Introduction to service-learning toolkit: Readings and resources for faculty.* Brown University: Author.

This collection of papers, compiled and made available by Campus Compact, addresses the fundamental challenges service-learning poses to the roles of teachers in academia. Service-learning calls educators to new levels of collaboration and experimentation as well as risk-taking in their work. Because of the difficulties that individual teachers and institutions encounter in implementing service-learning, this book has been designed as a practical guide to navigating this transition. It addresses many of the critical issues in theory and practice that are involved in service-learning. Chapters focus on understanding basic definitions, theory and teaching, community partnerships, and program modeling, among other issues. While this guide is intended for teachers in postsecondary education, many of these tools may be useful for work with younger students.

Claus, J., & Ogden, C. (Eds.). (1999). 198 pages. *Service-learning for youth empowerment and social change.* New York: Peter Lang.

This edited book presents theory and research on service-learning programs for youth. Throughout the volume, innovative programs are outlined and specific recommendations for program design are provided. An approach to service-learning is presented that combines community service, critical reflection, and social reform. Contributions include: "Beyond Test Scores and Standards: Service, Understanding, and Citizenship" / Schine; "In the Service of What? The Politics of Service-Learning" / Kahne and Westheimer; "Promoting Identity Development: Ten Ideas for School-Based Learning Programs" / Yates and Youniss; "An Empowering, Transformative Approach to Service" / Claus and Ogden; "Taking a Calculated Risk: Harnessing the Exuberance of Youth through Community Problem Solvers" / Halsted; "What's Love Got to Do With It? Teen Dancers on Community Service-Learning" / Bowers-Young and Lakes; "Ripples of Empowerment: A Personal Reflection" / Desmarais; "Service-Learning and the Making of Small 'd' Democrats" / Parsons; "Building Legacies: School Improvement and Youth Activism in an Urban Teacher Education Partnership" / Maloy, Sheehan, LaRoche, and Clark Jr.; "Empowering Teacher Education Students through Service-Learning: A Case Study" / Kinsely.

Conrad, D., & Hedin, D. (1987). 71 pages. *Youth service: A guidebook for developing and operating effective programs.* Washington, DC: Independent Sector.

This guidebook was developed as a resource for community leaders and educators interested in designing and promoting youth service programs. The book provides examples of community service programs and offers ideas and advice for designing, organizing, running, and promoting such programs. Attention is given to school-based programs, addressing both opportunities and barriers that exist in trying to implement service-learning programs in school contexts. The first section, entitled "What Youth Can Do," describes numerous ways in which youth can get involved in community service. The next section, "Program Models," focuses on models for integrating community service into youth agency and school programs. The next five sections ("Setting up the Projects," "Developing Your Own Projects," "Recruitment, Liability, and Transportation") offer practical advice for starting a program and keeping it running smoothly. The following section, "Learning from Service," provides suggestions to increase youth learning from service involvement, and the last two sections, "Rationale" and "Closing Note," summarize the goals and aims of community service. The guidebook also contains exercises for teachers and youth leaders, as well as sample administrative forms, a brief bibliography, and a listing of youth service resources.

Conrad, D., & Hedin, D. (1989). 38 pages. *High school community service: A review of research and programs.* Madison, WI: National Center on Effective Secondary Schools.

This document highlights community service programs in high schools and outlines recent efforts to make community service a part of the high school curriculum. The report summarizes current educational debates on service-learning, describes policies and practices of specific service-learning programs, summarizes research findings on the impact of service-learning, and highlights critical issues that confront educational researchers, policymakers, and practitioners interested in service-learning. This paper includes references and a list of resources for organizations interested in developing service programs.

Eberly, D. J. (Ed.). (1991). 60 pages. *National youth service: A democratic institution for the 21st century.* Washington, DC: National Service Secretariat Conference.

The proceedings from a conference on national youth service held at the Wingspread Conference Center in Racine, Wisconsin, in July 1991 are published in this volume. Chapter 1 provides a history of youth participation in the United States, documenting labor market trends, education, delinquency, and social problems. As a result of changes in technology and population characteristics, schools cannot be relied upon to meet all of the needs of youth. Voluntary national youth service offers an alternative means of preparing youth for civic roles. Chapter 2 explains how national youth service can benefit both youth and the nation as a whole and discusses ways to increase youth involvement in service. A list of conference participants is provided, along with biographical notes.

Ferrari, J. R., & Chapman, J. G. (Eds.). (1999). 161 pages. *Educating students to make a difference: Community-based service-learning.* Binghamton, NY: The Haworth Press.

This edited book provides helpful information for developing service-learning programs and courses. Case studies are provided to illustrate the ways in which service-learning can be integrated into the school curriculum. The book is divided into two main parts. Part 1 is entitled "Learning to Serve: Predispositions and Motivations," and part 2 is entitled "Service as Learning: Student, Faculty, and Community Outcomes."

Furco, A., & Billig, S. H. (Eds). (2002). 286 pages. *Service-learning: The essence of pedagogy.* Greenwich, CT: Information Age Publishing.

This edited book is the first volume in a proposed series entitled Advances in Service-Learning Research, which will discuss a variety of issues related to the design of effective research on service-learning. The editors suggest that better service-learning research is needed to understand the conditions that are necessary for effective programs and for changing school culture. This initial volume focuses on providing a solid understanding of service-learning from K–12 through higher education. The first section of the book seeks to define service-learning and to provide evidence exploring whether service-learning is better than community service. The second section of the book focuses on theoretical foundations for service-learning programs, including social trust theory, developmental contextualism, and program theory. The third section focuses on methodological issues in service-learning research, including qualitative and interview methods. The fourth section discusses the range of expected and desired outcomes that service-learning programs are designed to fulfill. The conclusion, written by the editors, identifies areas of service-learning that warrant further research attention.

Kendall, J. C. (Ed.). (1990). 625 pages. *Combining service and learning: A resource book for community and public service.* 3 Vols. Raleigh, NC: National Society for Internships and Experiential Education.

This three-volume series is a critical resource for designing and supporting community service-learning projects. Volume one focuses on theoretical and policy issues related to community service-learning. The volume is divided into five parts: "Essential Principles in Combining Service and Learning"; "Rationales and Theories for Combining Service and Learning"; Public Policy Issues and Guides"; Institutional Policy Issues and Guides"; and "History and Future of the Service-Learning Movement." The volume also contains an index and publications list. The second volume provides practical advice and ideas for programs and courses that combine service and learning. Volume two contains four parts: "Project Ideas for Service-Learners of All Ages: Suggestions for Developing and Nurturing School-Agency Relationships, Legal Issues, Models for Youth Programs, and Suggestions Regarding Recruitment"; "Profiles of College and University Service-Learning Programs"; "Profiles of Public Service Programs and Courses in K–12 Schools"; and "Descriptions of Community-Based Organizations, Government Programs, and Youth-Serving Agencies." The third volume provides a list of publications and references related to community service-learning.

Kenny, M. E., Simon, L. A. K., Kiley-Brabeck, K., & Lerner, R. M. (Eds). (2001). 452 pages. *Learning to serve: Promoting civil society through service-learning.* Norwell, MA: Kluwer.

This edited book discusses how colleges and universities can prepare students through service-learning to be active and engaged citizens. Service-learning is also described as a way for universities to fulfill their responsibilities to the community through outreach scholarship, which integrates research, teaching, and university-community partnership. This volume presents the history of service-learning and includes chapters written by representatives of twenty-two different colleges and universities that engage in various levels and types of community service activities. The volume concludes with four chapters that present the benefits and challenges of community service and university-community partnership as perceived by four youth-serving agencies, operating on local, state, and national levels. Overall, this book provides rich exemplars of the ways in which universities are seeking to fulfill their diverse missions and contribute to the development of a civil society through service-learning programs. The book should be of interest to parents, community leaders, teachers, and university professors and administrators.

Kinsley, C.W., & McPherson, K. (Eds.). (1995). 140 pages. *Enriching the curriculum through service-learning.* Alexandria, VA: Association for Supervision and Curriculum Development.

This is a practical guide to service-learning made up of six parts and a total of twenty-one contributions that describe specific service-learning projects in schools across the United States. Part 1 contributions emphasize the integration of service and academic learning for students in language arts classes, special education, and vocational education. Part 2 discusses ways in which the culture of the school can be transformed through service-learning, including the development of a caring school community and an appreciation of diversity. Part 3 focuses on service experiences that encourage teachers to facilitate learning, with part 4 focusing on the development of school and community partnerships. Part 5 highlights the importance of the reflection component of service-learning, with a list of service-learning resources being included in the final section, part 6.

McGuckin, F. (Ed.). (1998). 177 pages. *The reference shelf: Volunteerism.* New York: H.W. Wilson.

This book contains articles that provide a historical background and a variety of critical perspectives on service issues. The book is divided into four sections: Part 1, "Society's Responsibility and Commitment," explores current volunteer activity across multiple domains of need. Part 2, "Private Volunteering and AmeriCorps" provides examples of community partnerships, as well as a critique of AmeriCorps programs. Part 3, "Volunteerism Is Not Enough," looks critically at the limits of current volunteer efforts, including low rates of direct service and poor organization and management. Part 4, "Rewards of Volunteerism," discusses ways in which volunteers gain satisfaction from their service involvement.

Points of Light Foundation. (1997). 88 pages. *Agencies + schools = service-learning: A training toolbox.* Washington, DC: Author.

This manual is designed for agencies, nonprofit organizations, volunteer centers, and schools that wish to provide training for their staff in order to strengthen their service-learning programs. It also provides information for developing partnerships between agencies and schools. Nine chapters include information on preparing to run a training session, sample training agendas, definitions of service-learning, identifying opportunities for youth volunteers, and developing partnerships, as well as a list of resources and handouts that can be copied for participants. This manual has many ideas for training persons to work with youth involved in community service.

Radest, H. B. (1993). 216 pages. *Community service: Encounter with strangers.* Westport, CT: Praeger.

This book presents a discussion of the complexities of community service and the need to understand better the social and political implications of service, through "reflection, criticism and skepticism." The book begins with an introduction that raises questions concerning the goals of service and provides an overview of current service practice and its organizational and political roots. Next, Radest relates service to developmental psychology, schooling, and democracy. The book ends with a discussion of the moral and political conditions necessary to support a positive community service framework. This book analyzes community service from a critical conceptual perspective and may be of interest to individuals who are interested in the philosophical goals of community service.

Roehlkepartain, E. (1995). 27 pages. *Everyone wins when youth serve.* Washington, DC: Points of Light Foundation.

This booklet was developed by the Points of Light Foundation in conjunction with the National Youth Leadership Council as part of the foundation's initiative on Communities as Places of Caring. This initiative seeks to work with communities to increase opportunities for engaging youth in service-learning. The booklet defines service-learning and presents data that describe the benefits of youth service for community organizations, schools, the larger society, and the youth who serve. The booklet also addresses concerns that agencies may have about involving youth volunteers, describes the characteristics of effective programs, identifies first steps in developing opportunities for youth volunteers, and provides a checklist for organizations to assess their readiness for becoming involved in service-learning. This booklet is a helpful resource for organizations thinking about becoming involved in service-learning and is a tool for teachers and parents who are trying to engage community organizations in service-learning.

Roehlkepartain, E. C., Naftali, E. D., & Musegades, L. (2000). 197 pages. *Growing up generous: Engaging youth in giving and serving.* Minneapolis, MN: Search Institute.

This book is written for faith-based Jewish and Christian institutions that wish to develop a commitment to service among youth. The content is derived from a two-year study of the ways in which faith-based organizations develop habits of service and giving among young people. This research provides a base of suggestions for other organizations.

Schine, J. (1989). 22 pages. *Young adolescents and community service.* Washington, DC: Carnegie Council on Adolescent Development.

This document was written as a working paper for the Carnegie Council on Adolescent Development as part of its discussions on the value of community service for young adolescents. The author argues for involving adolescents in either school-based or community-based service programs. A description is provided of the Early Adolescent Helper Program at the City University of New York's Center for Advanced Study in Education, which has promoted youth service for young adolescents since 1982. Schine argues that community service programs that provide young adolescents with opportunities to participate in service and to experience the empowerment that comes with making a difference can help to address some of the problems facing society.

Schine, J. (Ed.). (1997). 212 pages. *Service-learning.* Chicago, IL: University of Chicago Press.

This yearbook, published by the National Society for the Study of Education, contains a collection of papers addressing issues relevant to educators, policymakers, and others involved in service-learning. Contributions are "Integrating Youth into Communities" / Kleinbard; "An International Perspective on Service-Learning" / Eberly; "Service-Learning: A Theoretical Model" / Sheckley and Keeton; "Research and Evaluation in Service-Learning: What Do We Need to Know?" / Lipka; "Service-Learning in Curriculum Reform" / Carter; "Service-Learning in the Comer School Development Program" / Haynes and Comer; "Service-Learning in the Classroom: Practical Issues" / Pardo; "Service-Learning in Higher Education" / Wutzdorff and Giles Jr.; Service-Learning in Teacher Preparation" / Scales and Koppelman; "Encouraging Cultural Competence in Service-Learning Practice" / Ward; "Service-Learning and Improved Academic Achievement" / Kunin; "The Role of the State" / Antonelli and Thompson; "Service-Learning as a Vehicle for Youth Development" / Zeldin and Tarlov; and "Looking Ahead: Issues and Challenges" / Schine. The book also contains a list of service resources, information regarding membership in the National Society for the Study of Education, and a list of the society's publications.

Search Institute. (2000). 184 pages. *An asset builder's guide to service-learning.* Minneapolis, MN: Author.

This book applies the assets framework, developed by the Search Institute, to the development of youth service-learning programs by educational, community, and religious organizations. It provides practical suggestions and concrete tools for creating service-learning projects and improving programs through the assets approach. The book is presented as a workbook that includes ideas and worksheets for use with service-learning programs. The central topics covered in this workbook include: how to work with different age groups, how to support and sustain youth involvement, program stages and steps, and a presentation of real-life examples from existing service-learning programs.

Stanton, T. K., Giles, D. E., & Cruz, N. I. (1999). 272 pages. *Service-learning: A movement's pioneers reflect on its origins, practice, and future.* San Francisco, CA: Jossey-Bass.

This book provides a history of service-learning by following the work of thirty-three advocates, scholars, and practitioners since the early 1960s. The book includes a discussion of several influential service-learning pioneers. It provides personal accounts of their service-learning work, their professional roles, and their rationales for combining service and learning within postsecondary education, as well as the challenges they faced in doing so. This book also describes the variety of service-learning practices developed by pioneers in the field and their evaluation of the results of their efforts. Recommendations for current policies and practice are offered and a listing of service-learning practice opportunities and a historical time line are provided.

Totten, S., & Pedersen, J. E. (Eds.). (1997). 378 pages. *Social issues and service at the middle level.* Boston, MA: Allyn & Bacon.

This edited book provides examples of outstanding community service programs throughout the United States. The book is intended as a reference for administrators, professors, and public school teachers. The eighteen essays in the book constitute two parts, "Social Issues" and "Service," which provide stimulating examples of how community service can be designed to increase social awareness and address critical social issues.

Wade, R. C. (Ed.). (1997). 379 pages. *Community service-learning: A guide to including service in the public school curriculum.* Albany: State University of New York Press.

This book is a comprehensive resource directed towards educators who want to integrate community service with the school curriculum. Part 1 contains seven chapters highlighting components of quality community service-learning programs. Part 2 provides examples of successful service-learning programs at the elementary, middle, and high school levels, with part 3 presenting the stories and perspectives of participants in community service-learning programs including students, agency members, teachers, parents, and administrators. The final section, part 4, addresses the future of service-learning in public schooling.

Waterman, A. S. (Ed.). (1997). 208 pages. *Service-learning: Applications from the research.* Mahwah, NJ: Lawrence Erlbaum.

This volume brings together the work of leading researchers in the area of service-learning and is a useful resource for both academics and service professionals who are interested in evaluating their programs and using research findings to guide the development of community service programs. A major focus of the book is to review and evaluate empirical research literature on service-learning programs. A second aim of the book is to present recommendations derived from research that provide guidance for planning, improving, and evaluating service-learning programs. The volume includes ten chapters. Following an introductory overview chapter written by Alan Waterman, part 1 focuses on service-learning methodologies. Part 2 presents research regarding the effectiveness of service-learning components, and part 3 provides research relating to service-learning contexts, covering rural and urban settings. The final chapter draws conclusions regarding the evaluation of service-learning.

Yates, M., & Youniss, J. (Eds.). (1999). 283 pages. *Roots of civic identity: International perspectives on community service and activism in youth.* New York: Cambridge University Press.

This edited book contains a collection of essays on youth community participation. Researchers from countries around the world present findings on service activities and political activism of youth in their countries. These findings challenge the image of "generation X" as socially uninvolved and uncaring and support the view that youth can learn to become active and concerned citizens through partici-

pation in community and civic activities. Youth can gain an understanding of politics and citizenship through participation in community and civic activities more effectively than through the study of
abstract ideas.

Youniss, J., & Yates, M. (1997). 173 pages. *Community service and social
responsibility in youth.* Chicago, IL: University of Chicago Press.

This is a scholarly book that presents a theoretical rationale for why
youth should engage in community service. The authors argue that
active participation in solving social problems helps to promote a sense
of personal and social identity among young people. The authors present
findings from their study of a class of high school juniors who participated in a mandatory service experience at a soup kitchen as part of a
required course on social justice. The authors maintain that the service
experience helped the young people to develop a sense of social responsibility and a belief that they could do something to make a political and
moral difference. They argue further that community service contributes to identity development, because it provides youth with a way to
connect with other generations, helps youth to understand their current
experiences in a broader social and historical context, and provides optimism for social change and a better future. The authors suggest that
community service can enhance the development of a personal and collective identity that includes feelings of personal agency and concern for
society's well-being.

RESOURCES FOR TEENAGERS AND THEIR PARENTS

DiGeronimo, T. F. (1995). 187 pages. *A student's guide to volunteering.*
Franklin Lakes, NJ: Career Press.

This book provides a guide for teenagers on how to become involved
in volunteer activity. It begins with a brief history of volunteer organizations and describes reasons why teens choose to become involved in
volunteer service. Opportunities for volunteer involvement in health
care, education, environmental protection, politics, substance abuse,
and in work with low-income populations are described, as well as the
personal characteristics required for successful and satisfying volunteerism in these settings. Brief accounts of volunteer experiences are
also provided by teens who have volunteered in each of these settings.
The book includes a directory of organizations in each state to contact

for information on volunteer opportunities and provides a list of national organizations.

Duper, L. L. (1996). 136 pages. *160 ways to help the world: Community service projects for young people.* New York: Facts on File.

An excellent resource for teachers and parents who are interested in helping youth to become involved in community service. The book provides step-by-step instructions for developing and implementing fun service projects that contribute to the community. Examples include starting a toy collection drive, planting trees or a garden, and sewing blankets for local homeless shelters. Advice is offered on how to plan and execute a project, and helpful hints are provided on how to obtain support from businesses, handle money, and generate publicity. A comprehensive index and list of community organizations are also included.

Erlbach, A. (1998). 64 pages. *The kid's volunteering book.* Minneapolis, MN: Lerner Publications.

This book is written for youth in the late elementary and middle school grades to help them become involved in volunteerism. The book provides twelve brief stories of youth who have volunteered in a variety of settings and activities, such as playing a clown in a children's hospital, landscaping following a hurricane, raising funds for a classmate with leukemia, and helping at an animal shelter. How to choose a volunteer project, how to apply for a volunteer position, and how to start your own volunteer efforts are discussed in additional chapters.

Goodman, A., & Smyth, F. (1994). 132 pages. *The big help book: 365 ways you can make a difference by volunteering.* New York: Simon & Schuster.

This book was written for children and early adolescents as part of The Big Help campaign of the Nickelodeon network. As the first television network focused on programming for children and teens, Nickelodeon sought to inspire young people to become active in their communities. The book includes advice on starting a volunteer group and ideas on large and small ways in which young people, by themselves or with their friends or family, can make a difference in improving their communities. Numerous suggestions are provided for ways in which young people can get involved in helping other children, the homeless, the elderly, animals, and in caring for the environment. Contact information is provided to connect with service activities, and brief profiles of young people engaged in each type of service activity are provided. More information on Nickelodeon's Big Help website is available in the Internet chapter in this book.

Karnes, F. A., & Bean, S. (1993). 159 pages. *Girls and young women leading the way.* Minneapolis, MN: Free Spirit.

Twenty biographies offer powerful examples of the leadership of girls and young women, ages eight to twenty-one, who have made a difference in their schools and communities through service and social action. The volume also includes suggestions on developing a leadership notebook, as well as ideas for leadership projects and resources and quotations from women leaders.

Lawson, D. M. (1998). 125 pages. *Volunteering: 101 ways you can improve the world.* San Diego, CA: ALTI Publishing.

This book describes the benefits of volunteering for people of all ages and answers 101 questions related to volunteering, including what keeps people from volunteering and other questions that volunteers confront on a daily basis. Questions are identified and answered in a one-page response. Questions fall into five categories, "Volunteering and You," "Volunteering and Life," "Volunteering with Others," "Volunteering with Corporations and Charities," and "Volunteering around the World." Examples of some of questions in the first category are, "How can I volunteer when I have no time to volunteer? Why should I volunteer? What's in it for me? How can I find out where to volunteer?" and "What can I possibly do? I don't feel that I have any talents." The book is written to promote volunteering and to serve as a guide for those who are already participating in volunteer activities.

Lewis, B. A. (1992). 175 pages. *Kids with courage: True stories about young people making a difference.* Minneapolis, MN: Free Spirit.

This book presents the stories of eighteen young people who have made a difference in the lives of others by following their hearts and standing up for their beliefs. Some of these youth have been involved in efforts to reduce crime, while others have taken social action to honor their ancestors, to increase the rights of youth and the disabled, or to help those without economic resources. Other youth relate stories of heroism in which they have saved the lives of others in situations posing risk and danger. These stories provide powerful examples for young people, demonstrating that they can make a real difference in the world if they choose to act and show courage.

Lewis, B. A. (1995). 175 pages. *The kid's guide to service projects: Over 500 service ideas for young people who want to make a difference.* Minneapolis, MN: Free Spirit.

This book covers more than 500 ideas for service projects for young people. The book is targeted to youth in middle and junior high school and briefly discusses the benefits of involvement in service activities. Ten steps to successful service projects are outlined and a list of ideas is provided. Youth are encouraged to pick a topic that interests them, such as animal rights, fighting crime, homeless people, the environment, politics and government, or senior citizens, and then use this book for ideas and resources to develop and carry out a service project.

Lewis, B. A. (1998). 211 pages. *The kid's guide to social action: How to solve the social problems you choose and turn creative thinking into positive action.* Minneapolis, MN: Free Spirit.

This is an excellent resource guide for youth who want to learn political action skills so they can solve social problems at community, state, and national levels. The book includes stories from youth who have been involved in and have made a contribution to changing their communities. In order to assist youth in becoming involved in service, addresses, phone numbers, and websites are provided of social action groups looking for youth volunteers. Skills that may be useful while participating in community service, such as letter writing, fundraising, and speechmaking, are also discussed.

Lewis, B. A. (1998). 277 pages. *What do you stand for?* Minneapolis, MN: Free Spirit.

This book, designed for early adolescents and teens eleven and older, provides activities for youth to evaluate themselves and their values. The self-reflective nature of these activities makes them suitable for integration with or as supplements to service-learning activities. The volume begins with activities designed to increase self-reflection and self-awareness. Each subsequent chapter focuses on character traits, such as caring, citizenship, courage, empathy, endurance, justice, leadership, loyalty, problem-solving, relationships, respect, responsibility, self-discipline, and wisdom. Each chapter includes character dilemmas, suggestions for activities or service projects, true stories of youth who present models of character in action, and resources for further investigation.

Mosaic Youth Center Board. (2001). 96 pages. *Step by step: A young person's guide to positive community change.* Minneapolis, MN: Search Institute.

This is a workbook for young people to help them set goals, identify strategies, and develop and implement plans to effect positive change in their communities and neighborhoods. Youth are taught a series of 6 steps for positive change, beginning with making decisions on the issues that are most important to them. The book may be helpful to youth and to youth organizations who wish to involve young people in community change.

Prudential. (1998). 15 pages. *Catch the spirit: A student's guide to community service.* Newark, NJ.

This pamphlet, presented by the Prudential Insurance Spirit of Community Initiative in cooperation with the U.S. Department of Education, provides information for young people who are interested in community service and want to make their communities better places to live. The booklet describes the variety of volunteer activities that volunteers can engage in; discusses how to determine the kind of volunteer project that matches the interests, skills, and commitment of the volunteer; provides a list of "Do's & don'ts of successful volunteering"; suggests local resources; and includes a listing of national organizations relevant to youth volunteers. The booklet can be obtained for free from Prudential Insurance or from the Consumer Information Center, Pueblo, Colorado (800-FED-INFO or www.pueblo.gsa.gov). More information on Prudential and this initiative is available in the organizations chapter of this book.

Waldman, J., & Cutherson, S. A. (2000). 192 pages. *Teens with courage to give: Young people who triumphed over tragedy and volunteered to make a difference.* Berkeley, CA: Conari Press.

In this book, thirty teens describe in their own words how they overcame their own challenges and went on to help other teens overcome adversity. These teens overcame physical challenges, such as cancer and amputation of a limb, or turned from paths of rebellion and legal difficulties to help other youth have more productive lives. A student who witnessed the Littleton, Colorado, shootings developed a teen drop-in center. A teenage mother now works for an organization dedicated to preventing teen pregnancy. This book provides important personal stories that may inspire teens to reach out and help others. Each chapter also provides the names and addresses of organizations that provide services to youth experiencing difficulties and organizations through which youth can serve others. The book includes a foreward written by Tom Culbertson, president and CEO of Youth Service America.

JOURNAL ARTICLES

Allen, J. P., Philliber, S., Herrling, S., & Kuperminc, G. P. (1997). Preventing teen pregnancy and academic failure: Experimental evaluation of a developmentally based approach. *Child Development, 68,* 729–742.

This study evaluated a national volunteer service program by comparing participants in Teen Outreach with a group of nonparticipants. Teen Outreach is a collaborative program between the Association of Junior Leagues International, local Junior League chapters, and school districts across the United States. The program was designed to prevent teenage pregnancy and school failure by involving high school students in volunteer service in their communities, coupled with classroom-based, curriculum-guided discussions in the school. The adolescents who participated in Teen Outreach evidenced lower rates of pregnancy, school failure, and academic suspension in comparison with teens assigned to a control group, even after accounting for student differences on background characteristics. These findings provide support for the effectiveness of the Teen Outreach Program specifically and more generally for the helpfulness of volunteer service as a means for preventing problem behaviors. This approach to promoting positive youth development through involvement in volunteer service emphasizes important developmental tasks of adolescence and offers a productive alternative to focusing upon problem behaviors of youth.

Allen, J. P., Kuperminc, G., Philliber, S., & Herre, K. (1994). Programmatic prevention of adolescent problem behaviors: The role of autonomy, relatedness, and volunteer service in the Teen Outreach Program. *American Journal of Community Psychology, 22,* 617–638.

This study explores the processes through which participation in a volunteer service program helps to prevent failure in school, suspension, and teenage pregnancy among youth. Data were collected from 1,020 students (aged eleven to nineteen years) who participated in a national replication of the Teen Outreach Program. Students were from sixty-six middle and high school sites. Differences across sites were examined using a prepost design and a comparison group of 1,013 age-matched students. At the middle school level, volunteer service programs that promoted feelings of autonomy among students, as well as opportunities to develop relationships with peers, were most effective in enhancing student feelings of success in reducing problem behaviors. This finding is consistent with developmental theory, which stresses the importance among early adolescents of gaining autonomy while also developing positive relationships with peers and caring adults. School programs that provided middle school students with opportunities to learn new skills and to choose the type of volunteer work they did were successful. Among high school students, these program characteristics were less important in determining whether students benefited from volunteer service. Implications of these findings for the development of volunteer service programs and other interventions aimed at reducing adolescent problem behaviors are discussed.

Astin, A. W., & Sax, L. J. (1998). How undergraduates are affected by service participation. *Journal of College Student Development, 39,* 251–263.

This study examined the impact of community service participation on the development of undergraduate college students. Data were collected from 3,450 freshmen (2,287 women and 1,163 men) who attended forty-two colleges receiving federal funding for community service programs. The findings indicate that participation in community service substantially enhances student development (e.g., life skill development, sense of civic responsibility), even after controlling for differences in individual student characteristics at the time of college entry.

Batchelder, T. H., & Root, S. (1994). Effects of an undergraduate program to integrate academic learning and service: Cognitive, pro-social cognitive, and identity outcomes. *Journal of Adolescence, 17,* 341–355.

This paper presents the findings of a study in which the authors investigated whether characteristics of service-learning (e.g., autonomy and instructional support for the experience) have an effect on cognitive, moral, and ego identity development among undergraduate college students. Ninety-six students in service-learning courses and other courses (control group) wrote responses to social problems at the beginning and end of their courses. In addition, students in the service-learning courses completed weekly journals and evaluations of their experiences. Students in the service-learning courses demonstrated significant gains on certain cognitive dimensions as well as increases in prosocial decision-making and reasoning and identity processes. The findings suggest that service-learning courses can promote gains in cognitive development among college students.

Billig, S. H. (2000). Research on K–12 school-based service-learning: The evidence builds. *Phi Delta Kappan, 81,* 658–664.

Service-learning programs in elementary and secondary schools have been growing in popularity and gaining support in school systems throughout the country. Although educators tend to support service-learning programs, research justifying the implementation of these programs is scarce. In this article, Billig compiles current research about service-learning programs and summarizes the benefits and "mediating factors" of these programs. According to Billig, the benefits of service-learning include a positive influence on the personal and social development of students, a positive effect on students' sense of civic responsibility, enhanced academic performance, a realistic outlook into career options, a positive influence on school climate, and a positive perception of youth among community members. Although there is increased research concerning service-learning programs, the author closes the article with a plea for more methodologically sound research efforts. This article is part of an entire issue of *Phi Delta Kappan* devoted to service-learning and is a great resource for readers looking for a current overview of youth service.

Boyer, E. (1987). Service: Linking school to life. *Community Education Journal, 15,* 7–9.

Based upon his study of American high schools, Boyer concluded that most school problems are related to feelings of isolation and lack of connection between what is learned at school and problems of the outside world. Youth often find it difficult to connect what they learn inside the classroom to the communities in which they live. Boyer proposes a plan requiring all students to participate in service activity. The requirement is called the "Carnegie unit" and encompasses not less than thirty hours of community service per year. The goal of Boyer's plan is to make students feel that they are assets to their communities, as well as autonomous individuals. Boyer provides some examples of successful service stories to illustrate the importance of this type of learning. Successful service activities benefit both the community and the school and involve students in reflection on the experience through writing or group discussion.

Brill, C. L. (1994). The effects of participation in service-learning on adolescents with disabilities. *Journal of Adolescence, 17,* 369–380.

This study examined whether participation in a service-learning program has positive effects for adolescents (aged twelve to twenty-one years) with disabilities. Thirteen special education teachers were surveyed concerning the effects of community service participation on students' social development behavior, attitudes, attendance, academic skills, adaptive behavior, and relationships with nondisabled peers. Adolescents with mild disabilities demonstrated the greatest gains in attendance and academic skills, and adolescents with moderate to profound disabilities demonstrated improvements in socialization and relationships with nondisabled peers.

Calabrese, R. L., & Schumer, R. (1986). The effects of service activities on adolescent alienation. *Adolescence, 21,* 675–687.

This pioneering study examined whether community service involvement has an impact on students' feelings of alienation. Fifty ninth grade students (thirty-three females and seventeen males) were assigned to either a community service group or a control group. Students assigned to community service were asked to plan, develop, and implement a community service project with the assistance of a teacher. Students in both the community service and the control group completed a measure of alienation. Student attendance, discipline, and grades were also evaluated before and after the community service activity. Students engaged in community service demonstrated a decrease in alienation following the initial ten weeks of service. Grades and behavior also showed improvement. Classes that did not continue community service after the first ten weeks subsequently reported gains in alienation that were similar to the control group. Students who continued in community service for a total of twenty weeks reported further drops in alienation. Overall, the findings suggest that community service activities may reduce levels of alienation and improve school behavior and grades.

Campbell, D. E. (2000). Social capital and service-learning. *Political Science and Politics, 33,* 641–645.

Campbell's article addresses the connection between service-learning and political interest and participation in the United States. While there are a growing number of political activities in high schools, the number of participants in such programs is on the decline. Campbell argues that service-learning is a means for encouraging youth to participate in politics and other aspects of community life. Service-learning can increase social capital, which can in turn increase "civic engagement," or participation in a range of community activities

Clary, E. G., & Snyder, M. (1991). The motivations to volunteer: Theoretical and practical considerations. *Current Directions in Psychological Science, 8,* 156–159.

This study explores motivations for engagement in volunteer activities. The authors identified six personal and social functions potentially served by volunteering and developed an inventory to assess them. In addition, the authors explore the role of motivation in the processes of volunteerism, especially decisions to begin volunteering and to continue to volunteer.

Conrad, D., & Hedin, D. (1991). School-based community service: What we know from research and theory. *Phi Delta Kappan, 72,* 743–749.

This article reviews research and theory on school-based community service. In November 1990, President Bush signed into law the National and Community Service Act. In support of this legislation, the authors put forth three arguments for the importance of community service including: (1) Fostering learning and social development, (2) Reforming society and preserving democratic processes, and (3) Reconnecting youth with the broader society.

DesMarais, J., Yang, Y., & Farzanehkia, F. (2000). Service-learning leadership development for youths. *Phi Delta Kappan, 81,* 678–641.

This article describes the ways in which service-learning can help youth to develop leadership skills, build character, and broaden awareness. The authors maintain that service-learning is one of the most influential ways for youth to learn leadership skills. In order for this to happen, however, power must be shared between young people and adults as they work together to accomplish community change. The authors maintain that service-learning programs are effective when there is a mutual, beneficial "partnership" and shared decision-making between young people and adults. It will be a challenge for adults to relinquish their power and allow youth to be decision-makers in service-learning programs.

Dunlap, M. R. (1998). Voices of students in multicultural service-learning settings. *Michigan Journal of Community Service-Learning, 5,* 58–67.

The author identified themes in journals written by thirty college students who were enrolled in a college course on child development and participated in a community-based service-learning placement in a multicultural setting. Three themes were identified in the students' journals: (1) students' philosophies regarding racial issues; (2) concerns about multicultural or race-related incidents; and (3) the resources they were able to use to give meaning to these experiences.

Eberly, D. J. (1993). National youth service: A developing institution. *NASSP Bulletin, 77,* 50–57.

This article traces the development of the national youth service movement, starting with the National Association of Secondary School Principals (NASSP) initiatives of the 1970s, extending through the passage of the National and Community Service Act in 1990. As a result of the passage of the National and Community Service Act, youth service became part of national policy. Service-learning activities have flourished in many schools. Mandatory community service has been instituted by some state and local school systems and is being considered by many others.

Eccles, J. S., & Barber, B. L. (1999). Student council, volunteering, basketball, or marching band: What kind of extracurricular involvement matters? *Journal of Adolescence Research, 14,* 10–43.

This study examined the potential advantages and disadvantages associated with participation in five types of extracurricular activities: (1) prosocial activities (e.g., church or volunteer activities), (2) team sports, (3) school involvement (e.g., student council), (4) performing arts, and (5) academic clubs. Participants were 1,259 adolescents, primarily of European American background. Results indicate that involvement in prosocial activities, including church and volunteer activities, is associated with positive academic outcomes and low rates of involvement in risky behaviors. In contrast, involvement with team sports was linked to both positive educational outcomes as well as high rates of involvement in drinking alcohol, a type of risky behavior. Two possible mediators of these associations were examined: peer associations and personal identity formation related to that activity. Results suggest that peer associations and the development of an activity-based identity (e.g., jock, brain, princess) help to explain the advantages and disadvantages of participation in different activities.

Furco, A. (1994). A conceptual framework for the institutionalization of youth service programs in primary and secondary education. *Journal of Adolescence, 17,* 395–409.

The author offers a conceptual framework that can serve as a basis for K–12 service programs. Nine possible ways to structure K–12 service programs are presented and twelve critical programmatic issues for ensuring successful program institutionalization are provided. Programmatic principles focus on program funding, recruitment, planning, development, marketing, transportation, legal aspects, assessment, and evaluation. The author suggests that this conceptual framework will help clarify conflicting models of youth service, reduce resistance to service programs, and develop more powerful and effective service programs.

Garber, M. P., & Heet, J. A. (2000). Free to choose service-learning. *Phi Delta Kappan, 81,* 676–677.

The authors describe what they view as the positive and negative aspects of service-learning programs. Service-learning is positive when it challenges students to see themselves as part of a larger community and helps them to recognize their responsibility to the community. The authors believe that service-learning can be a negative experience when students are required to participate in activities that go against their beliefs. Service-learning is most beneficial when students interact with others, when they are provided with positive role models, and when the parents choose schools that are consistent with their beliefs.

Giles Jr., D. E., & Eyler, J. (1994). The impact of a college community service laboratory on students' personal, social, and cognitive outcomes. *Journal of Adolescence, 17,* 327–339.

This study examined the impact of participation in a community service laboratory on personal, social, and cognitive outcomes. Results indicated that college student participants showed a significant increase in their belief that people can do something to make a difference and that they should be involved in community service (particularly in leadership and politics). Students' commitment to engage in volunteer service during the following semester also increased. Moreover, results indicated that students who participated in the community service laboratory were less likely to hold social service clients responsible for their problems.

Greenberg, R. (2000). Learn from those they serve. *Techniques, 75* (8), 18–21.

American high schools have seen an enormous growth in service-learning programs over the past fifteen years. This article describes a few of the numerous programs across the country where young volunteers are involved in community service. One example is CitySERVE in Columbus, Ohio, where projects include homebuilding, day care centers, community clean-up efforts, tutoring programs, free dental and eye clinics, and conflict resolution initiatives. Program participants recently restored a mural of the Great Depression, learning about an important era in history while simultaneously providing service to their community. In Charlotte County, Virginia, teachers work closely with high school students who tutor other students at risk of getting into trouble or dropping out of school. Volunteers learn what it feels like to help others and increase their sense of self-worth. A program in Williamson County, Tennessee, encourages students to volunteer at a day care for children of high school students and teachers. The program provides hands-on experience for those who are interested in careers in working with children as well as helping teenage mothers finish high school. Like many service-learning programs across the country, youth are not only taught the value of helping others, but also benefit from "hands-on learning."

Hamilton, S. F., & Fenzel, L. M. (1998). The impact of volunteer experience on adolescent social development: Evidence of program effects. *Journal of Adolescent Research, 3,* 65–80.

This study explores the impact of volunteerism on adolescent social development. Forty-four students, aged eleven to twenty-seven years, who had participated in either a childcare or community service project, completed a measure of social responsibility. Overall, students showed significant, but modest, gains in social responsibility. Girls, however, reported greater gains than did boys, and volunteers in community improvement projects gained more than students volunteering in childcare. The authors concluded that the general impact of volunteer experience on social development is positive but modest.

Hornbeck, D. (2000). Service-learning and reform in the Philadelphia Public Schools. *Phi Delta Kappan, 81,* 665.

The superintendent of the Philadelphia School District reports that Philadelphia is the first public school system in the country to integrate service-learning with learning objectives and academic principles in all schools across grades K–12. It is envisioned that by June 2002 "all students in the district will be required to produce a citizenship project as a condition for promotion to grades 5 and 9 and for graduation from high school." This means that students would have to participate in "real world" problem-solving as part of a service-learning project completed in grade school, middle school, and high school. The service-learning projects must meet district standards and involve "an essential question, active research and investigation, academic rigor and reflection, a real-world community connection, and applied problem solving in addressing an authentic school or community issue, need or problem through direct service or advocacy." With such rigorous scrutiny in the development and implementation of service-learning programs, students are expected to acquire the knowledge and skills to solve problems in their communities.

Johnson, A. M., & Notah, D. J. (1999). Service-learning: History, literature review, and a pilot study of eighth graders. *Elementary School Journal, 99,* 453–467.

This study investigated the effects of a service-learning curriculum on students' self-esteem and sense of personal responsibility. One hundred and fifty-six primarily Hispanic students in grades six to eight participated in the program. Quantitative data revealed no significant changes related to service participation. However, qualitative data (student reflective journals, a narrative essay, interviews, field notes, and observations) did suggest positive effects on students' self-esteem and responsibility. The authors discuss the results in light of the debate and recent litigation over mandatory community service.

Johnson, M. K., Beebe, T., Mortimer, J. T., & Snyder, M. (1998). Volunteerism in adolescence: A process perspective. *Journal of Research on Adolescence, 8,* 309–332.

This study addresses the questions "Who participates in volunteer work?" and "What are the effects of youth volunteerism?" Participants consisted of 100 ninth-grade students, chosen randomly from the Youth Development Study, a four-year longitudinal study of the developmental and psychological implications of work experience in adolescence. The results found that adolescent volunteering was significantly related to several educational, psychological, work-related, and attitudinal variables. Students who participate in volunteer activities have higher educational goals and aspirations, higher grade point averages, and more intrinsic motivation toward school than nonvolunteers.

Kennedy, E. M. (1991). National service and education for citizenship. *Phi Delta Kappan, 72,* 771–773.

Senator Kennedy suggests that adolescents enjoy being involved in community service and encourages school and agencies to help provide opportunities for community service. The National and Community Service Act of 1990, passed by the 101st Congress, helps to fund programs through which students from kindergarten through college provide service to their communities. A list of national resources for service-learning is provided.

Kielsmeier, J. C. (2000). A time to serve, a time to learn. *Phi Delta Kappan, 81,* 652–657.

Service is at an all-time high among youth, bringing meaning and purpose to many school programs. Many youth volunteer because they want to and not because they are forced to participate. Staff development and training for teachers have not kept up with program growth. Service-learning can have a strong and important impact on the youth of America, but in order to be effective, programs must have strong and well-prepared adult leaders and retain proper funding.

Kielsmeier, J., & Klopp, C. (2002). Service-learning: Positive youth development in the classroom and community. *Community Youth Development Journal, 3* (2), 33–39.

This article was published in a special issue of this journal, which is dedicated to increasing service-learning opportunities for youth in community agencies and youth serving organizations. The entire journal issue is valuable for persons interested in using service-learning as a means for promoting positive development among youth. This article describes five components of service-learning, youth voice/ownership, addressing a genuine community need, addressing specific learning objectives or curricula, reflection, and project process, and illustrates the application of these components to specific service projects. These five components of service-learning not only help communities and schools but also, most importantly, build a child's sense of identity and confidence.

Leming, J. S. (2001). Integrating a structured ethical reflection curriculum into high school community service experiences: Impact on students' sociomoral development. *Adolescence, 36* (141), 33–45.

In order to evaluate the effectiveness of reflection activities that focus on the ethical nature of community service, three groups of students were compared on measures of adolescent identity development before and after completion of the community service program. Students who completed the ethical reasoning component demonstrated greater gains in identity development than students who completed reflection with no ethical reasoning component and a control group of students who did not complete community service. The findings suggest that an ethical reasoning component in reflection helps students to think more systemically about situations from an ethical point of view.

LeSourd, S. J. (1997). Community service in a multicultural nation. *Theory into Practice, 36*, 157–163.

The author describes how service-learning experiences can foster connectedness to others, humane qualities, and a desire to construct the public good. In order for service-learning experience to achieve these effects, it must induce an emotional reaction from the student and be "carefully integrated into an academic structure." The author argues that service activities that increase interactions across social groups are necessary to prepare citizens for a pluralistic nation.

Middleton, E. B., & Kelly, K. R. (1996). Effects of community service on adolescent personality development. *Counseling and Values, 40*, 132–142.

This study explored the effects of participation in community service activities among 145 high school students aged fifteen to eighteen years. Although quantitative analyses provided limited evidence of change, qualitative analyses did suggest some positive changes. Students who participated in community service suggested that service participation enhanced their ability to help others, to develop new relationships, and to feel better about themselves.

Miller, F. (1994). Gender differences in adolescents' attitudes toward mandatory community service. *Journal of Adolescence, 17*, 381–393.

This study explored high school students' attitudes toward community service in general and their attitudes toward a mandatory community service requirement. Reasons underlying the students' attitudes toward mandatory service were also explored. Ninety-one male and female ninth- to twelfth-grade students read a script concerning a community service requirement being proposed by the state legislature and then responded to a series of questions concerning their attitudes, thoughts, and reasoning about the script. Female students were more positive than males about the mandatory service proposal. In general, students in upper grades gave more reasons both for and against the proposal than did students in lower grades.

Miller, G. M., & Neese, L. A. (1997). Self-esteem and reaching out: Implications for service-learning. *Professional School Counseling, 1,* 29–32.

This article describes service as a way of enhancing self-esteem among students. Through involvement in their communities, students are expected to develop a sense of caring for others and become aware of their own altruistic qualities. The authors provide a detailed description of a service-learning program in South Carolina, which was one of the original eight states to initiate service-learning in the schools. The authors suggest that service-learning is a positive option that counselors may wish to explore to benefit students and their communities.

Myers-Lipton, S. J. (1996). Effect of service-learning on college students' attitudes toward international understanding. *Journal of College Student Development, 37,* 659–668.

This study examined the effect of a two-year service-learning program (SLP), directed toward increasing international understanding and problem-solving. Twenty-five students performed a minimum of six hours of community service per week during the school semester, which was formally integrated into four academic courses. In addition, students participated in a month-long summer service-learning experience in Jamaica. Each service-learning class and two nonequivalent control groups (one composed of student volunteers and the other composed of the general student population) completed the International Understanding Scale before the SLP began, after the first summer service experience, and two years after the completion of the SLP. Overall, the students who were involved in SLP demonstrated greater gains in international understanding than other students.

O'Keefe, J. M. (1997). Children and community service: Character education in action. *Journal of Education, 179,* 47–62.

This article summarizes literature concerning school-based community service programs and discusses the potential of community service for developing student character. The author provides an in-depth examination of school-based community service programs offered at several urban Catholic schools and highlights the benefits of community service for the schools and the children. The models provided by these schools may be helpful to other schools, both private and public, that are interested in building student character through community service.

Putnam, R. (1995). Bowling alone: America's declining social capital. *Journal of Democracy, 6,* 65–77.

Robert Putnam's writings have been influential in providing a rationale for promoting service involvement among youth. Putnam begins by noting trends that American participation in government, politics, and community involvement have declined sharply over the past generation, and more so in the last decade. Participation in religious groups, labor unions, parent-teacher associations, and civic organization such as the Red Cross, Boy Scouts, Lions, and the Shriners, have all declined. In comparison with the past, Americans are less likely to join leagues, such as bowling, and more likely to go alone. These trends are of concern because there is less social interaction among community members and a greater detachment from civic responsibility. Putnam notes some countertrends with a rise in new forms of civic organization. For example, there has been a rapid growth in environmental and feminist groups, as well as the American Association of Retired Persons, which is now considered the largest private organization in the world. Although these "mass-membership" organizations have important political agendas, they do not generally provide for social interaction. Putnam argues that public policies and technological advances need to be examined regarding their impact on social networks. The structure of organizations and what attracts individuals to them need to be assessed, so we can once again become a "civic society."

Putnam, R. (2002). Bowling together. *The American Prospect, 13* (3).

Putnam compares America in 2002 with his description of civic engagement in 1995, presenting data from a survey administered between mid-October to mid-November 2001 that documents an increase in civic attitudes and behavior, especially trust in government.

Putnam maintains that opportunities for a "civic renewal" were created by the tragedies of September 11. He expresses the hope that government leaders will take advantage of the moment to support youth's involvement in political and social activity by increasing funding for AmeriCorps. Putnam's survey reveals an openness on the part of the U.S. citizenry to social justice and racial equity and suggests that policies should be initiated to increase multiculturalism and reduce ethnic and social class divisions and disparities.

Raskoff, S. A., & Sundeen, R. A. (2000). Community service programs in high schools. *Law and Contemporary Problems, 62,* 74–111.

This article examines high school community service programs as mechanisms of socialization and civic participation. The authors discuss the evolution of community service within schools and the rationales for program development. They then present a summary of program effects on student academic and personal development, according to available research findings. This is followed by an overview of key program elements and processes that are critical to successful outcomes. They also share results of surveys reporting student responses to high school service programs. Finally, the authors present their own three-year case study of high school community service in Los Angeles County, involving surveying and in-depth interviews with high school administrators and faculty, with community organizations in which students volunteer, and with participating students. Raskoff and Sundeen emphasize the importance of school-based community service programs in developing citizenship values. They recommend increased communication between schools and community organizations as an important step to improving students' service experiences.

Riley, R., & Wofford, H. (2000). The reaffirmation of the Declaration of Principles. *Phi Delta Kappan, 81,* 670–672.

In 1995, thirty states participated in a meeting called School Improvement: Strategies for Connecting Schools and Communities, which was sponsored by the U.S. Department of Education and the Corporation for National Service. The goal of the meeting was to find better ways to link schools and communities through service and six principles were identified to accomplish this. Examples of the ways in which these principles have been implemented across the country are presented in this article, authored by the secretary of education in the Clinton administration and the CEO of the Corporation for National Service. One high school in Virginia designed service projects that educated students on the dangers of drinking and driving, restored an American Indian burial ground, and repaired donated computers for community agencies. In another school in Wisconsin, students studied literature about domestic violence and wrote poems on this topic. Other examples are given, but the authors maintain that regardless of the school and location, everyone can get involved in implementing the six principles.

Rosenthal, S., Feiring, C., & Lewis, M. (1998). Political volunteering from late adolescence to young adulthood: Patterns and predictors. *Journal of Social Issues. Special Issue: Political development: Youth growing up in a global community, 54,* 477–493.

This study sought to identify characteristics that predict volunteerism among late adolescents. One hundred and five participants reported their volunteer involvement at ages eighteen and twenty-one. In addition, measures of cognitive ability, participation in social organizations, life stress, and family characteristics were completed concerning their lives from infancy through adolescence. Results indicated that most teens are involved in at least one volunteer activity during their adolescence, but that the rate of volunteerism in political activity increases substantially between the ages of eighteen to twenty-one. Cognitive ability, family cohesiveness, and membership in social organizations, such as the Boy Scouts, were the strongest predictors of volunteer activity during late adolescence. The results suggest that aspects of the social environment can provide incentives that increase volunteer activity.

Rutter, R. A., & Newmann, F. M. (1989). The potential of community service to enhance civic responsibility. *Social Education, 53,* 371–74.

In this article, the authors offer practical information for developing and implementing community service programs. In addition, they provide estimates of U.S. high school student participation in community service, describe the types of service programs and experiences offered to students, and provide evidence that service programs may not have realized their potential for increasing civic responsibility.

Scales, P. C., Blyth, D. A., Berkas, T. H., & Kielsmeier, J. C. (2000). The effects of service-learning on middle school students' social responsibility and academic success. *Journal of Early Adolescence, 20,* 332–358.

This paper reports findings from a study of 1,153 sixth- through eighth-grade students from three middle schools, one in Kentucky, one in Massachusetts, and one in Missouri. Students who had participated in service-learning were compared with students who had not been involved on levels of social responsibility and achievement. Findings suggest that involvement in service-learning can counter declines in social responsibility and negative school attitudes that occur among middle-school students. In comparison with nonservice students, those involved in service-learning maintained their level of concern for others and declined less in parent communication. Among those participating in service, being involved in service for more than thirty hours contributed to enhanced efficacy in helping others, and completion of a high number of reflection activities contributed to academic effort and a sustained positive view of school.

Schine, J. (1997). School-based service: Reconnecting schools, communities, and youth at the margin. *Theory into Practice, 36,* 170–175.

Schine argues that service-learning addresses developmental needs of early adolescents that may be overlooked in traditional school curricula. It is argued that inner city youth, in particular, may benefit from service-learning programs. Schine describes a student-initiated program that promotes understanding and communication between Dominican youth and local police. This program demonstrates how meaningful service activity can bring school and community together. Next, Schine describes several service-learning efforts sponsored by the urban National Helper's Network, noting ways that service-learning can empower those who serve, as well as those who are served. Schine reiterates the importance of quality service-learning programs that engage students and teachers in a context of richness and challenge. In order to be effective, service-learning programs must be carefully planned and integrated into the academic curriculum.

Schondel, C. K., & Boehm, K. E. (2000). Motivational needs of adolescent volunteers. *Adolescence, 35,* 335–344.

This scholarly article describes a study examining the personal and environmental factors that motivate adolescents to participate in volunteer opportunities. The authors administered a questionnaire to adolescents participating in a variety of volunteer activities. The adolescent volunteers at each site indicated that they experienced outside pressure to volunteer. Personal fulfillment gained from helping others, opportunities for social interaction, and the desire for recognition from others were additional reasons given for volunteering. The findings are consistent with the authors' predictions that adolescent volunteers are motivated by different factors than are adults.

Shumer, R. (1994). Community-based learning: Humanizing education. *Journal of Adolescence, 17,* 357–367.

This article presents a study of the secondary school Community-Based Learning Program (CBL). Program goals are: to bring community learning to the classroom, to reduce drop-out rates, and to promote citizenship through community involvement. Students participating in CBL were compared with non-CBL students from the same school. Researchers interviewed students and teachers, administered surveys, and conducted student case studies. Results revealed that CBL students had higher grades and school attendance than mainstream students. Students reported that doing community work and having college-aged tutors were the most important parts of the CBL program. This program provided many opportunities for close interaction with adults that are not available in traditional school settings. These personal relationships were found to be the most important positive factor for students.

Shumer, R. (1997). What research tells us about designing service-learning programs. *NASSP Bulletin, 81,* 18–24.

The author presents guidelines, derived from research, that can be used to design effective service-learning programs. Effective service-learning programs have clear goals with specific desired outcomes. Evaluation strategies are incorporated into the overall plan. Service projects involve activities that are meaningful to participants, take place over sufficient time to achieve an impact, and include a reflection component. Staff characteristics are also important. Teachers should be supportive of experiential learning. Moreover, successful service-learning programs are ones that elicit administrative support, encourage flexibility, provide staff development, and encourage collaboration by involving community partners in program planning, implementation, and evaluation.

Smolla, R. A. (1999). The constitutionality of mandatory public school community service programs. *Law and Contemporary Problems, 62,* 113–140.

This article discusses constitutionality questions raised by mandatory community service programs within public schools. Smolla divides constitutional concerns into two categories: global issues of required student service in schools and the inclusion or exclusion of specific agencies for student service involvement. Required service has been protested as a violation of the Thirteenth Amendment (involuntary servitude), the Fourteenth Amendment (due process), and the First Amendment (freedom of association, freedom against forced speech, and free exercise of religion). Issues of agency inclusion or exclusion have been debated in terms of the First Amendment (establishment clause) relating to student service involvement with religious or political organizations. Smolla examines constitutional bases for and against required service and agency inclusion or exclusion and summarizes court cases related to both issues.

Stukas, A. A., Clary, E. G., & Snyder, M. (1999). Service-learning: Who benefits and why? *Social Policy Report: Society for Research in Child Development, 13*, 1–19.

This paper was the headline piece of a social policy report issued by the Society for Research in Child Development. Goals of service-learning programs for students, institutions, and the community are reviewed. Research on "best practices" of service-learning is summarized. Based on the research literature the authors conclude that service-learning programs should: (1) support autonomy by encouraging students to have a voice in determining details of service activities, (2) be designed so that there is a match between the goals of service-learning and the activities offered, (3) attend to the relationships among all participants, and (4) provide opportunities for reflection.

Stukas, A. A., Snyder, M., & Clary, E. G. (1999). The effects of "mandatory volunteerism" on intentions to volunteer. *Psychological Science, 10*, 59–64.

The authors present findings from two studies which examined the effects of mandatory volunteerism on students' intentions to volunteer. The first study examined required service-learning among 371 undergraduate business students and the second study compared 63 undergraduates participating in voluntary and required service. Among students participating in mandatory community service, only those students who felt externally controlled stated that they were less likely to volunteer in the future.

Stukas, A. A., Switzer, G. E., Dew, M. A., Goycoolea, J. M., & Simmons, R. G. (1999). Parental helping models, gender, and service-learning. *Journal of Prevention and Intervention in the Community, 18*, 5–18.

Research suggests that girls, as well as students whose parents serve as models of helping, may be more likely to benefit from mandatory service-learning programs. The role of gender and the influence of parental helping models were examined in a survey of eighty-six seventh-grade students who completed a community service requirement during the school year. Girls reported more positive feelings about the service-learning program and indicated that they were more likely to volunteer in the future than did boys. Students whose parents provided models of helping also indicated a greater intention of volunteering in the future than those without parental helping models. Moreover, girls with parental helping models were more likely to have self-images of altruism than girls without parental helping models. The presence of parental helping models was not related to altruistic self-image among boys. The authors discuss the implications of their findings for the socialization of prosocial behavior among boys and girls.

Switzer, G. E., Simmons, R. G., Dew, M. A., Regalski, J. M., & Wang, C. (1995). The effect of a school-based helper program on adolescent self-image, attitudes and behavior. *Journal of Early Adolescence, 15,* 429–55.

This study sought to assess the effects of participation in a school-based helper program on the self-image, attitudes, and behaviors of early adolescents. One hundred and seventy-one seventh-grade students were assigned either to a helper program, through which students carried out volunteer helping activities, or to a control group. Results were gender-specific with boys in the helper program showing positive changes in self-esteem in comparison with girls and nonhelpers.

Tenenbaum, I. (2000). Building a framework for service-learning: The South Carolina experience. *Phi Delta Kappan, 81,* 666–669.

The author maintains that academic standards should be applied to service-learning programs and that well-trained professionals are needed to implement them. He explains how this has been accomplished in South Carolina, where service-learning and school-to-work programs have been integrated in the classroom and in "real world" situations. For example, in one rural school district, students applied their chemistry and math skills to help problem-solve the surrounding community's water quality. Based upon the students' findings, the community built a water tower through which 450 families were able to obtain water. South Carolina is one of eight states to receive financial support from W. K. Kellogg Foundation to create a Peer Consultant Initiative. Through this, practitioners and youth are trained in service-learning theory and practices. South Carolina has also supported service-learning training as part of teacher education programs.

Walker, T. (2002). Service as a pathway to political participation: What research tells us. *Applied Developmental Science,* 6 (4), 183–188.

In this study, the author examines the impact of community service on student participation in politics. Through an extensive review of research on service, Walker deduced that while service experiences increase the likelihood that students will serve their communities in the future, service does not automatically educate young people about politics or increase political participation. Many researchers believe this is due to the negativity associated with political organizations. The connections between service and politics need to be more fully developed in order to increase student engagement in political processes.

Weah, W., Simmons, V.C., & Hall, M. (2000). Service-learning and multicultural/multiethnic perspective. *Phi Delta Kappan, 81,* 673–675.

The authors describe the ways in which service-learning can increase multicultural learning and be relevant for diverse groups of students. Service projects can help youth connect with their heritage, address issues of race, achieve academic excellence, and build self-esteem. Some organizations, such as the National Indian Youth Leadership Project (NIYPL), United Negro Fund, and W. K. Kellogg Foundation, emphasize cultural diversity in service-learning. Service-learning can help students to challenge their fears about diversity and social inequalities and raise important questions about social equality. Service-learning is most productive when diverse people work together. Service-learning should seek to enable students to gain from their diverse traditions and cultures.

Yates, M., & Youniss, J. (1996). Community service and political-moral identity in adolescents. *Journal of Research on Adolescence, 6,* 271–284.

In this article, the authors present a theoretical framework for understanding how community service stimulates identity development in adolescents. The framework is rooted in Erik Erikson's (1968) writings, which stress the sociohistorical component of identity. Narratives from reflective essays of 132 Black parochial high school juniors who worked at a soup kitchen for the homeless as part of a school-based community service program are used to illustrate the framework. Findings from the analysis of student essays suggest that service experiences can stimulate student thinking and awareness concerning the political organization and moral structure of society.

Yates, M., & Youniss, J. (1996). A developmental perspective on community service in adolescence. *Social Development, 5*, 85–111.

In this article, the authors review forty-four studies concerning the benefits of community service for adolescent volunteers. The reviewed articles were published between 1952 and 1994. Overall the studies suggest that service activities can foster prosocial development among adolescents, including growth in feelings of agency, social relatedness, and moral-political awareness. Those service programs that offer intense experiences and provide opportunities for social interaction with those being served are most likely to enhance the prosocial development of the volunteers.

Yates, M., & Youniss, J. (1998). Community service and political identity development in adolescence. *Journal of Social Issues, 54*, 495–512.

This article addresses the relationship between political socialization and identity development. The authors seek to identify social processes, which foster youth involvement in political activities. Data from a study of Black urban adolescents who participated in a year-long service-learning program are used to illustrate factors that contribute to youth political commitment. The authors conclude that service experiences can help to foster political socialization and identity as youth think about the political implications of their experience and their roles and responsibilities as citizens.

Youniss, J., McLellan, J. A., & Yates, M. (1997). What we know about engendering civic identity. *American Behavioral Scientist, 40*, 620–631.

The authors review studies that show a link between participation in organized activities during the high school years and civic participation after fifteen or more years. Students who participated in high school government or community service projects were more likely to vote and to join community organizations as adults than were students who did not participate during high school. The authors argue that citizenship and civic identity, including a sense of agency and social responsibility, develop as a result of participation in civic and service activities during youth.

Youniss, J., McLellan, J. A., & Yates, M. (1999). Religion, community service, and identity in American youth. *Journal of Adolescence, 22,* 243–253.

In this paper, the authors explore the role of religion and community service in the identity development of adolescents. The authors present research findings that connect community service and religiosity. A review of research literature indicates that youth who believe that religion is important are more likely to participate in community service than youth who do not view religion as important. Youth who are involved in church-sponsored service articulate a religious rationale for their involvement in service, but are not service "nerds" nor adolescents who focus on a single issue. The authors conclude from this data that many adolescents both value religion and are involved in their schools and in the improvement of their communities.

Youniss, J., & Yates, M. (1999). Youth service and moral-civic identity: A case for everyday morality. *Educational Psychology Review, 11,* 361–376.

The authors review the literature on moral development in order to understand the role of service in enhancing the political-moral development of youth. Research suggests that youth activism, engagement in interpersonal relationships based upon mutual respect, and establishing a relationship with the broader society fulfill important developmental functions and are important for positive moral and civic development. The authors argue that participation in community service can contribute to respect for humanity and the development of a mature moral and civic identity that persists into adulthood.

Youniss, J., Yates, M., & Su, Y. (1997). Social integration: Community service and marijuana use in high school seniors. *Journal of Adolescent Research, 12,* 245–262.

This study compares adolescents who participate in community service with those who do not participate. Based upon self-report questionnaires, students were classified as belonging to one of four groups that reflect different attitudes toward school-adult norms and peer fun. The four groups were: (1) School—participants orientated toward school-adult norms but not peer fun, (2) Party—participants orientated toward peer fun but not school-adult norms, (3) All-around—participants orientated toward school-adult norms and peer fun, and (4) Neither—participants not orientated toward school-adult norms or peer fun. The four groups were compared on levels of participation in community service, religion, and politics. Students in the School and All-around groups participated in higher levels of community service, religion, and politics in comparison with students in the other two groups. Students in the Party group used marijuana more than students in the School group, but not more than students in the All-around group. The authors conclude that peer culture is related to participation in community service, marijuana use, and identification with school-adult norms.

VIDEO RESOURCES

All the Difference: Youth Service in Minnesota

Type: VHS
Length: 27 minutes
Cost: $20
Source: National Youth Leadership Council
1910 W. County Road B
St. Paul, MN 55113
(612) 631-3672, x1
http://www.nylc.org

Vignettes of service projects in schools throughout the state of Minnesota. Students from one of the schools filmed and edited the video.

At the Table: Youth Voices in Decision-Making

Type: VHS
Length: 14 minutes
Cost: $19.95
Source: The Innovation Center for Community & Youth Development
National 4-H Council
7100 Connecticut Avenue
Chevy Chase, MD 20815
(301) 961-2937
http://www.fourhcouncil.edu/cyd

This video helps to make a case for the involvement of youth in decision-making. In the first part of the video, young people explain why they want to participate in the decision-making processes of their organizations. Adults discuss some of their reservations about involving youth and explain how their actual experiences in working with young people have changed their opinions. The second part of the video describes some of the steps that organizations must take to make it possible for youth and adults to work in effective partnerships. This video was produced in conjunction with Youth on Board, the Youth Leadership Institute, the Center for Youth as Resources, and Community Partnerships with Youth and serves as a valuable tool in generating discussion about giving youth more responsibility in organizations and what it takes to do that.

Citizen Stories

Type: VHS
Length: 30 minutes
Cost: $20.00
Source: Close Up Foundation
             44 Canal Plaza
             Alexandria, VA 22314
             (800) 765-3131
             http://www.closeup.org

This video presents the stories of five individuals who have chosen to become involved in their communities to make a difference. It explains how they identified the problem, decided to address the issue, and how their efforts brought about positive community change. Citizens profiled in the video include a teen who feeds the homeless and Ralph Nader, who has fought full-time for consumer rights.

Community: An Intergenerational Friendship Program

Type: VHS
Length: 20 minutes
Cost: $35
Source: Bi-Folkal Productions, Inc.
             809 Williamson Street
             Madison, WI 53703
             (608) 251-2818
             http://www.bifolkal.org

This video promotes the idea of intergenerational visiting to potential volunteers, parents, funding agencies, and administrators of nursing facilities. It was developed by "Community," a model project in Phoenix, Arizona, through which students visit nursing homes as part of their school curriculum. Program guides, as well as this video, were produced to enable other schools and community organizations to set up successful intergenerational programs.

The Courage to Care: The Strength to Serve...

Type: VHS
Length: 15 minutes
Cost: $12.50
Source: Maryland Student Service Alliance
            Maryland State Department of Education
            200 West Baltimore Street
            Baltimore, MD 21201-2427
            (410) 767-0358
            http://sailor.lib.md.us/mssa

This video presents some of the essential elements involved in the preparation and implementation of effective service programs. The reflection component of service-learning is highlighted.

A Culture of Giving: Service-Learning in Native American Communities

Type: VHS
Length: 20 minutes
Cost: Free
Source: W. K. Kellogg Foundation
            One Michigan Avenue East
            Battle Creek, MI 49017-4058
            (269) 968-1611
            http://www.wkkf.org/

This video provides examples of service-learning projects completed in Native American communities in New Mexico and Northern Michigan. The video is narrated by Buffy Sainte-Marie and includes commentary from students and teachers concerning their experiences.

Democracy and Rights: One Citizen's Challenge

Type: VHS
Length: 32 minutes
Cost: $49.95
Source: Close Up Foundation
            44 Canal Plaza
            Alexandria, VA 22314
            (800) 765-3131
            http://www.closeup.org

This video provides valuable lessons in citizenship, courage, perseverance, and democratic social action. It portrays the story of the nine

Black students who climbed the stairs of Central High School in Little Rock, Arkansas, thereby taking the first step toward integration of the school.

Hidden Heroes: Youth Activism Today

Type: VHS
Length: 24 minute
Cost: $65
Source: Andrew Goodman Foundation, Inc.
            161 West 86th Street
            New York, NY 10024
            (212) 362-7265

This documentary video, released in 2000, presents the courageous accomplishments of youth to counter the negative youth images prevalent in the media. The film tells the stories of four youth groups from different parts of the country and what they have done to improve their communities by addressing critical social and economic issues. These youth provide examples of what young people can accomplish when they take leadership roles in working toward social change. The achievements of these young people are placed within the historical context of struggle and change within this country. A curriculum guide is provided that is useful for schools, colleges, churches, synagogues, and community organizations.

Learning In Deed: The Power of Service-Learning for American Schools

Type: VHS
Length: 19 minutes
Cost: Free
Source: National Commission on Service-Learning
            Education Development Center
            55 Chapel Street,
            Newton, MA 02458-1060
            (617) 618-2136
            http://www.servicelearningpartnership.org

This 2002 video was produced by the National Commission on Service-Learning, which recommends that service-learning be part of the school curriculum for all children from kindergarten through twelfth grade. Service-learning is described and its primary benefits are presented. The video was developed for educators, school board members, parents, and policymakers who want to become informed about service-learning and who might use the video to spread the word about the benefits of service-learning.

Learning That Matters: Service-Learning at Clemson University

Type: VHS
Length: 22 minutes
Cost: $15
Source: National Dropout Prevention Center
College of Health, Education, and Human Development
Clemson University
209 Martin Street
Clemson, SC 29634-0726
(864) 656-2599
http://www.dropoutprevention.org

Faculty members from Clemson University describe the challenges of implementing service-learning courses and discuss their solutions to these challenges.

Making the Case for Service-Learning

Type: VHS
Length: 12 minutes
Cost: $20
Source: National Youth Leadership Council
1910 W. County Road B
St. Paul, MN 55113
(612) 631-3672, x1
http://www.nylc.org

This 1996 video includes demonstrations of service-learning projects, explains the methodology of service-learning, and shows how service experiences can be integrated into school curriculum to enhance student learning and development.

Making the Connection Series

The following three videos were created in 1997 and 1998 as part of the training sessions of three state national demonstration projects in service-learning.

Driving Force or Afterthought

Type: VHS
Length: 26 minutes
Cost: $20, includes guidebook

Presents Rahima Wade, from the University of Iowa, describing four strategies for integrating service-learning into school curricula, including single subject, school-wide, district-wide, and thematic approaches.

Enriching Learning through Service

Type: VHS
Length: 35 minutes
Cost: $20, includes guidebook

Denise Schares, Ed.D., of the Vinton-Shellsburg School District in Vinton, Iowa, identifies practical steps for integrating community service with the academic curriculum. Includes ideas for projects, things to consider while developing a program. and thoughts on the future of service-learning.

Service-Learning at the District Level

Type: VHS
Length: 22 minutes
Cost: $20

This video featuring Rick Nelson, Youth Development Coordinator of the White Bear Lake Area Schools in Minnesota, demonstrates the benefits of service-learning and innovative program ideas and strategies.

All three of the above videos can be obtained from:

Source: National Youth Leadership Council
             1667 Snelling Avenue North, Suite D300
             St. Paul, MN 55108
             (651) 631-3672
             http://www.nylc.org/publications.cfm

Moments Frozen in Time

Type: VHS
Length: 14 minutes
Cost: $30
Source: Bi-Folkal Productions, Inc.
             809 Williamson St.
             Madison, WI 53703
             (608) 251-2818
             http://www.bifolkal.org

This video presents an intergeneration history project in which RSVP volunteers and ninth-grade students participate and collaborate. The video highlights the lessons learned by all involved.

Orientation for Youth: Aging and Nursing Homes

Type: VHS
Length: 40 minutes
Cost: $35

Source: Bi-Folkal Productions, Inc.
          809 Williamson Street
          Madison, WI 53703
          (608) 251-2818

This video is helpful for individuals interested in preparing youth for service in a nursing home facility. It can also be a useful tool for training teachers or group leaders who hope to prepare youth for intergenerational service.

Route to Reform: Service-Learning and School Improvement

Type: VHS
Cost: $20
Source: National Youth Leadership Council
          1667 Snelling Avenue North, Suite D300
          St. Paul, MN 55108
          (651) 631-3672
          http://www.nylc.org/publications.cfm

This 1994 video provides a glimpse of three exemplary interdisciplinary service-learning programs at the elementary, middle, and high school levels, located in Minnesota, Illinois, and Washington.

Service-Learning: Curriculum, Standards, and the Community

Type: VHS
Length: 36 minutes
Cost: $99
Source: The Master Teacher
          Leadership Lane
          P.O. Box 1207
          Manhattan, Kansas 66505-1207

This 1998 video is designed to help professionals develop effective service-learning programs that integrate community service, academic learning, civic consciousness and social development. Examples of community service projects across the country are highlighted, in conjunction with interviews of community leaders and teachers.

Service-Learning in Higher Education: A Portrait of Five Institutions

Type: VHS
Length: 20 minutes
Cost: $15
Source: National Dropout Prevention Center

College of Health, Education, and Human Development
Clemson University
209 Martin Street
Clemson, SC 29634-0726
(864) 656–2599
http://www.dropoutprevention.org

This video illustrates how service-learning has been developed and implemented at five varied college campuses, including a community college, a historically Black college, a land-grant university, a state university, and a private liberal arts college.

Taking the Reins Together: Youth/Adult Partnerships

Type: VHS
Length: 8 minutes
Cost: $19.95
Source: The Innovation Center for Community & Youth Development
            National 4-H Council
            7100 Connecticut Avenue
            Chevy Chase, MD 20815
            (301) 961-2937
            http://www.fourhcouncil.edu/cyd

This video was developed in conjunction with the National 4-H Council curriculum on Creating Youth/Adult Partnerships. The curriculum seeks to increase the ability of youth and adults to work together so that youth can attain meaningful leadership roles working with adults concerning issues of importance to youth. The video illustrates how a diverse group of youth and adults can collaborate as equal partners in addressing important concerns. Young people and adults discuss their experiences in working together in partnerships. This video is useful for helping youth and adults realize the power of youth/adult partnerships.

Youth Consultants: Putting It All Together

Type: VHS
Length: 22 minutes
Cost: $15
Source: National Dropout Prevention Center
            College of Health, Education, and Human Development
            Clemson University
            209 Martin Street
            Clemson, SC 29634-0726
            (864) 656-2599
            http://www.dropoutprevention.org

This video demonstrates how the voices of youth can be important in making the case for and developing service-learning in their schools, communities, and nation.

INTERNET SITES

Afterschool.gov
  http://www.afterschool.gov

A website sponsored by the U.S. federal government with a primary goal of providing a resource for teens and adults interested in ways youth can productively spend their out-of-school time. This website has several sections, including information for individuals interested in implementing programs for youth and addressing issues about funding and volunteers. There are two sections on the website that are geared especially for kids and teens. These pages include information on how to get involved in community service and volunteering. In addition, this website provides links to a number of governmental resources, updates on relevant legislation, organizations, and research and publications that are geared toward youth.

Ask ERIC
  http://www.askeric.org

Ask ERIC is a useful Internet service supported by the U.S. Department of Education's Educational Resource Information Center (ERIC) system, which provides education-related information and resources to teachers, librarians, counselors, administrators, parents, and students. The Ask ERIC website consists of a question-and-answer service, virtual library, and access to ERIC databases to search for research and information on a variety of topics related to education, including service-learning and community service. Through the question-and-answer service, anyone can post an education-related question and an email reply will be sent with resources and a bibliography list of current information that addresses the topic. The virtual library includes lesson plans, listservs and other education-related information and resources for professionals in the field of education.

Big Brothers Big Sisters of America
  http://www.bbbsa.org

The Big Brothers Big Sisters of America website includes information on the history of this youth-mentoring organization, as well as current news about Big Brothers Big Sisters. The website includes a frequently asked questions page that gives detailed information on the organization and access to two research studies examining the outcomes of the Big Brothers Big Sisters program. Information is also available on how to become involved in the local chapter. In addition, there are stories that exemplify the success of the program through personal narratives, as well as career opportunities available within the organization. Links to other youth and volunteer organizations and information on how to make contributions to the organization are also available on the website.

The Big Dummy's Guide to Service-Learning
   http://www.fiu.edu/~time4chg/Library/bigdummy.htm

The Big Dummy's Guide is a practical website for individuals who are interested in integrating service-learning into their courses, developing and implementing community service projects, or keeping informed about relevant issues related to volunteerism and service-learning (e.g., incorporating reflection into service and mandatory service programs). The website lists questions and answers asked by individuals interested in service-learning and includes 101 Ideas for Combining Service and Learning, a useful list of ideas for teachers who are interested in engaging in service-learning at the college or university level in specific subjects (e.g., art, history, political science). This site also includes a frequently asked questions page.

The Big Help
   http://www.nick.com/all_nick/specials/bighelp/

A nationwide, grassroots movement sponsored by the Nickelodeon television channel, The Big Help is a website for youth who want to know how to get involved in their communities. Each year, The Big Help has a different focus. For example, in 2001 the focus of its campaign was water. Kids can learn about how to monitor, clean, and preserve water supplies. The website gives a list of tips and suggestions as to how kids can make a difference. The Big Help also encourages youth to volunteer time to improve their communities. The Big Helpmobile travels across the country to aquariums and zoos to provide education to youth about these important issues. Interested individuals can learn from the website when the Big Helpmobile will be in their area. The website also provides a Big Help toolkit for youth interested in engaging in their own service projects.

Campus Compact
   http://www.compact.org

The Campus Compact website includes a variety of resources for students, faculty, presidents of colleges and universities, and administrators involved in service-learning programs. Information regarding upcoming events, best practices and model programs, news about service-learning, examples of syllabi, and job postings are also available. This website includes links to other websites on service-learning, national service, service opportunities for students, higher education, diversity-related sites, policymaking opportunities for students, and links to other state compacts.

Campus Outreach Opportunity League (COOL)
http://www.cool2serve.org

The Campus Outreach Opportunity League (COOL) website includes information on the organization and training opportunities for individuals who want to implement community service programs on college campuses. To identify community service opportunities, an online resource center is accessible on the website. In addition, a calendar of events is posted, along with the COOL leadership curriculum and an alumni network.

Children's Express News
http://www.cenews.org

Children's Express is an international media organization that aims to provide children with a means to voice their opinions. Children from ages eight to eighteen use the organization in a variety of ways, but can report and/or edit stories that are broadcasted on television, in newspapers, on the radio, and online. There are currently 750 children who work directly for the organization, but thousands who use it to express their views online on current hot issues. The website is user-friendly and encourages interaction from the children. Online weekly polls encourage youth to have opinions about important issues. The homepage is filled with links to articles written by children about such issues as race, education, current events, politics, and so on. Children's Express encourages its readers to respond to articles and to give feedback about the organization and the website in general. It also provides instructions on how to submit an article to the organization so it may be published in some form. The Children's Express recently joined partnership with the W. K. Kellogg Foundation to explore diversity and current issues through the eyes of children. The website provides ways to support and become involved in Children's Express. In the future, Children's Express hopes to pave a more permanent presence for themselves worldwide in both developed and developing nations to encourage freedom of expression for children everywhere.

City Cares
http://www.citycares.org

The national City Cares website gives access to local City Cares affiliates. Local City Cares affiliates include: Atlanta; Baltimore; Boston; Chicago; Dallas, Texas; Los Angeles; Miami; Nashville; New York; Orlando, Florida; Phoenix, Arizona; San Diego, California; San Francisco; Seattle; Washington, D.C.; and the United Kingdom. The site gives information about the national umbrella organization and the services that each local City Cares affiliate provides. Individuals can locate local volunteer opportunities and examples of projects, serve-a-thons and special volunteer activities, and how to start a local City Cares organization.

CommunityService
http://www.communityservice.org

This website provides a matching service for individuals interested in volunteering with nonprofit organizations that are in need of volunteers. Individuals can go to the website to search for volunteer opportunities that match their interest or experience in areas of health, education, and arts and culture by entering their zip code. In addition, interested individuals can search for volunteer events in their community. Communityservice.org also offers a free email account for volunteers. Nonprofit organizations can use the website to post volunteer opportunities and events and to post profiles of their organizations. The website also includes reviews of organizations and volunteer opportunities and a journal section, which allows volunteers to share their experiences with others online.

Compendium of Assessment and Research Tools (CART)
http://cart.rmcdenver.com

CART is a free, accessible database that individuals can use online to search for tools or instruments for use in the assessment and research of service-learning and other educational or development programs for youth. Instruments are available to assist in assessing the design and implementation of programs (e.g., program characteristics, program quality, teacher's role, student engagement, and sources of support); the school, family, and community contexts in which the program takes place; and the outcomes of the program (e.g., academic-related, youth development, social, career development, citizenship, school, and community outcomes). For each instrument or assessment tool, the database gives information on the population it was used with, a description of the measure, and how to obtain the measure. Some measures are free of charge, while others are copyrighted and require permission and a fee.

Connect for Kids
  http://www.connectforkids.org

Connect for Kids is an Internet site designed for all adults who are interested in promoting healthy communities for youth. The Connect for Kids website is a comprehensive resource for adults who are interested in becoming active citizens and striving to better their communities for families and children. On the website, information can be accessed on more than thirty topics, ranging from youth development and community service to welfare reform and health issues that affect children. Individuals can access facts and statistics through reports and research, opinion polls, and book reviews on these relevant topics. The website includes a news section for current events, ideas for action that parents and families can take in their communities, as well as a list of organizations and calendar of events. The site provides listings according to state and is updated weekly. A features section links to articles that explain the relevance of issues that impact youth (e.g., children's mental health, out-of-school programs, the teen years). Individuals can also subscribe to weekly and monthly newsletters via email.

The Corporation for National Service
  http://www.nationalservice.org

This website gives an overview of national service programs, including information on how youth and adults can get involved in AmeriCorps, Learn and Serve America, and SeniorCorps. Service resources are available for members and alumni of AmeriCorps programs, as well as for project directors and administrators of national service programs. The website also includes current news and research about the impact of service programs and grant information and applications. In addition, state-by-state profiles of service programs; information on job listings, fellowships, and internships; and links to related service websites are also available on the website.

Directory of State Service Commission Web Sites
  http://members.aol.com/amostberg/page/service-sites.htm

The website lists state service organizations with Internet sites for each state, prepared by the Corporation for National Service.

Earth Force
  http://www.earthforce.org

The Earth Force website gives details on how youth can get involved in a range of programs to improve the environment (e.g., Get Out Spoke'n Campaign). Individuals can access a range of curriculum materials, including making neighborhoods more bike-friendly, and how to help youth learn to protect a river. In addition, the Earth Force website includes a variety of links to other organizations that promote environmental awareness and action, youth leadership, service-learning and community service, and government and bicycle-related organizations. Youth can also order products online for water monitoring through GREEN's online catalog.

Family Cares
  http://www.familycares.org

Family Cares is an online resource for parents who are interested in making a difference in their communities by engaging in family service projects. The overall mission of Family Cares, which is a program of the Child Charitable Development Association, is to promote caring in children through opportunities to help others. The website includes examples and details of family service projects and activities for young people. In addition, there are resources available on the site for parents to assist them in teaching their kids about social issues, including homelessness and hunger. Anyone can access the Family Cares Internet site free of charge.

Global Youth Action Network
  http://www.youthlink.org

The Global Youth Action Network provides an opportunity for youth and agencies that serve youth to share resources and information with the goal to increase youth action and engagement. This website provides resources for youth to speak out on important issues. Youth can fill out a National Youth Platform survey that indicates what issues are of the greatest concern to them, as well as their ideas about potential solutions. Once 1,000 surveys are collected in each country, the results are presented by the National Youth Action Council to the leader of that country. The website also provides information about awards given by this organization to youth who take action in their communities. Ideas for creating and implementing projects or community youth action summits are provided online in the *Youth Action Guide*. The website also provides an extensive database for youth and youth organizations to search for services, events, platforms, and organizations throughout the world. Finally, opportunities are posted for youth to get involved, special events, internships and jobs, scholarships and awards, as well as many other resources.

Hearts and Minds
http://www.heartsandminds.org

The Hearts and Minds website is a helpful resource for information on volunteering, social issues, nonprofit organizations, and self-help and support groups. For example, in the volunteering section, there are links to organizations and charities to which individuals can make donations, as well as resources for nonprofit organizations. In addition, there are links for organizations under specific topics/issues, including poverty and homelessness, the environment, tolerance (racism and human rights), labor and responsible business, and democracy. The website also includes inspirational quotes and articles on a variety of topics.

HEAVEN—Helping, Educate, Activate, Volunteer, and Empower via the Net
http://www.vergant.com/heavens

Established in 1997, HEAVEN (Helping, Educate, Activate, Volunteer, and Empower via the Net) is a nonprofit website that aims to use technology and the Internet to engage youth in learning about important issues and to improve their communities. The ANGELS (America's Network of Givers, Educators, Learners and Servers) program is an educational program for youth that utilizes the Internet to engage in community service for underserved areas. Over the course of the semester, youth learn invaluable skills in computers, as well as building skills in writing and community organizing to engage in a project to improve their community and to address a global issue. The ANGELS program is currently operating in New York City's schools. Examples of websites that youth have developed through this program are available on the HEAVEN website. In addition, the Y2 Connect section of the website gives detailed information on the digital divide and the importance of access to technology.

Idealist

http://www.idealist.org

Idealist is an Internet website sponsored by Action without Borders. Individuals can access and search a database of over 20,000 nonprofit and volunteer organizations internationally. On the Idealist website is a nonprofit career center, which includes job and internship openings, assistance on resumes, information about fellowships and academic programs in public service, volunteer and work opportunities abroad, and information for high school students who are interested in public service. In addition, the website has a frequently asked questions page regarding volunteerism and links to useful resources for nonprofit organizations to help manage their programs. Individuals can subscribe to a newsletter, *Ideas in Action*, via email that includes resources, articles, and updates on conferences relevant to volunteer and other nonprofit organizations. All services are free of charge.

Learning In Deed

http://www.learningindeed.org

Sponsored by the W. K. Kellogg Foundation, the Learning In Deed website is an excellent resource for up-to-date information on service-learning. This website contains information for students, educators, researchers, and policymakers interested in K–12 service-learning. The website also includes a newsroom for the latest information on the Learning In Deed initiative, tools and resources for teachers, students, and researchers, including current research, funding opportunities and resources, and a research network. Policymakers can learn about current legislation and activities across the United States. In addition, the website links to other useful service-learning resources and organizations.

Make-A-Difference Day

http://www.usaweekend.com/diffday/

An annual event every fourth Saturday in October, Make-A-Difference Day is a one-day, nationwide community service event sponsored by USA Today's Weekend magazine and partnered with the Points of Light Foundation. The website includes a database individuals can access to find volunteer opportunities. In addition, the website has a project idea generator for those who are trying to develop and implement their own service project for Make-A-Difference Day. The website includes a timeline, frequently asked questions page, and information about how to register and purchase merchandise and about awards for projects.

Mighty Media, Inc.

http://www.mightymedia.com

Mighty Media is a comprehensive, interactive online educational network geared toward young people in kindergarten through the 12th grade, teachers, and school administrators in the U.S. and internationally. The website focuses on addressing involvement in the areas of environmental education, service-learning, human rights, art, cultural diversity, and health education. Included in this educational network is access to various interactive forums. Teacher Talk is a site where teachers can interact and share ideas online. The Educational Resource Center includes information for teachers and school administrators on integrating social action in the classroom, including curriculum and lesson plans on various topics (e.g., environment, human rights, and service-learning) accessible on the site. The Key Pals Club is an online pen pal service to connect youth with other young people in different parts of the world to learn about other cultures. Through the Mighty Mentors program, teachers pair up via email to lend support and share ideas about teaching.

The service-learning-based program Youth In Action includes a description of the purpose of the program, a list of forum topics youth can discuss, links to organizations in which youth can become involved, and an online application that includes details about Youth In Action. The website also includes a web page, Bring the Noise, where kids can voice their opinions about important social issues in their communities and schools. Users have to register to access the full services of the website.

The National Mentoring Partnership

http://www.mentoring.org

The National Mentoring Partnership is a program that promotes mentoring and serves as a resource for current mentors or for individuals who wish to become mentors. The site includes descriptions of how to become a mentor and ideas and tips on how to improve your mentoring relationship. Further instructions provided by the organization include how to run a mentoring program in one's own community and how to take action within one's community. Anybody can join the National Mentoring Program online; however, there is a member fee. Members have access to current news about mentoring, information on training opportunities, a listserv for members, and a member directory. The site provides access to research findings on mentoring, best practices, information on how to obtain training materials, a frequently asked questions page, and an online store.

The National Service-Learning Clearinghouse
http://www.servicelearning.org

The National Service-Learning Clearinghouse offers a useful website that includes extensive information on service-learning, research reports, and several databases to search for information on service-learning from kindergarten to higher education. Partnered with Learn and Serve America, this website has links to many relevant service-learning resources and organizations. Available resources include a frequently asked questions page, publications, bibliographies, videos, and newsletters. Individuals can subscribe to a listserv to connect with other professionals interested in service-learning.

The National Service-Learning Partnership
http://www.service-learningpartnership.org

The National Service-Learning Partnership website is a tool for those who seek to promote service-learning and make it a standard in a youth's educational development. The website encourages interested persons to enroll in the partnership and receive information from the chair as well as legislative updates from Congress. A newsletter is offered by emailing the website, as are monthly electronic alerts about policy education efforts. The website offers a number of resources ranging from advocacy assistance to policy advocacy education workshops.

National Service Resource Center
http://nsrc.etr.org

The National Service Resource Center is a website for programs funded by the Corporation for National Service. Individuals can find information regarding community service. Some of the services the website provides include a database to search for books, videos, curriculum, multimedia, and bibliographies; a service to order publications; a listing of a number of electronic discussion groups that are relevant for individuals interested in community service; and email addresses of individuals who can provide technical assistance. Other resources available on the website include a calendar of upcoming trainings and information about organizations that provide training and technical assistance to service organizations. Online documents and sample forms for organizations

(e.g., applications, interview, evaluation, mission statements, and certificates) are also downloadable from the site. The website has also posted
its newsletter, *The Resource Connection,* as well as links to other service-
related organizations.

Peace Corps Kids World
  http://www.peacecorps.gov/kids

The Peace Corps Kids World website is an informative and easily
accessible place for youth to learn about the Peace Corps and the work
of Peace Corps volunteers, including the history of the Peace Corps,
what volunteers do, and where volunteers serve. In addition, this website has a section that allows youth to explore all of the different places
around the world that Peace Corps volunteers provide service, including
Africa, the Pacific, South and Central America, the Caribbean, and Asia.
For each country, there is information about the language, geography,
climate, and local customs. In another section of the website, young people can learn about the holidays, food, schools, and what a typical day is
like in a particular country. In addition, there is a section of the website
dedicated to the art of storytelling in different cultures around the
world. Furthermore, young people can learn about ways to make a difference in their life through service to the community or schools. There
is also information and resources that teachers can access to include in
the curriculum.

Pitch In: A Celebration of Voluntary Action
  http://www.pitchin.org

Pitch In is a Canadian-based electronic magazine (e-zine) equipped
with lively music geared toward youth who volunteer. Pitch In, which is
sponsored by Young People's Press (a Canadian news service for youth),
posts articles written by youth about their experiences volunteering in
the community. Young people interested in contributing articles to the
Pitch In e-zine can email the editor on the website. The website
includes an overview of the site and links to other e-zines geared toward
youth, youth organizations that provide information and opportunities
(e.g., internships and volunteer opportunities), and websites dedicated
to social issues (e.g., antiracism, disabilities, and health). The website
offers a unique feature that enables young people to send electronic
greeting cards to individuals to thank them for volunteering in their
community.

Planet Repair.org

http://www.planetrepair.org

Developed with support from the U.S. Environmental Protection Agency (EPA) and the Academy for Educational Development, the Planet Repair website provides information and resources for youth to learn about environmental and conservation issues and to learn how to become involved in their communities. Four different environmental issues are addressed: water resources, beaches and the sun, air pollution, and chemical exposure. Individuals can search for an activity in one of these topic areas to implement in their community. In addition, the website includes a message board to share ideas and a toolbox of creative ideas to make your environmental service activity a success.

Project America

http://www.project.org

Based on the premise that each individual can positively impact the community through service, Project America is designed to encourage community service in corporations, foundations, communities, and individuals. The site includes an action guide describing specific service options, as well as a link to how to become involved in one's community. Resources and a link to past publications by the organizations are also included on the site. Finally, a link is provided so that the reader can find information about Make-A-Difference Day. The organization also supports helping students find alternative spring break opportunities in which they can engage in service.

Project Learning Tree

http://www.plt.org

The Project Learning Tree website is useful and informative for teachers. Available on the website are descriptions of the organization's programs, which include environmental service projects for grades pre-K through 12. Teachers can access curriculum examples of the environmental service projects. A calendar of events, newsletter, and an educator exchange are also useful resources for teachers implementing environmental education service projects in their classrooms.

Search Institute

http://www.search-institute.org

The Search Institute affords parents, teachers and school administrators, and community members and agencies with a range of resources to build developmental assets for young people. Included on the website is a full description of the assets framework, tools, and resources for developing or promoting assets; research publications using the assets framework; and surveys. In addition, the website has other publications and research on other topics of interest to parents, teachers, and community members, including an article on involving families in service. Interested individuals can establish connections with other people building assets through an online bulletin board.

SERVEnet

http://www.servenet.org

Affiliated with Youth Service America, SERVEnet is a comprehensive website designed to increase the number and quality of service opportunities to improve the lives of children. The site is an excellent resource for finding organizations looking for volunteers. In order to find volunteer opportunities, one can enter one's zip code, city, state, areas of interest and availability, and then the computer will generate openings. Nonprofit organizations can use SERVEnet's resources to find volunteers, best practices for volunteers, research, and funding opportunities. In addition, the site contains articles on community service and volunteering, youth service statistics, job opportunities, access to online publications, and links to relevant resources for volunteers and organizations. Individuals can also subscribe to SERVEnet's newsletter and join a listserv to communicate with other individuals interested in service.

Sierra Club

http://www.sierraclub.org

The Sierra Club's website contains information on current and important environmental issues, as well as beautiful places to protect and explore around the world. Links on the site provide information regarding political issues involving environmental issues, background information on the group, and instructions on how to join the Sierra Club or contribute to the cause. To encourage individuals to take action, a special section of the site has a "hot issue" of the week, as well as a list of other pressing environmental issues, such as clean water, population issues, global warming, energy, trade, endangered species, and the wildlands. For each topic, the site includes ways to contact congressmen and other means to voice opinions and explore ways in which youth can become involved to make a difference in the protection of the environment. Individuals interested in participating in a Sierra Club outing can search an online database by location, type of outing, and date of trip. For each trip, one can find extensive information and links about the details and itinerary of the trip, as well as links to learn more about the locations and environmental issues. Individuals can also access the John Muir exhibit, an educational website that details the founding of the Sierra Club by John Muir and the importance of the Sierra Club activities. In addition, there are links to a number of other useful environmental education websites and resources for environmental educators.

Students in Service to America
 http://www.studentsinservicetoamerica.org

This website is sponsored by the National Service-Learning Clearinghouse and contains a number of links that provide information on service-learning organizations, sources of funding, resources for program evaluation, partnership opportunities, programs for student recognition, and reflection practices.

Teachers Network
 http://www.teachnet.org

The Teachers Network website is a useful resources for teachers who are interested in creative, web-based ideas about how to integrate service-learning in the curriculum. The website provides examples of specific lessons that are detailed from start to finish. These plans also include how the curriculum is aligned with learning standards and ideas for assessment. On the website, individuals can search for lesson plans by subject and grade level. In addition to curriculum examples, the website provides a great deal of information and resources for teachers, including videos, grant information, a book store, online bulletin boards to discuss important issues for teachers, and a helpline for new teachers.

The Teenager's Guide to the Real World Online
 http://www.bygpub.com/books/tg2rw/volunteer.htm

This website is the online resource and companion to the book, *Teenager's Guide to the Real World*. The website includes a section entitled, "20 Ways for Teenagers to Help Other People by Volunteering," which is an extensive list of volunteer ideas for youth. Some ideas include: homeless shelters; literacy activities; working in hospitals, animal shelters, environmental organizations; political campaigns; and creating websites for community organizations. The list of ideas includes a summary of the activities and links to organizations and resources in which youth can locate more information on volunteer opportunities. In addition, there are other links to charitable organizations, internships, and volunteer opportunities.

UCLA Service-Learning Clearinghouse Project
http://www.gseis.ucla.edu/slc/

This website is primarily designed as a useful resource for individuals interested in learning more about service-learning in higher education. The UCLA Service Learning Clearinghouse Project is one of the partners of the Learn and Serve America National Service-Learning Clearinghouse and is funded through the Corporation for National Service. The website provides access to a number of different resources on the following topics: service-learning basics, examples of model programs, course syllabi, instructional resources, evaluation and research, funding opportunities, tips for faculty and administrators, and extensive links to other service-learning oriented programs. One of the other topics covered on the website is a kindergarten through higher education partnership section, which highlights publications and links to other online organizations that are geared toward providing teacher education in support of service-learning and developing service-learning programs in elementary, middle, and high schools.

UNICEF's Voices of Youth
http://www.unicef.org/voy/

Available on UNICEF's website, Voices of Youth is an electronic discussion for individuals who want to communicate about issues that can make the world a better place. Ideas are shared online by youth and adults on important global issues, including children's rights, education, violence, abuse, health, and the environment. Youth can give their opinions on a range of social issues impacting children worldwide. There are three different forums of Voices of Youth: the Meeting Place, where people give their views on current issues that impact youth; The Learning Place, a global learning project where youth and adults in different locations around the world can find activities and projects to work on together; and the Teachers' Place, where teachers and other educators can use the network for educational projects and as a place to share ideas and information on education and children's rights. There is a forum of online classrooms where student groups are connected to one another to discuss relevant social issues. The website is also available in French and Spanish.

USA Freedom Corps
   http://www.usafreedomcorps.gov

This website explains the purpose of the USA Freedom Corps, founded by President Bush in 2002. Americans are encouraged to think about their responsibilities to their communities and to volunteer their time and talents. Through this website, students and adults can use the Volunteer Network to identify service opportunities that match their interests and geographic location. The website also offers a link to *Students in Service to America,* a guidebook developed by the USA Freedom Corps, the U.S. Department of Education, and the Corporation for National and Community Service for use by educators and others who want to engage young people in service. (This guidebook is also available at www.studentsinservicetoamerica.org.) The website is offered in Spanish and contains weekly updates, and it has separate sections designated for organizations and for volunteers.

Volunteer Match
   http://www.volunteermatch.org

The Volunteer Match website gives people a way to find and post volunteer opportunities online. Anyone who wants to find opportunities may do so by entering in his or her zip code. This website will find opportunities within a certain distance, time, and category. Some examples of available volunteer categories include education and literacy, arts and culture, homeless and housing, animals, children and youth, politics, and religion. A person can also find opportunities by city with City Match, which provides access to opportunities in approximately thirty cities. A person can also search for a particular organization that is of interest. This website also provides virtual volunteering, which lets people who cannot physically go out and volunteer have an opportunity to get involved from their home or office. In order for an organization to post their opportunities, a representative from the organization must register and become a member.

Youth Action Network
   http://www.teaching.com/youth/

The Youth Action Network website is a tool for giving youth a voice about important social issues. First, there are many links a young person can access in order to learn about issues such as energy, gays and lesbians, and education. Then, youth are able to express views about the issues either through a discussion forum or by voting on a certain issue.

After learning and talking about issues, the youth can then go to four different links—petitions, surveys, the media, and the government—to find out how to take action. With these links, youth are able to have their opinions heard. The website also enables people to sign in on the guest book and leave their contact information for their organization.

Youth Cyberstation
  http://www.pch.gc.ca/cyberstation/html

This website is separated into five zones: Volunteer Zone, Skills Zone, Opportunity Zone, Action Zone, and the Info Zone that provides youth with information and resources about volunteerism and service in Canada. For example, the Volunteer Zone gives information about the importance of volunteering and the reasons why youth should volunteer. The Action Zone provides tips and recommendations on how youth can take action and get involved. In addition, there are many links throughout the site to volunteer organizations and other resources on volunteering. The website is also available in French.

Glossary

Community service This generally means volunteering in the community or within a school setting, such as tutoring younger children. The focus in on the benefits of the service on the recipients, with little focus on the learning of the service provider. The term has also been used in the criminal justice system, as when an offender is sentenced to some unpaid work in the community in exchange for time in jail.

Corporation for National Service Created in 1993 as part of the National and Community Service Trust Act, this federal agency seeks to increase opportunities for young people and adults to provide service to their communities in the United States.

Experiential education An approach to learning that begins with a real-life experience that is processed in ways that the individual constructs or gains new knowledge or insight. It emphasizes learning by doing. Experiential education includes a number of different teaching and learning activities, including service-learning, internships, outdoor education, and problem-based learning.

Internship An applied experience in which students practice the skills they have learned in the classroom. This is often an essential component of a professional training program in which a professional-in-training practices skills under supervision prior to assuming more responsibility and independence. The goals of internships tend to be professional, in contrast with academic, personal, and civic goals emphasized in service-learning.

Mandatory service Some high schools require students to complete community service or service-learning in order to obtain a degree. The requirement may include a specific number of hours of service or completion of a project or service course. Whether or not service should be mandatory is a topic of controversy, which has also been the focus of several lawsuits.

National and Community Service Act of 1990 This legislation creates a new federal agency, the Commission on National and Community Service, and a nonpartisan, nonprofit organization, the Points of Light Foundation, which seek to expand service initiatives across the country.

National and Community Service Trust Act of 1993 This federal legislation establishes the Corporation for National Service to operate three initiatives, Learn and Serve America, AmeriCorps, and the National Senior Services Corp.

National service Voluntary service, generally completed on a full-time basis. The service meets a national human or environmental need and is generally carried out by youthful citizens. AmeriCorps is an example of a national service program, which is financed nationally but is operated by the local community.

Reflection The ability to stand back from an experience and to think about and identify connections between the experience, actions and their effects, factors that led to positive or negative effects, or factors that may have contributed to the need for action. Opportunities for connecting service experiences with academic, social, personal, and civic learning can be created through reflection experiences.

Service-learning The integration of learning with service to others. Learning and service are blended in order that each activity is enriched by the other. The service meets real community needs, as students gain in academic, personal, civic, or social development. Reflection is considered an essential component to promote learning. Service-learning can be voluntary or mandatory, can be part-time or full-time, and can be paid or unpaid. Service-learning can be distinguished from other forms of experiential education by its emphasis on mutual benefit to the service provider and recipient.

Volunteer A person who performs a service or good deed of her own free will and without pay. There is no explicit focus on academic or civic learning or personal or professional development to be gained by the volunteer.

Index

About the Authors

MAUREEN E. KENNY is Associate Professor in the Department of Counseling in Developmental and Educational Psychology at Boston College.

LAURA A. GALLAGHER is affiliated with the Family Insititute at Notrhwestern University.